Python Reinforcement Learning Projects

Eight hands-on projects exploring reinforcement learning algorithms using TensorFlow

Sean Saito
Yang Wenzhuo
Rajalingappaa Shanmugamani

Packt>

BIRMINGHAM - MUMBAI

Python Reinforcement Learning Projects

Commissioning Editor: Pravin Dhandre
Acquisition Editor: Divya Poojari
Content Development Editor: Snehal Kolte
Technical Editor: Dharmendra Yadav
Copy Editor: Safis Editing
Project Coordinator: Manthan Patel
Proofreader: Safis Editing
Indexer: Tejal Daruwale Soni
Graphics: Jisha Chirayil
Production Coordinator: Deepika Naik

First published: September 2018

Production reference: 1280918

Published by Packt Publishing Ltd.
Livery Place
35 Livery Street
Birmingham
B3 2PB, UK.

ISBN 978-1-78899-161-2

www.packtpub.com

Mapt

mapt.io

Mapt is an online digital library that gives you full access to over 5,000 books and videos, as well as industry leading tools to help you plan your personal development and advance your career. For more information, please visit our website.

Why subscribe?

- Spend less time learning and more time coding with practical eBooks and Videos from over 4,000 industry professionals

- Improve your learning with Skill Plans built especially for you

- Get a free eBook or video every month

- Mapt is fully searchable

- Copy and paste, print, and bookmark content

Packt.com

Did you know that Packt offers eBook versions of every book published, with PDF and ePub files available? You can upgrade to the eBook version at www.packt.com and as a print book customer, you are entitled to a discount on the eBook copy. Get in touch with us at customercare@packtpub.com for more details.

At www.packt.com, you can also read a collection of free technical articles, sign up for a range of free newsletters, and receive exclusive discounts and offers on Packt books and eBooks.

Contributors

About the authors

Sean Saito is the youngest ever Machine Learning Developer at SAP and the first bachelor hired for the position. He currently researches and develops machine learning algorithms that automate financial processes. He graduated from Yale-NUS College in 2017 with a Bachelor of Science degree (with Honours), where he explored unsupervised feature extraction for his thesis. Having a profound interest in hackathons, Sean represented Singapore during Data Science Game 2016, the largest student data science competition. Before attending university in Singapore, Sean grew up in Tokyo, Los Angeles, and Boston.

Writing this book is a daunting task for any 23-year-old, and hence I would like to thank many people who made this possible. My greatest words of gratitude belong to my mother and brother for giving me as much love, understanding, and guidance as anyone can fathom. Many thanks also goes to my closest friends and mentors, all from whom I've acquired much knowledge and wisdom, for their encouragement and advice.

Yang Wenzhuo works as a Data Scientist at SAP, Singapore. He got a bachelor's degree in computer science from Zhejiang University in 2011 and a PhD in machine learning from National University of Singapore in 2016. His research focuses on optimization in machine learning and deep reinforcement learning. He has published papers on top machine learning/computer vision conferences including ICML and CVPR, and operations research journals including Mathematical Programming.

Rajalingappaa Shanmugamani is currently working as an Engineering Manager for a Deep learning team at Kairos. Previously, he worked as a Senior Machine Learning Developer at SAP, Singapore and worked at various startups in developing machine learning products. He has a Masters from Indian Institute of Technology—Madras. He has published articles in peer-reviewed journals and conferences and submitted applications for several patents in the area of machine learning. In his spare time, he coaches programming and machine learning to school students and engineers.

I thank my spouse Ezhil, mom, dad, family and friends for their immense support. I thank all the teachers, colleagues and mentors from whom I have learned a lot. I thank the coauthors Wen and Sean making their contributions a pleasure to read. I thank the publishing team from Packt especially Snehal for encouraging at difficult times.

About the reviewer

Jalaj Thanaki is an experienced data scientist with a history of working in the information technology, publishing, and finance industries. She is the author of *Python Natural Language Processing*, published by Packt Publishing. Her research interest lies in natural language processing, machine learning, deep learning, and big data analytics. Besides being a data scientist, Jalaj is also a social activist, traveler, and nature lover.

Packt is searching for authors like you

If you're interested in becoming an author for Packt, please visit `authors.packtpub.com` and apply today. We have worked with thousands of developers and tech professionals, just like you, to help them share their insight with the global tech community. You can make a general application, apply for a specific hot topic that we are recruiting an author for, or submit your own idea.

Table of Contents

Preface

Reinforcement learning is one of the most exciting and rapidly growing fields in machine learning. This is due to the many novel algorithms developed and incredible results published in recent years.

In this book, you will learn about the core concepts of RL including Q-learning, policy gradients, Monte Carlo processes, and several deep reinforcement learning algorithms. As you make your way through the book, you'll work on projects with datasets of various modalities including image, text, and video. You will gain experience in several domains, including gaming, image processing, and physical simulations. You'll explore technologies such as TensorFlow and OpenAI Gym to implement deep learning reinforcement learning algorithms that also predict stock prices, generate natural language, and even build other neural networks.

By the end of this book, you will have hands-on experience with eight reinforcement learning projects, each addressing different topics and/or algorithms. We hope these practical exercises will provide you with better intuition and insight about the field of reinforcement learning and how to apply its algorithms to various problems in real life.

Who this book is for

Python Reinforcement Learning Projects is for data analysts, data scientists, and machine learning professionals who have a working knowledge of machine learning techniques and are looking to explore emerging fields within machine learning such as reinforcement learning. Individuals who want to work on hands-on implementation projects will also find this book useful.

What this book covers

Chapter 1, *Up and Running with Reinforcement Learning*, introduces AI, RL, deep learning, the history/applications of the field, and other relevant topics. It will also provide a high-level overview of fundamental deep learning and TensorFlow concepts, especially those relevant to RL.

Chapter 2, *Balancing Cart Pole*, will have you implement your first RL algorithms in Python and TensorFlow to solve the cart pole balancing problem.

Chapter 3, *Playing Atari Games*, will get you creating your first deep RL algorithm to play ATARI games.

Chapter 4, *Simulating Control Tasks*, provides a brief introduction to actor-critic algorithms for continuous control problems. You will learn how to simulate classic control tasks, look at how to implement basic actor-critic algorithms, and understand the state-of-the-art algorithms for control.

Chapter 5, *Building Virtual Worlds in Minecraft*, takes the advanced concepts covered in previous chapters and applies them to Minecraft, a game more complex than those found on ATARI.

Chapter 6, *Learning to Play Go*, has you building a model that can play Go, the popular Asian board game that is considered one of the world's most complicated games.

Chapter 7, *Creating a Chatbot*, will teach you how to apply deep RL in natural language processing. Our reward function will be a future-looking function, and you will learn how to think in terms of probability when creating this function.

Chapter 8, *Generating a Deep Learning Image Classifier*, introduces one of the latest and most exciting advancements in RL: generating deep learning models using RL. We explore the cutting-edge research produced by Google Brain and implement the algorithms introduced.

Chapter 9, *Predicting Future Stock Prices*, discusses building an agent that can predict stock prices.

Chapter 10, *Looking Ahead*, concludes the book by discussing some of the real-world applications of reinforcement learning and introducing potential areas of future academic work.

To get the most out of this book

The examples covered in this book can be run on Windows, Ubuntu, or macOS. All the installation instructions are covered. A basic knowledge of Python and machine learning is required. It's preferred that you have GPU hardware, but it's not necessary.

Download the example code files

You can download the example code files for this book from your account at `www.packt.com`. If you purchased this book elsewhere, you can visit `www.packt.com/support` and register to have the files emailed directly to you.

You can download the code files by following these steps:

1. Log in or register at `www.packt.com`.
2. Select the **SUPPORT** tab.
3. Click on **Code Downloads & Errata**.
4. Enter the name of the book in the **Search** box and follow the onscreen instructions.

Once the file is downloaded, please make sure that you unzip or extract the folder using the latest version of:

- WinRAR/7-Zip for Windows
- Zipeg/iZip/UnRarX for Mac
- 7-Zip/PeaZip for Linux

The code bundle for the book is also hosted on GitHub at `https://github.com/PacktPublishing/Python-Reinforcement-Learning-Projects`. In case there's an update to the code, it will be updated on the existing GitHub repository.

We also have other code bundles from our rich catalog of books and videos available at `https://github.com/PacktPublishing/`. Check them out!

Conventions used

There are a number of text conventions used throughout this book.

CodeInText: Indicates code words in text, database table names, folder names, filenames, file extensions, pathnames, dummy URLs, user input, and Twitter handles. Here is an example: "The gym-minecraft package has the same interface as other Gym environments."

A block of code is set as follows:

```
import logging
import minecraft_py
logging.basicConfig(level=logging.DEBUG)
```

Any command-line input or output is written as follows:

```
python3 -m pip install gym
python3 -m pip install pygame
```

Bold: Indicates a new term, an important word, or words that you see on screen. For example, words in menus or dialog boxes appear in the text like this. Here is an example: "Select **System info** from the **Administration** panel."

Warnings or important notes appear like this.

Tips and tricks appear like this.

Get in touch

Feedback from our readers is always welcome.

General feedback: If you have questions about any aspect of this book, mention the book title in the subject of your message and email us at customercare@packtpub.com.

Errata: Although we have taken every care to ensure the accuracy of our content, mistakes do happen. If you have found a mistake in this book, we would be grateful if you would report this to us. Please visit www.packt.com/submit-errata, selecting your book, clicking on the Errata Submission Form link, and entering the details.

Piracy: If you come across any illegal copies of our works in any form on the Internet, we would be grateful if you would provide us with the location address or website name. Please contact us at copyright@packt.com with a link to the material.

If you are interested in becoming an author: If there is a topic that you have expertise in and you are interested in either writing or contributing to a book, please visit authors.packtpub.com.

Reviews

Please leave a review. Once you have read and used this book, why not leave a review on the site that you purchased it from? Potential readers can then see and use your unbiased opinion to make purchase decisions, we at Packt can understand what you think about our products, and our authors can see your feedback on their book. Thank you!

For more information about Packt, please visit packt.com.

1
Up and Running with Reinforcement Learning

What will **artificial intelligence** (**AI**) look like in the future? As applications of AI algorithms and software become more prominent, it is a question that should interest many. Researchers and practitioners of AI face further relevant questions; how will we realize what we envision and solve known problems? What kinds of innovations and algorithms are yet to be developed? Several subfields in machine learning display great promise toward answering many of our questions. In this book, we shine the spotlight on reinforcement learning, one such, area and perhaps one of the most exciting topics in machine learning.

Reinforcement learning is motivated by the objective to learn from the environment by interacting with it. Imagine an infant and how it goes about in its environment. By moving around and acting upon its surroundings, the infant learns about physical phenomena, causal relationships, and various attributes and properties of the objects he or she interacts with. The infant's learning is often motivated by a desire to accomplish some objective. such as playing with surrounding objects or satiating some spark of curiosity. In reinforcement learning, we pursue a similar endeavor; we take a computational approach toward learning about the environment. In other words, our goal is to design algorithms that learn through their interactions with the environment in order to accomplish a task.

What use do such algorithms provide? By having a generalized learning algorithm, we can offer effective solutions to several real-world problems. A prominent example is the use of reinforcement learning algorithms to drive cars autonomously. While not fully realized, such use cases would provide great benefits to society, for reinforcement learning algorithms have empirically proven their ability to surpass human-level performance in several tasks. One watershed moment occurred in 2016 when DeepMind's AlphaGo program defeated 18-time Go world champion Lee Sedol four games to one. AlphaGo was essentially able to learn and surpass three millennia of Go wisdom cultivated by humans in a matter of months. Recently, reinforcement learning algorithms have been shown to be effective in playing more complex, real-time multi-agent games such as Dota. The same algorithms that power these game-playing algorithms have also succeeded in controlling robotic arms to pick up objects and navigating drones through mazes. These examples suggest not only what these algorithms are capable of, but also what they can potentially accomplish down the road.

Introduction to this book

This book offers a practical guide for those eager to learn about reinforcement learning. We will take a hands-on approach toward learning about reinforcement learning by going through numerous examples of algorithms and their applications. Each chapter focuses on a particular use case and introduces reinforcement learning algorithms that are used to solve the given problem. Some of these use cases rely on state-of-the-art algorithms; hence through this book, we will learn about and implement some of the best-performing algorithms and techniques in the industry.

The projects increase in difficulty/complexity as you go through the book. The following table describes what you will learn from each chapter:

Chapter name	The use case/problem	Concepts/algorithms/technologies discussed and used
Balancing Cart Pole	Control horizontal movement of a cart to balance a vertical bar	OpenAI Gym framework, Q-Learning
Playing Atari Games	Play various Atari games at human-level proficiency	Deep Q-Networks
Simulating Control Tasks	Control agents in a continuous action space as opposed to a discrete one	**Deterministic policy gradients** (**DPG**), **Trust Region Policy Optimization** (**TRPO**), multi-tasking
Building Virtual Worlds in Minecraft	Navigate a character in the virtual world of Minecraft	Asynchronous Advantage Actor-Critic (**A3C**)

Learning to Play Go	Go, one of the oldest and most complex board games in the world	Monte Carlo tree search, policy and value networks
Creating a Chatbot	Generating natural language in a conversational setting	Policy gradient methods, **Long Short-Term Memory** (**LSTM**)
Auto Generating a Deep Learning Image Classifier	Create an agent that generates neural networks to solve a given task	Recurrent neural networks, policy gradient methods (REINFORCE)
Predicting Future Stock Prices	Predict stock prices and make buy and sell decisions	Actor-Critic methods, time-series analysis, experience replay

Expectations

This book is best suited for the reader who:

- Has intermediate proficiency in Python
- Possesses a basic understanding of machine learning and deep learning, especially for the following topics:
    - Neural networks
    - Backpropagation
    - Convolution
    - Techniques for better generalization and reduced overfitting
- Enjoys a hands-on, practical approach toward learning

Since this book serves as a practical introduction to the field, we try to keep theoretical content to a minimum. However, it is advisable for the reader to have basic knowledge of some of the fundamental mathematical and statistical concepts on which the field of machine learning depends. These include the following:

- Calculus (single and multivariate)
- Linear algebra
- Probability theory
- Graph theory

Having some experience with these subjects would greatly assist the reader in understanding the concepts and algorithms we will cover throughout this book.

Hardware and software requirements

The ensuing chapters will require you to implement various reinforcement learning algorithms. Hence a proper development environment is necessary for a smooth learning journey. In particular, you should have the following:

- A computer running either macOS or the Linux operating system (for those on Windows, try setting up a Virtual Machine with a Linux image)
- A stable internet connection
- A GPU (preferably)

We will exclusively use the Python programming language to implement our reinforcement learning and deep learning algorithms. Moreover, we will be using Python 3.6. A list of libraries we will be using can be found on the official GitHub repository, located at (`https://github.com/PacktPublishing/Python-Reinforcement-Learning-Projects`). You will also find the implementations of every algorithm we will cover in this book.

Installing packages

Assuming you have a working Python installation, you can install all the required packages using the `requirements.txt` file found in our repository. We also recommend you create a `virtualenv` to isolate your development environment from your main OS system. The following steps will help you construct an environment and install the packages:

```
# Install virtualenv using pip
$ pip install virtualenv

# Create a virtualenv
$ virtualenv rl_projects

# Activate virtualenv
$ source rl_projects/bin/activate

# cd into the directory with our requirements.txt
(rl_projects) $ cd /path/to/requirements.txt

# pip install the required packages
(rl_projects) $ pip install -r requirements.txt
```

And now you are all set and ready to start! The next few sections of this chapter will introduce the field of reinforcement learning and will also provide a refresher on deep learning.

What is reinforcement learning?

Our journey begins with understanding what reinforcement learning is about. Those who are familiar with machine learning may be aware of several learning paradigms, namely **supervised learning** and **unsupervised learning**. In supervised learning, a machine learning model has a supervisor that gives the ground truth for every data point. The model learns by minimizing the distance between its own prediction and the ground truth. The dataset is thus required to have an annotation for each data point, for example, each image of a dog and a cat would have its respective label. In unsupervised learning, the model does not have access to the ground truths of the data and thus has to learn about the distribution and patterns of the data without them.

In reinforcement learning, the agent refers to the model/algorithm that learns to complete a particular task. The agent learns primarily by receiving **reward signals**, which is a scalar indication of how well the agent is performing a task.

Suppose we have an agent that is tasked with controlling a robot's walking movement; the agent would receive positive rewards for successfully walking toward a destination and negative rewards for falling/failing to make progress.

Moreover, unlike in supervised learning, these reward signals are not given to the model immediately; rather, they are returned as a consequence of a sequence of **actions** that the agent makes. Actions are simply the things an agent can do within its **environment**. The environment refers to the world in which the agent resides and is primarily responsible for returning reward signals to the agent. An agent's actions are usually conditioned on what the agent perceives from the environment. What the agent perceives is referred to as the **observation** or the **state** of the environment. What further distinguishes reinforcement learning from other paradigms is that the actions of the agent can alter the environment and its subsequent responses.

For example, suppose an agent is tasked with playing Space Invaders, the popular Atari 2600 arcade game. The environment is the game itself, along with the logic upon which it runs. During the game, the agent queries the environment to make an observation. The observation is simply an array of the (210, 160, 3) shape, which is the screen of the game that displays the agent's ship, the enemies, the score, and any projectiles. Based on this observation, the agent makes some actions, which can include moving left or right, shooting a laser, or doing nothing. The environment receives the agent's action as input and makes any necessary updates to the state.

For instance, if a laser touches an enemy ship, it is removed from the game. If the agent decides to simply move to the left, the game updates the agent's coordinates accordingly. This process repeats until a **terminal state**, a state that represents the end of the sequence, is reached. In Space Invaders, the terminal state corresponds to when the agent's ship is destroyed, and the game subsequently returns the score that it keeps track of, a value that is calculated based on the number of enemy ships the agent successfully destroys.

> Note that some environments do not have terminal states, such as the stock market. These environments keep running for as long as they exist.

Let's recap the terms we have learned about so far:

Term	Description	Examples
Agent	A model/algorithm that is tasked with learning to accomplish a task.	Self-driving cars, walking robots, video game players
Environment	The world in which the agent acts. It is responsible for controlling what the agent perceives and providing feedback on how well the agent is performing a particular task.	The road on which a car drives, a video game, the stock market
Action	A decision the agent makes in an environment, usually dependent on what the agent perceives.	Steering a car, buying or selling a particular stock, shooting a laser from the spaceship the agent is controlling
Reward signal	A scalar indication of how well the agent is performing a particular task.	Space Invaders score, return on investment for some stock, distance covered by a robot learning to walk
Observation/state	A description of the environment as can be perceived by the agent.	Video from a dashboard camera, the screen of the game, stock market statistics
Terminal state	A state at which no further actions can be made by the agent.	Reaching the end of a maze, the ship in Space Invaders getting destroyed

Put formally, at a given timestep, t, the following happens for an agent, P, and environment, E:

```
- P queries E for some observation sₜ
- P decides to take action aₜ based on observation sₜ
- E receives aₜ and returns reward rₜ based on the action
- P receives rₜ
- E updates sₜ to sₜ₊₁ based on aₜ and other factors
```

How does the environment compute r_t and s_{t+1}? The environment usually has its own algorithm that computes these values based on numerous input/factors, including what action the agent takes.

Sometimes, the environment is composed of multiple agents that try to maximize their own rewards. The way gravity acts upon a ball that we drop from a height is a good representation of how the environment works; just like how our surroundings obey the laws of physics, the environment has some internal mechanism for computing rewards and the next state. This internal mechanism is usually hidden to the agent, and thus our job is to build agents that can learn to do a good job at their respective tasks, despite this uncertainty.

In the following sections, we will discuss in more detail the main protagonist of every reinforcement learning problem—the agent.

The agent

The goal of a reinforcement learning agent is to learn to perform a task well in an environment. Mathematically, this means to maximize the cumulative reward, R, which can be expressed in the following equation:

$$R = r_0 + \gamma^1 r_1 + \cdots + \gamma^t r_t$$

We are simply calculating a weighted sum of the reward received at each timestep. γ is called the **discount factor**, which is a scalar value between 0 and 1. The idea is that the later a reward comes, the less valuable it becomes. This reflects our perspectives on rewards as well; that we'd rather receive $100 now rather than a year later shows how the same reward signal can be valued differently based on its proximity to the present.

Because the mechanics of the environment are not fully observable or known to the agent, it must gain information by performing an action and observing how the environment reacts to it. This is much like how humans learn to perform certain tasks as well.

Suppose we are learning to play chess. While we don't have all the possible moves committed to memory or know exactly how an opponent will play, we are able to improve our proficiency over time. In particular, we are able to become proficient in the following:

- Learning how to react to a move made by the opponent
- Assessing how good of a position we are in to win the game
- Predicting what the opponent will do next and using that prediction to decide on a move
- Understanding how others would play in a similar situation

In fact, reinforcement learning agents can learn to do similar things. In particular, an agent can be composed of multiple functions and models to assist its decision-making. There are three main components that an agent can have: the policy, the value function, and the model.

Policy

A policy is an algorithm or a set of rules that describe how an agent makes its decisions. An example policy can be the strategy an investor uses to trade stocks, where the investor buys a stock when its price goes down and sells the stock when the price goes up.

More formally, a policy is a function, usually denoted as π, that maps a state, s_t, to an action, a_t:

$$a_t = \pi(s_t)$$

This means that an agent decides its action given its current state. This function can represent anything, as long as it can receive a state as input and output an action, be it a table, graph, or machine learning classifier.

For example, suppose we have an agent that is supposed to navigate a maze. We shall further assume that the agent knows what the maze looks like; the following is how the agent's policy can be represented:

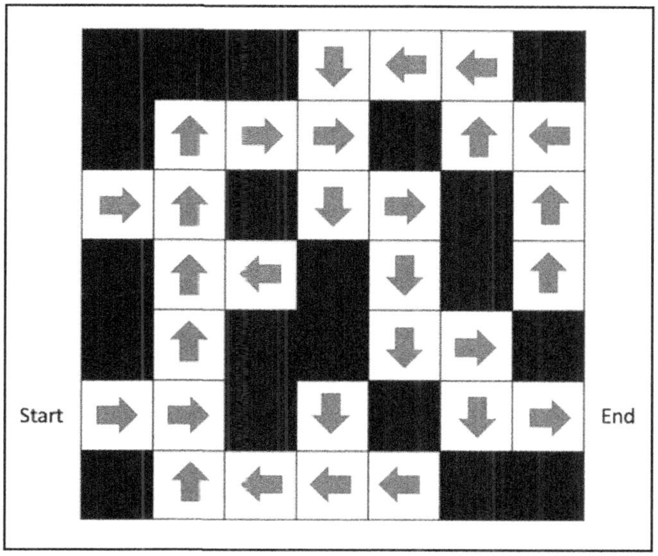

Figure 1: A maze where each arrow indicates where an agent would go next

Each white square in this maze represents a state the agent can be in. Each blue arrow refers to the action an agent would take in the corresponding square. This essentially represents the agent's policy for this maze. Moreover, this can also be regarded as a deterministic policy, for the mapping from the state to the action is deterministic. This is in contrast to a stochastic policy, where a policy would output a probability distribution over the possible actions given some state:

$$\pi(a_t \mid s_t) = P(a_t \mid s_t)$$

Here, $\pi(a_t \mid s_t)$ is a normalized probability vector over all the possible actions, as shown in the following example:

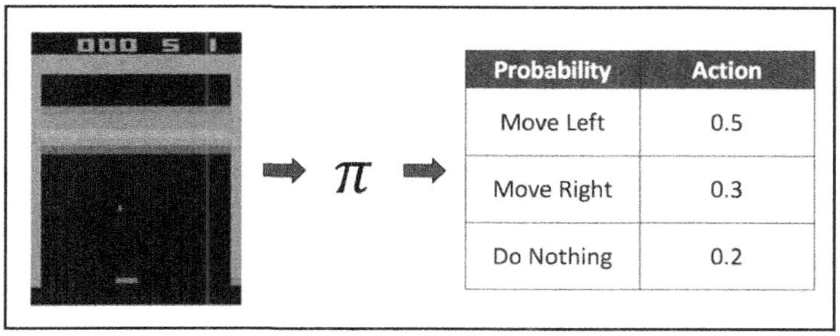

Probability	Action
Move Left	0.5
Move Right	0.3
Do Nothing	0.2

Figure 2: A policy mapping the game state (the screen) to actions (probabilities)

The agent playing the game of Breakout has a policy that takes the screen of the game as input and returns a probability for each possible action.

Value function

The second component an agent can have is called the **value function**. As mentioned previously, it is useful to assess your position, good or bad, in a given state. In a game of chess, a player would like to know the likelihood that they are going to win in a board state. An agent navigating a maze would like to know how close it is to the destination. The value function serves this purpose; it predicts the expected future reward an agent would receive in a given state. In other words, it measures whether a given state is desirable for the agent. More formally, the value function takes a state and a policy as input and returns a scalar value representing the expected cumulative reward:

$$v(s, \pi) = E\left[R|s, \pi\right] = E\left[r_0 + \gamma r_1 + \cdots + \gamma^t r_t | s, \pi\right]$$

Take our maze example, and suppose the agent receives a reward of -1 for every step it takes. The agent's goal is to finish the maze in the smallest number of steps possible. The value of each state can be represented as follows:

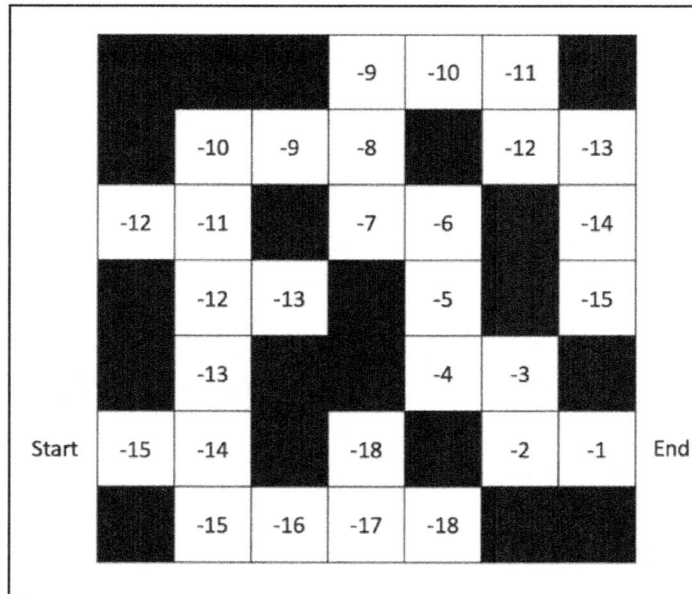

			-9	-10	-11		
	-10	-9	-8		-12	-13	
-12	-11		-7	-6		-14	
	-12	-13		-5		-15	
	-13			-4	-3		
Start	-15	-14		-18		-2	-1	End
	-15	-16	-17	-18			

Figure 3: A maze where each square indicates the value of being in the state

Each square basically represents the number of steps it takes to get to the end of the maze. As you can see, the smallest number of steps required to reach the goal is 15.

How can the value function help an agent perform a task well, other than informing us of how desirable a given state is? As we will see in the following sections, value functions play an integral role in predicting how well a sequence of actions will do even before the agent performs them. This is similar to chess players imagining how well a sequence of future actions will do in improving his or her chances of winning. To do this, the agent also needs to have an understanding of how the environment works. This is where the third component of an agent, the **model**, becomes relevant.

Model

In the previous sections, we discussed how the environment is not fully known to the agent. In other words, the agent usually does not have an idea of how the internal algorithm of the environment looks. The agent thus needs to interact with it to gain information and learn how to maximize its expected cumulative reward. However, it is possible for the agent to have an internal replica, or a model, of the environment. The agent can use the model to predict how the environment would react to some action in a given state. A model of the stock market, for example, is tasked with predicting what the prices will look like in the future. If the model is accurate, the agent can then use its value function to assess how desirable future states look. More formally, a model can be denoted as a function, M, that predicts the probability of the next state given the current state and an action:

$$M(s_t, a_t) = P(s_{t+1} \mid s_t, a_t)$$

In other scenarios, the model of the environment can be used to enumerate possible future states. This is commonly used in turn-based games, such as chess and tic-tac-toe, where the rules and scope of possible actions are clearly defined. Trees are often used to illustrate the possible sequence of actions and states in turn-based games:

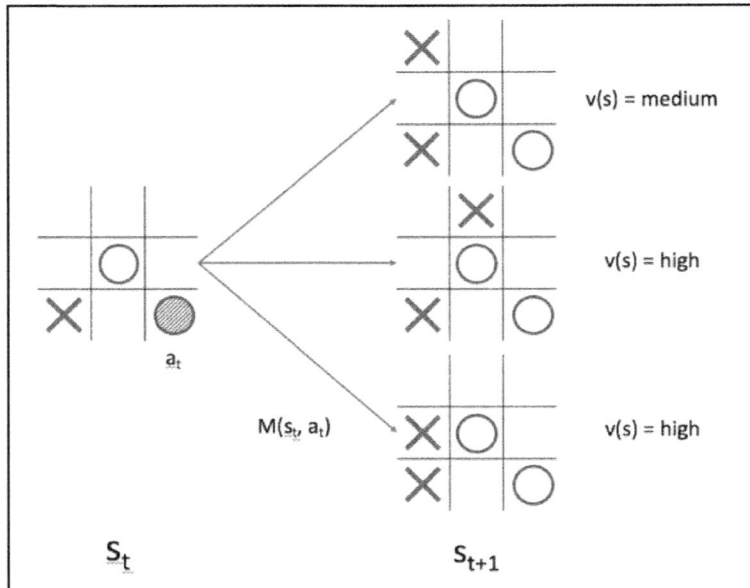

Figure 4: A model using its value function to assess possible moves

In the preceding example of the tic-tac-toe game, $M(s_t, a_t)$ denotes the possible states that taking the a_t action (represented as the shaded circle) could yield in a given state, s_t. Moreover, we can calculate the value of each state using the agent's value function. The middle and bottom states would yield a high value since the agent would be one step away from victory, whereas the top state would yield a medium value since the agent needs to prevent the opponent from winning.

Let's review the terms we have covered so far:

Term	Description	What does it output?
Policy	The algorithm or function that outputs decisions the agent makes	A scalar/single decision (deterministic policy) or a vector of probabilities over possible actions (stochastic policy)
Value Function	The function that describes how good or bad a given state is	A scalar value representing the expected cumulative reward
Model	An agent's representation of the environment, which predicts how the environment will react to the agent's actions	The probability of the next state given an action and current state, or an enumeration of possible states given the rules of the environment

In the following sections, we will use these concepts to learn about one of the most fundamental frameworks in reinforcement learning: the Markov decision process.

Markov decision process (MDP)

A Markov decision process is a framework used to represent the environment of a reinforcement learning problem. It is a graphical model with directed edges (meaning that one node of the graph points to another node). Each node represents a possible state in the environment, and each edge pointing out of a state represents an action that can be taken in the given state. For example, consider the following MDP:

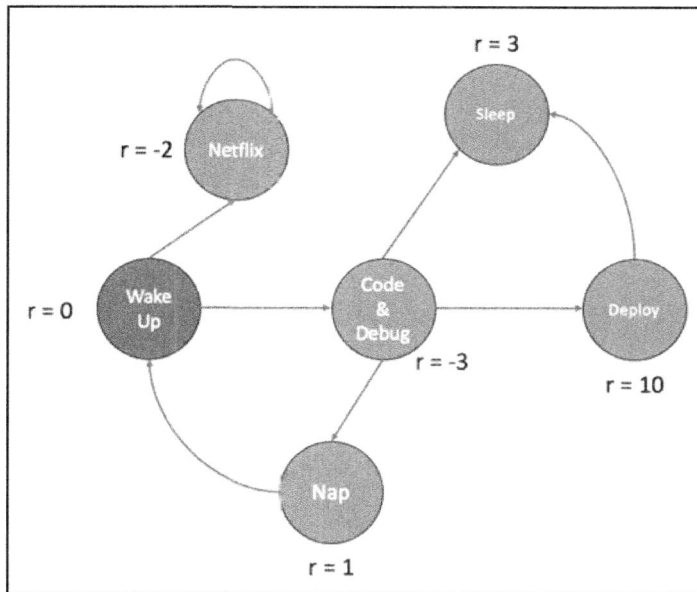

Figure 5: A sample Markov Decision Process

The preceding MDP represents what a typical day of a programmer could look like. Each circle represents a particular state the programmer can be in, where the blue state (**Wake Up**) is the initial state (or the state the agent is in at *t*=0), and the orange state (**Publish Code**) denotes the terminal state. Each arrow represents the transitions that the programmer can make between states. Each state has a reward that is associated with it, and the higher the reward, the more desirable the state is.

We can tabulate the rewards as an adjacency matrix as well:

State\action	Wake Up	Netflix	Code and debug	Nap	Deploy	Sleep
Wake Up	N/A	-2	-3	N/A	N/A	N/A
Netflix	N/A	-2	N/A	N/A	N/A	N/A
Code and debug	N/A	N/A	N/A	1	10	3
Nap	0	N/A	N/A	N/A	N/A	N/A
Deploy	N/A	N/A	N/A	N/A	N/A	3
Sleep	N/A	N/A	N/A	N/A	N/A	N/A

The left column represents the possible states and the top row represents the possible actions. N/A means that the action is not performable from the given state. This system basically represents the decisions that a programmer can make throughout their day.

When the programmer wakes up, they can either decide to work (code and debug the code) or watch Netflix. Notice that the reward for watching Netflix is higher than that of coding and debugging. For the programmer in question, watching Netflix seems like a more rewarding activity, while coding and debugging is perhaps a chore (which, I hope, is not the case for the reader!). However, both actions yield negative rewards, even though our objective is to maximize our cumulative reward. If the programmer chooses to watch Netflix, they will be stuck in an endless loop of binge-watching, which continuously lowers the reward. Rather, more rewarding states will become available to the programmer if they decide to code diligently. Let's look at the possible trajectories, which are the sequence of actions, the programmer can take:

- Wake Up | Netflix | Netflix | ...
- Wake Up | Code and debug | Nap | Wake Up | Code and debug | Nap | ...
- Wake Up | Code and debug | Sleep
- Wake Up | Code and debug | Deploy | Sleep

Both the first and second trajectories represent infinite loops. Let's calculate the cumulative reward for each, where we set $\gamma = 0.9$:

- $R = 0 + 0.9 * -2 + 0.9^2 * -2 + 0.9^3 * -2 \cdots < 0$
- $R = 0 + 0.9 * -3 + 0.9^2 * 1 + 0.9^3 + 0.0 + 0.9^4 * -3 + 0.9^5 * 1 + \cdots < 0$
- $R = 0 + 0.9 * -3 + 0.9^2 * 3 = -0.27$
- $R = 0.0 + 0.9 * -3 + 0.9^2 * 10 + 0.9^3 * 3 = 7.587$

It is easy to see that both the first and second trajectories, despite not reaching a terminal state, will never return positive rewards. The fourth trajectory yields the highest reward (successfully deploying code is a highly rewarding accomplishment!).

What we have calculated are the value functions for four policies that a programmer can take to go through their day. Recall that the value function is the expected cumulative reward starting from a given state and following a policy. We have observed four possible policies and have evaluated how each leads to a different cumulative reward; this exercise is also called **policy evaluation**. Moreover, the equations we have applied to calculate the expected rewards are also known as **Bellman expectation equations**. The Bellman equations are a set of equations used to evaluate and improve policies and value functions to help a reinforcement learning agent learn better. Though a thorough introduction to Bellman equations is outside the scope of this book, they are foundational to building a theoretical understanding of reinforcement learning. We encourage the reader to look into this further.

> While we will not cover Bellman equations in depth, we highly recommend the reader to do so in order to build a solid understanding of reinforcement learning. For more information, refer to *Reinforcement Learning: An Introduction* by Richard S. Sutton and Andrew Barto (reference at the end of this chapter).

Now that you have learned about some the key terms and concepts of reinforcement learning, you may be wondering how we teach a reinforcement learning agent to maximize its reward, or in other words, find that the fourth trajectory is the best. In this book, you will be working on solving this question for numerous tasks and problems, all using deep learning. While we encourage you to be familiar with the basics of deep learning, the following sections will serve as a light refresher to the field.

Deep learning

Deep learning has become one of the most popular and recognizable fields of machine learning and computer science. Thanks to an increase in both available data and computational resources, deep learning algorithms have successfully surpassed previous state-of-the-art results in countless tasks. For several domains, including image recognition and playing Go, deep learning has even exceeded the capabilities of mankind.

It is thus not surprising that many reinforcement learning algorithms have started to utilize deep learning to bolster performance. Many of the reinforcement learning algorithms from the beginning of this chapter rely on deep learning. This book, too, will revolve around deep learning algorithms used to tackle reinforcement learning problems.

The following sections will serve as a refresher on some of the most fundamental concepts of deep learning, including neural networks, backpropagation, and convolution. However, if are unfamiliar with these topics, we highly encourage you to seek other sources for a more in-depth introduction.

Neural networks

A neural network is a type of computational architecture that is composed of layers of perceptrons. A perceptron, first conceived in the 1950s by Frank Rosenblatt, models the biological neuron and computes a linear combination of a vector of input. It also outputs a transformation of the linear combination using a non-linear activation, such as the sigmoid function. Suppose a perceptron receives an input vector of $x \in R^n$. The output, a, of the perceptron, would be as follows:

$$a(x) = \sigma(\sum_i^n w_i x_i + b)$$

$$\sigma(z) = \frac{1}{1 + e^{-z}}$$

Where $w = (w_1, \dots, w_n)$ are the weights of the perceptron, b is a constant, called the **bias**, and σ is the sigmoid activation function that outputs a value between 0 and 1.

Perceptrons have been widely used as a computational model to make decisions. Suppose the task was to predict the likelihood of sunny weather the next day. Each x_i would represent a variable, such as the temperature of the current day, humidity, or the weather of the previous day. Then, $a(x)$ would compute a value that reflects how likely it is that there will be sunny weather tomorrow. If the model has a good set of values for w, it is able to make accurate decisions.

In a typical neural network, there are multiple layers of neurons, where each neuron in a given layer is connected to all neurons in the prior and subsequent layers. Hence these layers are also referred to as **fully-connected layers**. The weights of a given layer, l, can be represented as a matrix, W^l:

$$W^l = \begin{bmatrix} w_{11}^l & w_{12}^l & w_{13}^l & \cdots & w_{1n}^l \\ w_{21}^l & w_{22}^l & w_{23}^l & \cdots & w_{2n}^l \\ \vdots & \vdots & \vdots & \ddots & \vdots \\ w_{d1}^l & w_{d2}^l & w_{d3}^l & \cdots & w_{dn}^l \end{bmatrix}$$

$$B = (b_1, b_2, \ldots, b_n)$$

Where each w_{ij} denotes the weight between the i neuron of the previous layer and the j neuron of this layer. B^l denotes a vector of biases, one for each neuron in the l layer. Hence, the activation, a^l, of a given layer, l, can be defined as follows:

$$a^l(x) = \sigma(W^l a^{l-1}(x) + B^l)$$

$$a^0(x) = x$$

Where $a^0(x)$ is just the input. Such neural networks with multiple layers of neurons are called **multilayer perceptrons (MLP)**. There are three components in an MLP: the input layer, the hidden layers, and the output layer. The data flows from the input layer, transformed through a series of linear and non-linear functions in the hidden layers, and is outputted from the output layer as a decision or a prediction. Hence this architecture is also referred to as a feed-forward network. The following diagram shows what a fully-connected network would look like:

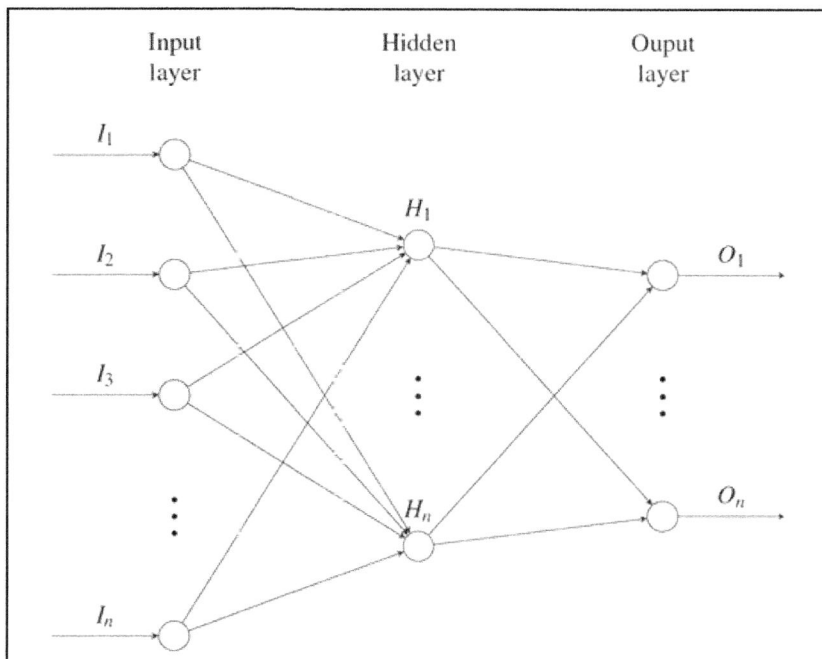

Figure 6: A sketch of a multilayer perceptron

Backpropagation

As mentioned previously, a neural network's performance depends on how good the values of *W* are (for simplicity, we will refer to both the weights and biases as *W*). When the whole network grows in size, it becomes untenable to manually determine the optimal weights for each neuron in every layer. Therefore, we rely on backpropagation, an algorithm that iteratively and automatically updates the weights of every neuron.

To update the weights, we first need the ground truth, or the target value that the neural network tries to output. To understand what this ground truth could look like, we formulate a sample problem. The MNIST dataset is a large repository of 28x28 images of handwritten digits. It contains 70,000 images in total and serves as a popular benchmark for machine learning models. Given ten different classes of digits (from zero to nine), we would like to identify which digit class a given images belongs to. We can represent the ground truth of each image as a vector of length 10, where the index of the class (starting from 0) is marked as 1 and the rest are 0s. For example, an image, *x*, with a class label of five would have the ground truth of $y(x) = (0, 0, 0, 0, 0, 1, 0, 0, 0, 0)$, where *y* is the target function we approximate.

What should the neural network look like? If we take each pixel in the image to be an input, we would have 28x28 neurons in the input layer (every image would be flattened to become a 784-dimensional vector). Moreover, because there are 10 digit classes, we have 10 neurons in the output layer, each neuron producing a sigmoid activation for a given class. There can be an arbitrary number of neurons in the hidden layers.

Let *f* represent the sequence of transformations that the neural network computes, parameterized by the weights, *W*. *f* is essentially an approximation of the target function, *y*, and maps the 784-dimensional input vector to a 10 dimensional output prediction. We classify the image according to the index of the largest sigmoid output.

Now that we have formulated the ground truth, we can measure the distance between it and the network's prediction. This error is what allows the network to update its weights. We define the error function *E(W)* as follows:

$$E(W) = \frac{1}{2n} \sum_{i}^{n} \| y(x_i) - f_W(x_i) \|^2$$

The goal of backpropagation is to minimize *E* by finding the right set of *W*. This minimization is an optimization problem whereby we use gradient descent to iteratively compute the gradients of *E* with respect to *W* and propagate them through the network starting from the output layer.

Unfortunately, an in-depth explanation of backpropagation is outside the scope of this introductory chapter. If you are unfamiliar with this concept, we highly encourage you to study it first.

Convolutional neural networks

Using backpropagation, we are now able to train large networks automatically. This has led to the development of increasingly complex neural network architectures. One example is the **convolutional neural network (CNN)**. There are mainly three types of layers in a CNN: the convolutional layer, the pooling layer, and the fully-connected layer. The fully-connected layer is identical to the standard neural network discussed previously. In the convolutional layer, weights are part of convolutional kernels. Convolution on a two-dimensional array of image pixels is defined as the following:

$$C(u,v) = \sum_v \sum_u f(u,v)g(x-u, y-v)$$

Where $f(u, v)$ is the pixel intensity of the input at coordinate (u, v), and $g(x-u, y-v)$ is the weight of the convolutional kernel at that location.

A convolutional layer comprises a stack of convolutional kernels; hence the weights of a convolutional layer can be visualized as a three-dimensional box as opposed to the two-dimensional array that we defined for fully-connected layers. The output of a single convolutional kernel applied to an input is also a two-dimensional mapping, which we call a filter. Because there are multiple kernels, the output of a convolutional layer is again a three-dimensional box, which can be referred to as a volume.

Finally, the pooling layer reduces the size of the input by taking $m*m$ local patches of pixels and outputting a scalar. The max-pooling layer takes $m*m$ patches and outputs the greatest value among the patch of pixels.

Given an input volume of the (32, 32, 3) shape—corresponding to height, width, and depth (channels)—a max-pooling layer with a pooling size of 2x2 will output a volume of the (16, 16, 3) shape. The input to the CNN are usually images, which can also be viewed as volumes where the depth corresponds to RGB channels.

The following is a depiction of a typical convolutional neural network:

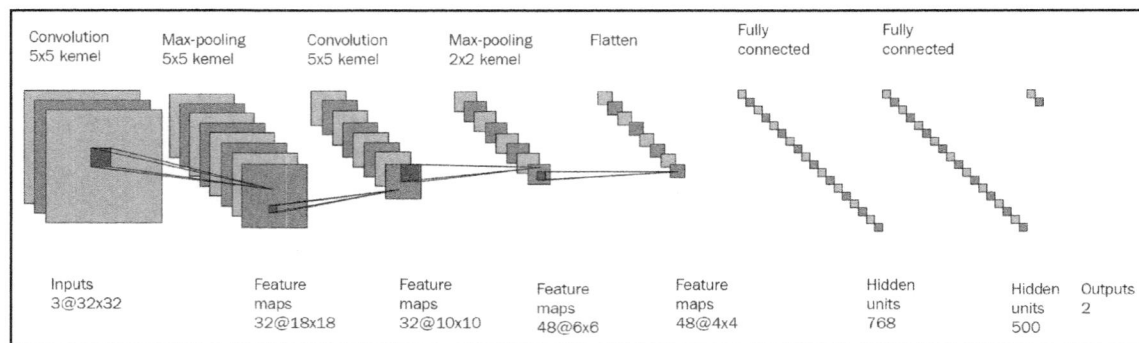

Convolution 5x5 kemel	Max-pooling 5x5 kemel	Convolution 5x5 kemel	Max-pooling 2x2 kemel	Flatten	Fully connected	Fully connected	
Inputs 3@32x32	Feature maps 32@18x18	Feature maps 32@10x10	Feature maps 48@6x6	Feature maps 48@4x4	Hidden units 768	Hidden units 500	Outputs 2

Figure 7: An example convolutional neural network

Advantages of neural networks

The main advantage of a CNN over a standard neural network is that the former is able to learn visual and spatial features of the input, while for the latter such information is lost due to flattening input data into a vector. CNNs have made significant strides in the field of computer vision, starting with increased classification accuracies of MNIST data and object recognition, semantic segmentation, and other domains. CNNs have many applications in real life, from facial detection in social media to autonomous vehicles. Recent approaches have also applied CNNs to natural language processing and text classification tasks to produce state-of-the-art results.

Now that we have covered the basics of machine learning, we will go through our first implementation exercise.

Implementing a convolutional neural network in TensorFlow

In this section, we will implement a simple convolutional neural network in TensorFlow to solve an image classification task. As the rest of this book will be heavily reliant on TensorFlow and CNNs, we highly recommend that you become sufficiently familiar with implementing deep learning algorithms using this framework.

TensorFlow

TensorFlow, developed by Google in 2015, is one of the most popular deep learning frameworks in the world. It is used widely for research and commercial projects and boasts a rich set of APIs and functionalities to help researchers and practitioners develop deep learning models. TensorFlow programs can run on GPUs as well as CPUs, and thus abstract the GPU programming to make development more convenient.

Throughout this book, we will be using TensorFlow exclusively, so make sure you are familiar with the basics as you progress through the chapters.

> Visit https://www.tensorflow.org/ for a complete set of documentation and other tutorials.

The Fashion-MNIST dataset

Those who have experience with deep learning have most likely heard about the MNIST dataset. It is one of the most widely-used image datasets, serving as a benchmark for tasks such as image classification and image generation, and is used by many computer vision models:

Figure 8: The MNIST dataset (reference at end of chapter)

There are several problems with MNIST, however. First of all, the dataset is too easy, since a simple convolutional neural network is able to achieve 99% test accuracy. In spite of this, the dataset is used far too often in research and benchmarks. The F-MNIST dataset, produced by the online fashion retailer Zalando, is a more complex, much-needed upgrade to MNIST:

Figure 9: The Fashion-MNIST dataset (taken from https://github.com/zalandoresearch/fashion-mnist, reference at the end of this chapter)

Instead of digits, the F-MNIST dataset includes photos of ten different clothing types (ranging from t-shirts to shoes) compressed in to 28x28 monochrome thumbnails. Hence, F-MNIST serves as a convenient drop-in replacement to MNIST and is increasingly gaining popularity in the community. Hence we will train our CNN on F-MNIST as well. The preceding table maps each label index to its class:

Index	Class
0	T-shirt/top
1	Trousers
2	Pullover
3	Dress
4	Coat
5	Sandal
6	Shirt
7	Sneaker
8	Bag
9	Ankle boot

In the following subsections, we will design a convolutional neural network that will learn to classify data from this dataset.

Building the network

Multiple deep learning frameworks have already implemented APIs for loading the F-MNIST dataset, including TensorFlow. For our implementation, we will be using Keras, another popular deep learning framework that is integrated with TensorFlow. The Keras datasets module provides a highly convenient interface for loading the datasets as numpy arrays.

Finally, we can start coding! For this exercise, we only need one Python module, which we will call cnn.py. Open up your favorite text editor or IDE, and let's get started.

Our first step is to declare the modules that we are going to use:

```
import logging
import os
import sys

logger = logging.getLogger(__name__)

import tensorflow as tf
import numpy as np
from keras.datasets import fashion_mnist
from keras.utils import np_utils
```

The following describes what each module is for and how we will use it:

Module(s)	Purpose
logging	For printing statistics as we run the code
os, sys	For interacting with the operating system, including writing files
tensorflow	The main TensorFlow library
numpy	An optimized library for vector calculations and simple data processing
keras	For downloading the F-MNIST dataset

We will implement our CNN as a class called SimpleCNN. The __init__ constructor takes a number of parameters:

```
class SimpleCNN(object):

    def __init__(self, learning_rate, num_epochs, beta, batch_size):
        self.learning_rate = learning_rate
        self.num_epochs = num_epochs
        self.beta = beta
        self.batch_size = batch_size
        self.save_dir = "saves"
        self.logs_dir = "logs"
        os.makedirs(self.save_dir, exist_ok=True)
        os.makedirs(self.logs_dir, exist_ok=True)
        self.save_path = os.path.join(self.save_dir, "simple_cnn")
        self.logs_path = os.path.join(self.logs_dir, "simple_cnn")
```

The parameters our SimpleCNN is initialized with are described here:

Parameter	Purpose
learning_rate	The learning rate for the optimization algorithm
num_epochs	The number of epochs it takes to train the network
beta	A float value (between 0 and 1) that controls the strength of the L2-penalty
batch_size	The number of images to train on in a single step

Moreover, save_dir and save_path refer to the locations where we will store our network's parameters. logs_dir and logs_path refer to the locations where the statistics of the training run will be stored (we will show how we can retrieve these logs later).

Methods for building the network

Now, in this section, we will see two methods that can be used to build the function, which are:

- build method
- fit method

build method

The first method we will define for our SimpleCNN class is the build method, which is responsible for building the architecture of our CNN. Our build method takes two pieces of input: the input tensor and the number of classes it should expect:

```
def build(self, input_tensor, num_classes):
    """
    Builds a convolutional neural network according to the input shape and
the number of classes.
    Architecture is fixed.

    Args:
        input_tensor: Tensor of the input
        num_classes: (int) number of classes

    Returns:
        The output logits before softmax
    """
```

We will first initialize tf.placeholder, called is_training. TensorFlow placeholders are like variables that don't have values. We only pass them values when we actually train the network and call the relevant operations:

```
with tf.name_scope("input_placeholders"):
    self.is_training = tf.placeholder_with_default(True, shape=(),
name="is_training")
```

The tf.name_scope(...) block allows us to name our operations and tensors properly. While this is not absolutely necessary, it helps us organize our code better and will help us to visualize the network. Here, we define a tf.placeholder_with_default called is_training, which has a default value of True. This placeholder will be used for our dropout operations (since dropout has different modes during training and inference).

Naming your operations and tensors is considered a good practice. It helps you organize your code.

Our next step is to define the convolutional layers of our CNN. We make use of three different kinds of layers to create multiple layers of convolutions: `tf.layers.conv2d`, `tf.max_pooling2d`, and `tf.layers.dropout`:

```
with tf.name_scope("convolutional_layers"):
    conv_1 = tf.layers.conv2d(
        input_tensor,
        filters=16,
        kernel_size=(5, 5),
        strides=(1, 1),
        padding="SAME",
        activation=tf.nn.relu,
    kernel_regularizer=tf.contrib.layers.l2_regularizer(scale=self.beta),
        name="conv_1")
    conv_2 = tf.layers.conv2d(
        conv_1,
        filters=32,
        kernel_size=(3, 3),
        strides=(1, 1),
        padding="SAME",
        activation=tf.nn.relu,
    kernel_regularizer=tf.contrib.layers.l2_regularizer(scale=self.beta),
        name="conv_2")
    pool_3 = tf.layers.max_pooling2d(
        conv_2,
        pool_size=(2, 2),
        strides=1,
        padding="SAME",
        name="pool_3"
    )
    drop_4 = tf.layers.dropout(pool_3, training=self.is_training,
name="drop_4")

    conv_5 = tf.layers.conv2d(
        drop_4,
        filters=64,
        kernel_size=(3, 3),
        strides=(1, 1),
        padding="SAME",
        activation=tf.nn.relu,
    kernel_regularizer=tf.contrib.layers.l2_regularizer(scale=self.beta),
        name="conv_5")
```

```
    conv_6 = tf.layers.conv2d(
        conv_5,
        filters=128,
        kernel_size=(3, 3),
        strides=(1, 1),
        padding="SAME",
        activation=tf.nn.relu,
    kernel_regularizer=tf.contrib.layers.l2_regularizer(scale=self.beta),
        name="conv_6")
    pool_7 = tf.layers.max_pooling2d(
        conv_6,
        pool_size=(2, 2),
        strides=1,
        padding="SAME",
        name="pool_7"
    )
    drop_8 = tf.layers.dropout(pool_7, training=self.is_training,
name="drop_8")
```

Here are some explanations of the parameters:

Parameter	Type	Description
filters	int	Number of filters output by the convolution.
kernel_size	Tuple of int	The shape of the kernel.
pool_size	Tuple of int	The shape of the max-pooling window.
strides	int	The number of pixels to slide across per convolution/max-pooling operation.
padding	str	Whether to add padding (SAME) or not (VALID). If padding is added, the output shape of the convolution remains the same as the input shape.
activation	func	A TensorFlow activation function.
kernel_regularizer	op	Which regularization to use for the convolutional kernel. The default value is None.
training	op	A tensor/placeholder that tells the dropout operation whether the forward pass is for training or for inference.

In the preceding table, we have specified the convolutional architecture to have the following sequence of layers:

CONV | CONV | POOL | DROPOUT | CONV | CONV | POOL | DROPOUT

However, you are encouraged to explore different configurations and architectures. For example, you could add batch-normalization layers to improve the stability of training.

Finally, we add the fully-connected layers that lead to the output of the network:

```
with tf.name_scope("fully_connected_layers"):
    flattened = tf.layers.flatten(drop_8, name="flatten")
    fc_9 = tf.layers.dense(
        flattened,
        units=1024,
        activation=tf.nn.relu,
    kernel_regularizer=tf.contrib.layers.l2_regularizer(scale=self.beta),
        name="fc_9"
    )
    drop_10 = tf.layers.dropout(fc_9, training=self.is_training,
name="drop_10")
    logits = tf.layers.dense(
        drop_10,
        units=num_classes,
    kernel_regularizer=tf.contrib.layers.l2_regularizer(scale=self.beta),
        name="logits"
    )

return logits
```

`tf.layers.flatten` turns the output of the convolutional layers (which is 3-D) into a single vector (1-D) so that we can pass them through the `tf.layers.dense` layers. After going through two fully-connected layers, we return the final output, which we define as `logits`.

Notice that in the final `tf.layers.dense` layer, we do not specify an `activation`. We will see why when we move on to specifying the training operations of the network.

Next, we implement several helper functions. `_create_tf_dataset` takes two instances of `numpy.ndarray` and turns them into TensorFlow tensors, which can be directly fed into a network. `_log_loss_and_acc` simply logs training statistics, such as loss and accuracy:

```
def _create_tf_dataset(self, x, y):
    dataset = tf.data.Dataset.zip((
            tf.data.Dataset.from_tensor_slices(x),
            tf.data.Dataset.from_tensor_slices(y)
        )).shuffle(50).repeat().batch(self.batch_size)
    return dataset

def _log_loss_and_acc(self, epoch, loss, acc, suffix):
    summary = tf.Summary(value=[
        tf.Summary.Value(tag="loss_{}".format(suffix),
simple_value=float(loss)),
        tf.Summary.Value(tag="acc_{}".format(suffix),
simple_value=float(acc))
```

```
    ])
    self.summary_writer.add_summary(summary, epoch)
```

fit method

The last method we will implement for our `SimpleCNN` is the `fit` method. This function triggers training for our CNN. Our `fit` method takes four input:

Argument	Description
X_train	Training data
y_train	Training labels
X_test	Test data
y_test	Test labels

The first step of `fit` is to initialize `tf.Graph` and `tf.Session`. Both of these objects are essential to any TensorFlow program. `tf.Graph` represents the graph in which all the operations for our CNN are defined. You can think of it as a sandbox where we define all the layers and functions. `tf.Session` is the class that actually executes the operations defined in `tf.Graph`:

```
def fit(self, X_train, y_train, X_valid, y_valid):
    """
    Trains a CNN on given data

    Args:
        numpy.ndarrays representing data and labels respectively
    """
    graph = tf.Graph()
    with graph.as_default():
        sess = tf.Session()
```

We then create datasets using TensorFlow's Dataset API and the `_create_tf_dataset` method we defined earlier:

```
train_dataset = self._create_tf_dataset(X_train, y_train)
valid_dataset = self._create_tf_dataset(X_valid, y_valid)

# Creating a generic iterator
iterator = tf.data.Iterator.from_structure(train_dataset.output_types,
                                           train_dataset.output_shapes)
next_tensor_batch = iterator.get_next()

# Separate training and validation set init ops
train_init_ops = iterator.make_initializer(train_dataset)
valid_init_ops = iterator.make_initializer(valid_dataset)
```

```
input_tensor, labels = next_tensor_batch
```

`tf.data.Iterator` builds an iterator object that outputs a batch of images every time we call `iterator.get_next()`. We initialize a dataset each for the training and testing data. The result of `iterator.get_next()` is a tuple of input images and corresponding labels.

The former is `input_tensor`, which we feed into the `build` method. The latter is used for calculating the loss function and backpropagation:

```
num_classes = y_train.shape[1]

# Building the network
logits = self.build(input_tensor=input_tensor, num_classes=num_classes)
logger.info('Built network')

prediction = tf.nn.softmax(logits, name="predictions")
loss_ops = tf.reduce_mean(tf.nn.softmax_cross_entropy_with_logits_v2(
    labels=labels, logits=logits), name="loss")
```

`logits` (the non-activated outputs of the network) are fed into two other operations: `prediction`, which is just the softmax over `logits` to obtain normalized probabilities over the classes, and `loss_ops`, which calculates the mean categorical cross-entropy between the predictions and the labels.

We then define the backpropagation algorithm used to train the network and the operations used for calculating accuracy:

```
optimizer = tf.train.AdamOptimizer(learning_rate=self.learning_rate)
train_ops = optimizer.minimize(loss_ops)

correct = tf.equal(tf.argmax(prediction, 1), tf.argmax(labels, 1),
name="correct")
accuracy_ops = tf.reduce_mean(tf.cast(correct, tf.float32),
name="accuracy")
```

We are now done building the network along with its optimization algorithms. We use `tf.global_variables_initializer()` to initialize the weights and operations of our network. We also initialize the `tf.train.Saver` and `tf.summary.FileWriter` objects. The `tf.train.Saver` object saves the weights and architecture of the network, whereas the latter keeps track of various training statistics:

```
initializer = tf.global_variables_initializer()

logger.info('Initializing all variables')
sess.run(initializer)
logger.info('Initialized all variables')
```

```
sess.run(train_init_ops)
logger.info('Initialized dataset iterator')
self.saver = tf.train.Saver()
self.summary_writer = tf.summary.FileWriter(self.logs_path)
```

Finally, once we have set up everything we need, we can implement the actual training loop. For every epoch, we keep track of the training cross-entropy loss and accuracy of the network. At the end of every epoch, we save the updated weights to disk. We also calculate the validation loss and accuracy every 10 epochs. This is done by calling sess.run(...), where the arguments to this function are the operations that the sess object should execute:

```
logger.info("Training CNN for {} epochs".format(self.num_epochs))
for epoch_idx in range(1, self.num_epochs+1):
    loss, _, accuracy = sess.run([
        loss_ops, train_ops, accuracy_ops
    ])
    self._log_loss_and_acc(epoch_idx, loss, accuracy, "train")

    if epoch_idx % 10 == 0:
        sess.run(valid_init_ops)
        valid_loss, valid_accuracy = sess.run([
            loss_ops, accuracy_ops
        ], feed_dict={self.is_training: False})
        logger.info("=====================> Epoch {}".format(epoch_idx))
        logger.info("\tTraining accuracy: {:.3f}".format(accuracy))
        logger.info("\tTraining loss: {:.6f}".format(loss))
        logger.info("\tValidation accuracy: {:.3f}".format(valid_accuracy))
        logger.info("\tValidation loss: {:.6f}".format(valid_loss))
        self._log_loss_and_acc(epoch_idx, valid_loss, valid_accuracy,
"valid")

    # Creating a checkpoint at every epoch
    self.saver.save(sess, self.save_path)
```

And that completes our fit function. Our final step is to create the script for instantiating the datasets, the neural network, and then running training, which we will write at the bottom of cnn.py.

We will first configure our logger and load the dataset using the Keras fashion_mnist module, which loads the training and testing data:

```
if __name__ == "__main__":
    logging.basicConfig(stream=sys.stdout,
                        level=logging.DEBUG,
                        format='%(asctime)s %(name)-12s %(levelname)-8s %(message)s')
```

```
logger = logging.getLogger(__name__)

logger.info("Loading Fashion MNIST data")
(X_train, y_train), (X_test, y_test) = fashion_mnist.load_data()
```

We then apply some simple preprocessing to the data. The Keras API returns `numpy` arrays of the `(Number of images, 28, 28)` shape.

However, what we actually want is `(Number of images, 28, 28, 1)`, where the third axis is the channel axis. This is required because our convolutional layers expect input that have three axes. Moreover, the pixel values themselves are in the range of `[0, 255]`. We will divide them by 255 to get a range of `[0, 1]`. This is a common technique that helps stabilize training.

Furthermore, we turn the labels, which are simply an array of label indices, into one-hot encodings:

```
logger.info('Shape of training data:')
logger.info('Train: {}'.format(X_train.shape))
logger.info('Test: {}'.format(X_test.shape))

logger.info('Adding channel axis to the data')
X_train = X_train[:,:,:,np.newaxis]
X_test = X_test[:,:,:,np.newaxis]

logger.info("Simple transformation by dividing pixels by 255")
X_train = X_train / 255.
X_test = X_test / 255.

X_train = X_train.astype(np.float32)
X_test = X_test.astype(np.float32)
y_train = y_train.astype(np.float32)
y_test = y_test.astype(np.float32)
num_classes = len(np.unique(y_train))

logger.info("Turning ys into one-hot encodings")
y_train = np_utils.to_categorical(y_train, num_classes=num_classes)
y_test = np_utils.to_categorical(y_test, num_classes=num_classes)
```

We then define the input to the constructor of our `SimpleCNN`. Feel free to tweak the numbers to see how they affect the performance of the model:

```
cnn_params = {
    "learning_rate": 3e-4,
    "num_epochs": 100,
    "beta": 1e-3,
    "batch_size": 32
```

}

And finally, we instantiate `SimpleCNN` and call its `fit` method:

```
logger.info('Initializing CNN')
simple_cnn = SimpleCNN(**cnn_params)
logger.info('Training CNN')
simple_cnn.fit(X_train=X_train,
               X_valid=X_test,
               y_train=y_train,
               y_valid=y_test)
```

To run the entire script, all you need to do is run the module:

```
$ python cnn.py
```

And that's it! You have successfully implemented a convolutional neural network in TensorFlow to train on the `F-MNIST` dataset. To track the progress of the training, you can simply look at the output in your terminal/editor. You should see an output that resembles the following:

```
$ python cnn.py
Using TensorFlow backend.
2018-07-29 21:21:55,423 __main__ INFO Loading Fashion MNIST data
2018-07-29 21:21:55,686 __main__ INFO Shape of training data:
2018-07-29 21:21:55,687 __main__ INFO Train: (60000, 28, 28)
2018-07-29 21:21:55,687 __main__ INFO Test: (10000, 28, 28)
2018-07-29 21:21:55,687 __main__ INFO Adding channel axis to the data
2018-07-29 21:21:55,687 __main__ INFO Simple transformation by dividing
pixels by 255
2018-07-29 21:21:55,914 __main__ INFO Turning ys into one-hot encodings
2018-07-29 21:21:55,914 __main__ INFO Initializing CNN
2018-07-29 21:21:55,914 __main__ INFO Training CNN
2018-07-29 21:21:58,365 __main__ INFO Built network
2018-07-29 21:21:58,562 __main__ INFO Initializing all variables
2018-07-29 21:21:59,284 __main__ INFO Initialized all variables
2018-07-29 21:21:59,639 __main__ INFO Initialized dataset iterator
2018-07-29 21:22:00,880 __main__ INFO Training CNN for 100 epochs
2018-07-29 21:24:23,781 __main__ INFO ====================> Epoch 10
2018-07-29 21:24:23,781 __main__ INFO Training accuracy: 0.406
2018-07-29 21:24:23,781 __main__ INFO Training loss: 1.972021
2018-07-29 21:24:23,781 __main__ INFO Validation accuracy: 0.500
2018-07-29 21:24:23,782 __main__ INFO Validation loss: 2.108872
2018-07-29 21:27:09,541 __main__ INFO ====================> Epoch 20
2018-07-29 21:27:09,541 __main__ INFO Training accuracy: 0.469
2018-07-29 21:27:09,541 __main__ INFO Training loss: 1.573592
2018-07-29 21:27:09,542 __main__ INFO Validation accuracy: 0.500
2018-07-29 21:27:09,542 __main__ INFO Validation loss: 1.482948
```

```
2018-07-29 21:29:57,750 __main__ INFO =====================> Epoch 30
2018-07-29 21:29:57,750 __main__ INFO Training accuracy: 0.531
2018-07-29 21:29:57,750 __main__ INFO Training loss: 1.119335
2018-07-29 21:29:57,750 __main__ INFO Validation accuracy: 0.625
2018-07-29 21:29:57,750 __main__ INFO Validation loss: 0.905031
2018-07-29 21:32:45,921 __main__ INFO =====================> Epoch 40
2018-07-29 21:32:45,922 __main__ INFO Training accuracy: 0.656
2018-07-29 21:32:45,922 __main__ INFO Training loss: 0.896715
2018-07-29 21:32:45,922 __main__ INFO Validation accuracy: 0.719
2018-07-29 21:32:45,922 __main__ INFO Validation loss: 0.847015
```

Another thing to check out is TensorBoard, a visualization tool developed by the developers of TensorFlow, to graph the model's accuracy and loss. The `tf.summary.FileWriter` object we have used serves this purpose. You can run TensorBoard with the following command:

```
$ tensorboard --logdir=logs/
```

`logs` is where our `SimpleCNN` model writes the statistics to. TensorBoard is a great tool for visualizing the structure of our `tf.Graph`, as well as seeing how statistics such as accuracy and loss change over time. By default, the TensorBoard logs can be accessed by pointing your browser to `localhost:6006`:

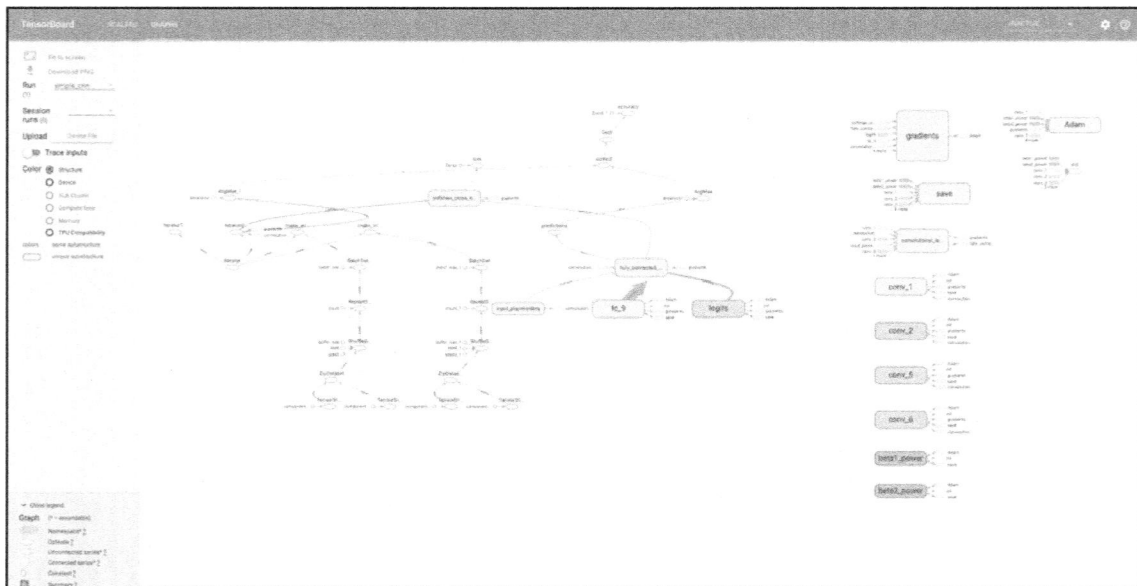

Figure 10: TensorBoard and its visualization of our CNN

Congratulations! We have successfully implemented a convolutional neural network using TensorFlow. However, the CNN we implemented is rather rudimentary, and only achieves mediocre accuracy—the challenge to the reader is to tweak the architecture to improve its performance.

Summary

In this chapter, we took our first step in the world of reinforcement learning. We covered some of the fundamental concepts and terminology of the field, including the agent, the policy, the value function, and the reward. We also covered basic topics in deep learning and implemented a simple convolutional neural network using TensorFlow.

The field of reinforcement learning is vast and ever-expanding; it would be impossible to cover all of it in a single book. We do, however, hope to equip you with the practical skills and the necessary experience to navigate this field.

The following chapters will consist of individual projects—we will use a combination of reinforcement learning and deep learning algorithms to tackle several tasks and problems. We will build agents that will learn to play Go, explore the world of Minecraft, and play Atari video games. We hope you are ready to embark on this exciting learning journey!

References

Sutton, Richard S., and Andrew G. Barto. *Reinforcement learning: An introduction*. MIT press, 1998.

Y. LeCun, L. Bottou, Y. Bengio, and P. Haffner. *Gradient-based learning applied to document recognition*. Proceedings of the IEEE, 86(11):2278-2324, November 1998.

Xiao, Han, Kashif Rasul, and Roland Vollgraf. *Fashion-mnist: a novel image dataset for benchmarking machine learning algorithms*. arXiv preprint arXiv:1708.07747 (2017).

Balancing CartPole

In this chapter, you will learn about the CartPole balancing problem. The CartPole is an inverted pendulum, where the pole is balanced against gravity. Traditionally, this problem is solved by control theory, using analytical equations. However, in this chapter, we will solve the problem with machine learning.

The following topics will be covered in this chapter:

- Installing OpenAI Gym
- The different environments of Gym

OpenAI Gym

OpenAI is a non-profit organization dedicated to researching artificial intelligence. Visit `https://openai.com` for more information about the mission of OpenAI. The technologies developed by OpenAI are free for anyone to use.

Gym

Gym provides a toolkit to benchmark AI-based tasks. The interface is easy to use. The goal is to enable reproducible research. Visit `https://gym.openai.com` for more information about Gym. An agent can be taught inside of the `gym`, and learn activities such as playing games or walking. An environment is a library of problems.

The standard set of problems presented in the gym are as follows:

- CartPole
- Pendulum
- Space Invaders
- Lunar Lander

- Ant
- Mountain Car
- Acrobot
- Car Racing
- Bipedal Walker

Any algorithm can work out in the gym by training for these activities. All of the problems have the same interface. Therefore, any general reinforcement learning algorithm can be used through the interface.

Installation

The primary interface of the gym is used through Python. Once you have Python3 in an environment with the `pip` installer, the gym can be installed as follows:

```
sudo pip install gym
```

Advanced users that want to modify the source can compile from the source by using the following commands:

```
git clone https://github.com/openai/gym
cd gym
pip install -e .
```

A new environment can be added to the `gym` with the source code. There are several environments that need more dependencies. For macOS, install the dependencies by using the following command:

```
brew install cmake boost boost-python sdl2 swig wget
```

For Ubuntu, use the following commands:

```
apt-get install -y python-numpy python-dev cmake zlib1g-dev libjpeg-dev
xvfb libav-tools xorg-dev python-opengl libboost-all-dev libsdl2-dev swig
```

Once the dependencies are there, install the complete `gym` as follows:

```
pip install 'gym[all]'
```

This will install most of the environments that are required.

Running an environment

Any gym environment can be initialized and run by using a simple interface. Let's start by importing the gym library, as follows:

1. First we import the gym library:

```
import gym
```

2. Next, create an environment by passing an argument to gym.make. In the following code, CartPole is used as an example:

```
environment = gym.make('CartPole-v0')
```

3. Next, reset the environment:

```
environment.reset()
```

4. Then, start an iteration and render the environment, as follows:

```
for dummy in range(100):
    environment.render()
    environment.step(environment.action_space.sample())
```

Also, change the action space at every step, to see CartPole moving. Running the preceding program should produce a visualization. The scene should start with a visualization, as follows:

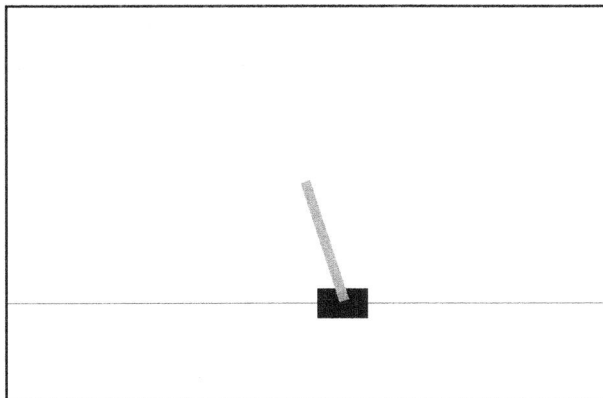

The preceding image is called a **CartPole**. The CartPole is made up of a cart that can move horizontally and a pole that can move rotationally, with respect to the center of the cart.

The pole is pivoted to the cart. After some time, you will notice that the pole is falling to one side, as shown in the following image:

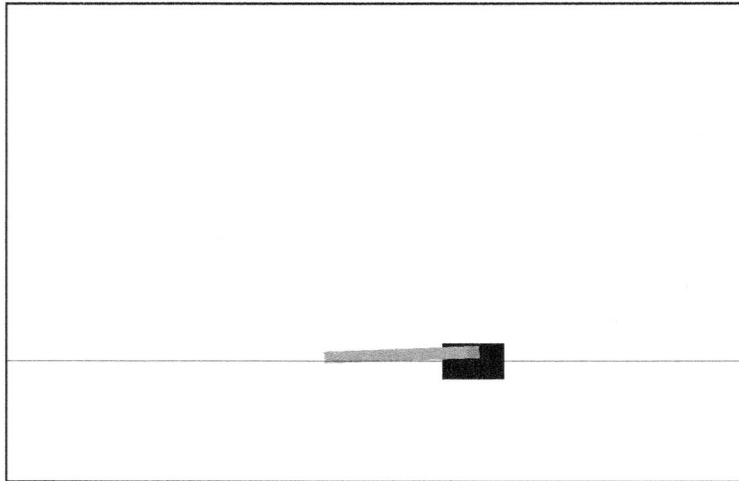

After a few more iterations, the pole will swing back, as shown in the following image. All of the movements are constrained by the laws of physics. The steps are taken randomly:

Other environments can be seen in a similar way, by replacing the argument of the gym environment, such as `MsPacman-v0` or `MountrainCar-v0`. For other environments, other licenses may be required. Next, we will go through the rest of the environments.

Atari

To play Atari games, any environment can be invoked. The following code refers to the game Space Invaders:

```
environment = gym.make( SpaceInvaders-v0')
```

Once the preceding command has executed, you will see the following screen:

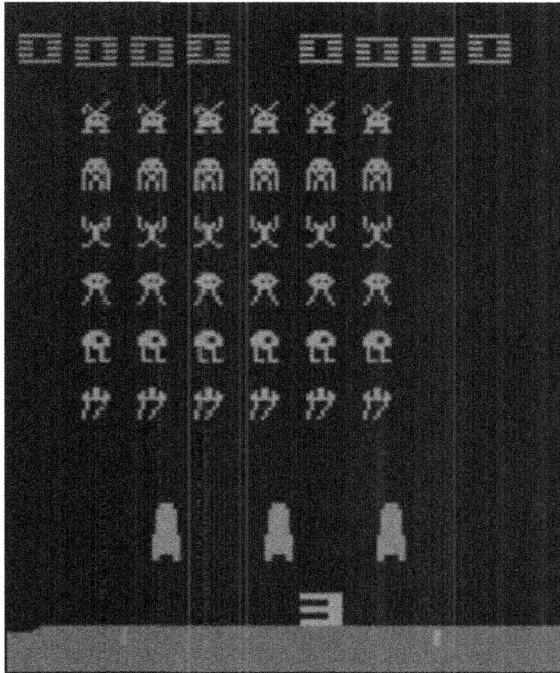

An Atari game can be played in this environment.

Algorithmic tasks

There are algorithmic tasks that can be learned through reinforcement learning. A copy environment can be invoked, as follows:

```
environment = gym.make( Copy-v0')
```

The process of copying a string is shown in the following screenshot:

```
Total length of input instance: 4, step: 0

Observation Tape     :   BAB
Output Tape          :
Targets              :   CBAB
```

MuJoCo

MuJoCo stands for **multi-joint dynamics with contact**. It's a simulation environment for robots and multi-body dynamics:

```
environment = gym.make('Humanoid-v2')
```

The following is a visualization for the simulation of a humanoid:

Simulation of a humanoid

There are robots and other objects that can be simulated in this environment.

Robotics

A robotics environment can also be created, as follows:

```
environment = gym.make('HandManipulateBlock-v0')
```

The following is a visualization of a robot hand:

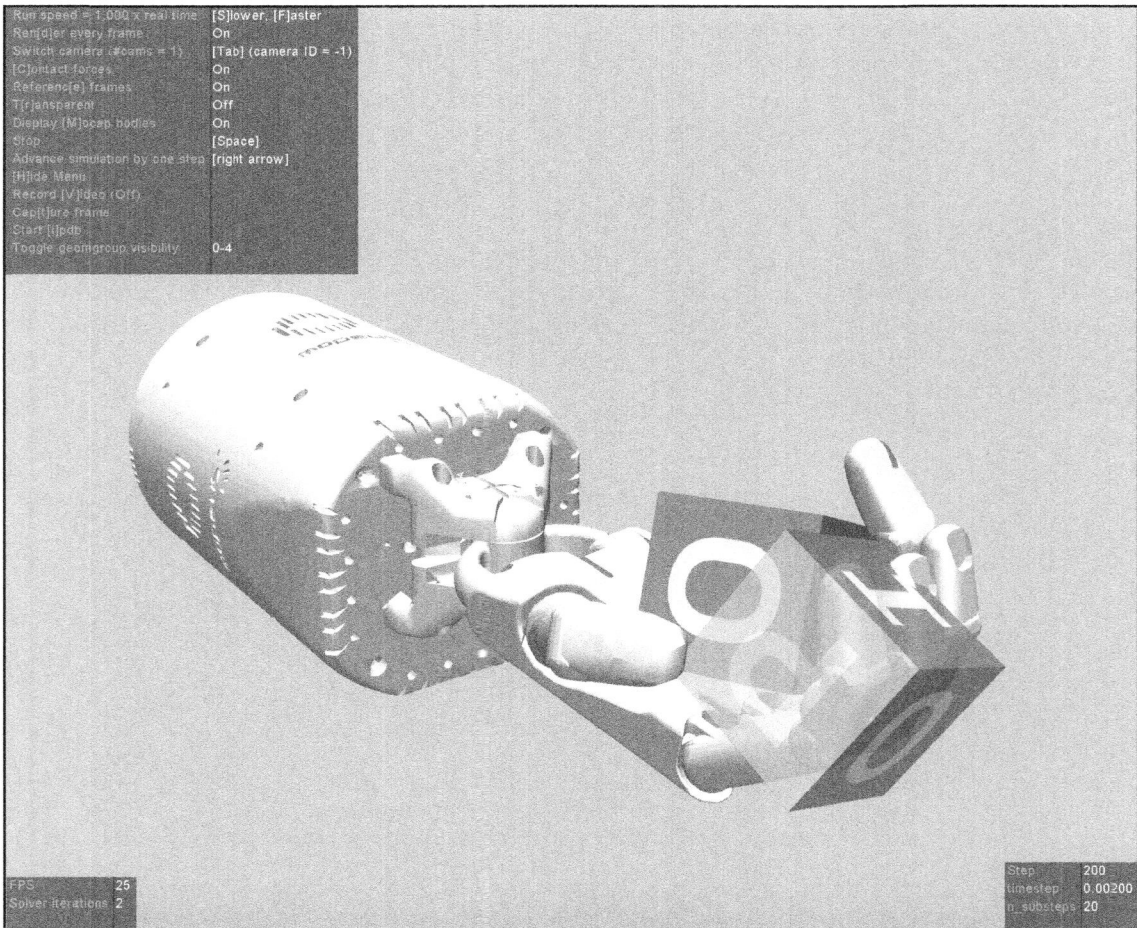

There are several environments in which OpenAI Gym can be used.

Markov models

The problem is set up as a reinforcement learning problem, with a trial and error method. The environment is described using `state_values state_values (?)`, and the `state_values` are changed by actions. The actions are determined by an algorithm, based on the current `state_value`, in order to achieve a particular `state_value` that is termed a **Markov model**. In an ideal case, the past `state_values` does have an influence on future `state_values`, but here, we assume that the current `state_value` has all of the previous `state_values` encoded. There are two types of `state_values`; one is observable, and the other is non-observable. The model has to take non-observable `state_values` into account, as well. That is called a **Hidden Markov model**.

CartPole

At each step of the cart and pole, several variables can be observed, such as the position, velocity, angle, and angular velocity. The possible `state_values` of the cart are moved right and left:

1. `state_values`: Four dimensions of continuous values.
2. `Actions`: Two discrete values.
3. The dimensions, or space, can be referred to as the `state_value` space and the action space. Let's start by importing the required libraries, as follows:

   ```
   import gym
   import numpy as np
   import random
   import math
   ```

4. Next, make the environment for playing CartPole, as follows:

   ```
   environment = gym.make('CartPole-v0')
   ```

5. Next, define the number of buckets and the number of actions, as follows:

   ```
   no_buckets = (1, 1, 6, 3)
   no_actions = environment.action_space.n
   ```

6. Next, define the `state_value_bounds`, as follows:

   ```
   state_value_bounds = list(zip(environment.observation_space.low,
   environment.observation_space.high))
   state_value_bounds[1] = [-0.5, 0.5]
   state_value_bounds[3] = [-math.radians(50), math.radians(50)]
   ```

7. Next, define the `action_index`, as follows:

```
action_index = len(no_buckets)
```

8. Next define the `q_value_table`, as follows:

```
q_value_table = np.zeros(no_buckets + (no_actions,))
```

9. Next, define the minimum exploration rate and the minimum learning rate:

```
min_explore_rate = 0.01
min_learning_rate = 0.1
```

10. Next, define the maximum episodes, the maximum time steps, the streak to the end, the solving time, the discount, and the number of streaks, as constants:

```
max_episodes = 1000
max_time_steps = 250
streak_to_end = 120
solved_time = 199
discount = 0.99
no_streaks = 0
```

11. Next, define the `select` action that can decide the action, as follows:

```
def select_action(state_value, explore_rate):
    if random.random() < explore_rate:
        action = environment.action_space.sample()
    else:
        action = np.argmax(q_value_table[state_value])
    return action
```

12. Next, select the explore state, as follows:

```
def select_explore_rate(x):
    return max(min_explore_rate, min(1, 1.0 -
math.log10((x+1)/25)))
```

13. Next, select the learning rate, as follows:

```
def select_learning_rate(x):
    return max(min_learning_rate, min(0.5, 1.0 -
math.log10((x+1)/25)))
```

14. Next, `bucketize` the `state_value`, as follows:

```
def bucketize_state_value(state_value):
    bucket_indexes = []
    for i in range(len(state_value)):
        if state_value[i] <= state_value_bounds[i][0]:
            bucket_index = 0
        elif state_value[i] >= state_value_bounds[i][1]:
            bucket_index = no_buckets[i] - 1
        else:
            bound_width = state_value_bounds[i][1] -
state_value_bounds[i][0]
            offset =
(no_buckets[i]-1)*state_value_bounds[i][0]/bound_width
            scaling = (no_buckets[i]-1)/bound_width
            bucket_index = int(round(scaling*state_value[i] -
offset))
        bucket_indexes.append(bucket_index)
    return tuple(bucket_indexes)
```

15. Next, train the episodes, as follows:

```
for episode_no in range(max_episodes):
    explore_rate = select_explore_rate(episode_no)
    learning_rate = select_learning_rate(episode_no)

    observation = environment.reset()

    start_state_value = bucketize_state_value(observation)
    previous_state_value = start_state_value

    for time_step in range(max_time_steps):
        environment.render()
        selected_action = select_action(previous_state_value,
explore_rate)
        observation, reward_gain, completed, _ =
environment.step(selected_action)
        state_value = bucketize_state_value(observation)
        best_q_value = np.amax(q_value_table[state_value])
        q_value_table[previous_state_value + (selected_action,)] +=
learning_rate * (
                reward_gain + discount * (best_q_value) -
q_value_table[previous_state_value + (selected_action,)])
```

16. Next, print all of the relevant metrics for the training process, as follows:

```
print('Episode number : %d' % episode_no)
print('Time step : %d' % time_step)
print('Selection action : %d' % selected_action)
print('Current state : %s' % str(state_value))
print('Reward obtained : %f' % reward_gain)
print('Best Q value : %f' % best_q_value)
print('Learning rate : %f' % learning_rate)
print('Explore rate : %f' % explore_rate)
print('Streak number : %d' % no_streaks)

if completed:
    print('Episode %d finished after %f time steps' %
(episode_no, time_step))
    if time_step >= solved_time:
        no_streaks += 1
    else:
        no_streaks = 0
    break

previous_state_value = state_value

if no_streaks > streak_to_end:
    break
```

17. After training for a period of time, the CartPole will be able to balance itself, as shown in the following image:

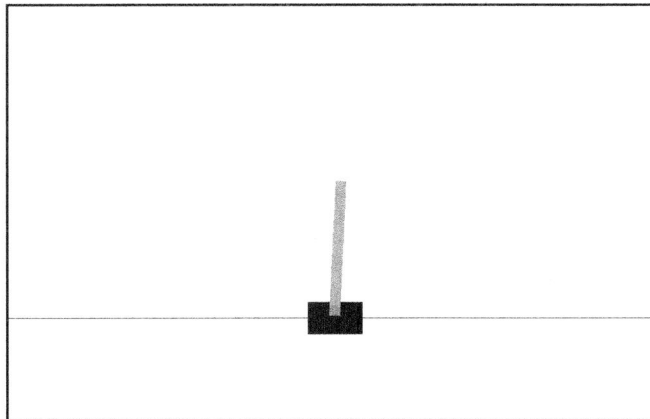

You have learned a program that will stabilize the CartPole.

Summary

In this chapter, you learned about the OpenAI Gym, used in reinforcement learning projects. You saw several examples of the training platform provided out of the box. Then, we formulated the problem of the CartPole, and made the CartPole balance by using a trial and error approach.

In the next chapter, you will learn how to play Atari games by using the Gym and a reinforcement learning approach.

3
Playing Atari Games

an a machine learn how to play video games by itself and beat human players? Solving this problem is the first step toward general **artificial intelligence (AI)** in the field of gaming. The key technique to creating an AI player is **deep reinforcement learning**. In 2015, Google's DeepMind, one of the foremost AI/machine learning research teams (who are famous for building AlphaGo, the machine that beat Go champion Lee Sedol) proposed the deep Q-learning algorithm to build an AI player that can learn to play Atari 2600 games, and surpass a human expert on several games. This work made a great impact on AI research, showing the possibility of building general AI systems.

In this chapter, we will introduce how to use gym to play Atari 2600 games, and then explain why the deep Q-learning algorithm works and how to implement it using TensorFlow. The goal is to be able to understand deep reinforcement learning algorithms and how to apply them to solve real tasks. This chapter will be a solid foundation to understanding later chapters, where we will be introducing more complex methods.

The topics that we will cover in this chapter are as follows:

- Introduction to Atari games
- Deep Q-learning
- Implementation of DQN

Introduction to Atari games

Atari, Inc. was an American video game developer and home computer company founded in 1972 by Nolan Bushnell and Ted Dabney. In 1976, Bushnell developed the Atari video computer system, or Atari VCS (later renamed Atari 2600). Atari VCS was a flexible console that was capable of playing the existing Atari games, which included a console, two joysticks, a pair of paddles, and the combat game cartridge. The following screenshot depicts an Atari console:

Atari 2600 has more than 500 games that were published by Atari, Sears, and some third parties. Some famous games are Breakout, Pac-Man, Pitfall!, Atlantis, Seaquest, and Space Invaders.

As a direct result of the North American video game crash of 1983, Atari, Inc. was closed and its properties were split in 1984. The home computing and game console divisions of Atari were sold to Jack Tramiel under the name Atari corporation in July 1984.

For readers who are interested in playing Atari games, here are several online Atari 2600 emulator websites where you can find many popular Atari 2600 games:

- http://www.2600online.com/

- http://www.free80sarcade.com/all2600games.php

- http://www.retrogames.cz/index.php

Because our goal is to develop an AI player for these games, it is better to play with them first and understand their difficulties. The most important thing is to: relax and have fun!

Building an Atari emulator

OpenAI gym provides an Atari 2600 game environment with a Python interface. The games are simulated by the arcade learning environment, which uses the Stella Atari emulator. For more details, read the following papers:

- MG Bellemare, Y Naddaf, J Veness, and M Bowling, *The arcade learning environment: An evaluation platform for general agents*, journal of Artificial Intelligence Research (2012)
- Stella: A Multi-Platform Atari 2600 VCS emulator, `http://stella.sourceforge.net/`

Getting started

If you don't have a full install of OpenAI `gym`, you can install the Atari environment dependencies via the following:

```
pip install gym[atari]
```

This requires the `cmake` tools. This command will automatically compile the arcade learning environment and its Python interface, `atari-py`. The compilation will take a few minutes on a common laptop, so go have a cup of coffee.

After the Atari environment is installed, try the following:

```
import gym
atari = gym.make('Breakout-v0')
atari.reset()
atari.render()
```

If it runs successfully, a small window will pop up, showing the screen of the game `Breakout`, as shown in the following screenshot:

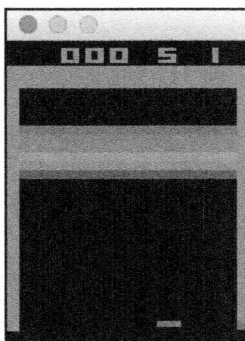

The meaning of the v0 suffix in the `Breakout` rom name will be explained later. We will use `Breakout` to test our algorithm for training an AI game player. In `Breakout`, several layers of bricks lie on the top of the screen. A ball travels across the screen, bouncing off the top and side walls of the screen. When a brick is hitted, the ball bounces away and the brick is destroyed, giving the player several points according to the color of the brick. The player loses a turn when the ball touches the bottom of the screen. In order to prevent this from happening, the player has to move the paddle to bounce the ball back.

Atari VCS uses a joystick as the input device for controlling Atari 2600 games. The total number of inputs that a joystick and a paddle can make is 18. In the `gym` Atari environment, these actions are labeled as the integers ranged from 0 to 17. The meaning of each action is as follows:

0	1	2	3	4	5
NO OPERATION	FIRE	UP	RIGHT	LEFT	DOWN
6	7	8	9	10	11
UP+RIGHT	UP+LEFT	DOWN+RIGHT	DOWN+LEFT	UP+FIRE	RIGHT+FIRE
12	13	14	15	16	17
LEFT+FIRE	DOWN+FIRE	UP+RIGHT+FIRE	UP+LEFT+FIRE	DOWN+RIGHT+FIRE	DOWN+LEFT+FIRE

One can use the following code to get the meanings of the valid actions for a game:

```
actions = atari.env.get_action_meanings()
```

For `Breakout`, the actions include the following:

```
[0, 1, 3, 4] or ['NOOP', 'FIRE', 'RIGHT', 'LEFT']
```

To get the number of the actions, one can also use the following:

```
num_actions = atari.env.action_space.n
```

Here, the member variable, `action_space`, in `atari.env` stores all the information about the valid actions for a game. Typically, we only need to know the total number of valid actions.

We now know how to access the action information in the Atari environment. But, how do you control the game given these actions? To take an action, one can call the `step` function:

```
observation, reward, done, info = atari.step(a)
```

The input argument, `a`, is the action you want to execute, which is the index in the valid action list. For example, if one wants to take the LEFT action, the input should be 3 not 4, or if one takes no action, the input should be 0. The `step` function returns one of the following four values:

- `Observation`: An environment-specific object representing your observation of the environment. For Atari, it is the screen image of the frame after the action is executed.
- `Reward`: The amount of reward achieved by the action.
- `Done`: Whether it's time to reset the environment again. In Atari, if you lost your last life, `done` will be true, otherwise it is false.
- `Info`: Diagnostic information useful for debugging. It is not allowed to use this information in the learning algorithm, so usually we can ignore it.

Implementation of the Atari emulator

We are now ready to build a simple Atari emulator using gym. As with other computer games, the keyboard input used to control Atari games is as shown here:

w	*a*	*s*	*d*	*space*
UP	LEFT	DOWN	RIGHT	FIRE

To detect the keyboard inputs, we use the `pynput.keyboard` package, which allows us to control and monitor the keyboard (`http://pythonhosted.org/pynput/`). If the `pynput` package is not installed, run the following:

```
pip install pynput
```

`pynput.keyboard` provides a keyboard listener used to capture keyboard events. Before creating a keyboard listener, the `Listener` class should be imported:

```
import gym
import queue, threading, time
from pynput.keyboard import Key, Listener
```

Besides the `Listener` class, the other packages, such as `gym` and `threading`, are also necessary in this program.

The following code shows how to use `Listener` to capture keyboard inputs, that is, where one of the *w*, *a*, *s*, *d*, and *space* keys is pressed:

```
def keyboard(queue):
    def on_press(key):
        if key == Key.esc:
            queue.put(-1)
        elif key == Key.space:
            queue.put(ord(' '))
        else:
            key = str(key).replace("'", '')
            if key in ['w', 'a', 's', 'd']:
                queue.put(ord(key))

    def on_release(key):
        if key == Key.esc:
            return False

    with Listener(on_press=on_press, on_release=on_release) as listener:
        listener.join()
```

Actually, a keyboard listener is a Python `threading.Thread` object, and all callbacks will be invoked from the thread. In the `keyboard` function, the listener registers two callbacks: `on_press` , which is invoked when a key is pressed and `on_release` invoked when a key is released. This function uses a synchronized queue to share data between different threads. When *w*, *a*, *s*, *d*, or *space* is pressed, its ASCII value is sent to the queue, which can be accessed from another thread. If *esc* is pressed, a termination signal, -, is sent to the queue. Then, the listener thread stops when *esc* is released.

Starting a keyboard listener has some restrictions on macOS X; that is, one of the following should be true:

- The process must run as root
- The application must be white-listed under enable access for assistive devices

For more information, visit `https://pythonhosted.org/pynput/keyboard.html`.

Atari simulator using gym

The other part of the emulator is the `gym` Atari simulator:

```
def start_game(queue):
    atari = gym.make('Breakout-v0')
    key_to_act = atari.env.get_keys_to_action()
    key_to_act = {k[0]: a for k, a in key_to_act.items() if len(k) > 0}
    observation = atari.reset()
    import numpy
    from PIL import Image
    img = numpy.dot(observation, [0.2126, 0.7152, 0.0722])
    img = cv2_resize_image(img)
    img = Image.fromarray(img)
    img.save('save/{}.jpg'.format(0))
    while True:
        atari.render()
        action = 0 if queue.empty() else queue.get(block=False)
        if action == -1:
            break
        action = key_to_act.get(action, 0)
        observation, reward, done, _ = atari.step(action)
        if action != 0:
            print("Action {}, reward {}".format(action, reward))
        if done:
            print("Game finished")
            break
        time.sleep(0.05)
```

The first step is to create an `Atari` environment using `gym.make`. If you are interested in playing other games such as Seaquest or Pitfall, just change Breakout-v0 to Seaquest-v0 or `Pitfall-v0`. Then, `get_keys_to_action` is called to get the `key to action` mapping, which maps the ASCII values of *w*, *a*, *s*, *d*, and *space* to internal actions. Before the Atari simulator starts, the `reset` function must be called to reset the game parameters and memory, returning the first game screen image. In the main loop, `render` is called to render the Atari game at each step. The input action is pulled from the queue without blocking. If the action is the termination signal, -1, the game quits. Otherwise, this action is taken at the current step by running `atari.step`.

To start the emulator, run the following code:

```
if __name__ == "__main__":
    queue = queue.Queue(maxsize=10)
    game = threading.Thread(target=start_game, args=(queue,))
    game.start()
    keyboard(queue)
```

Press the **fire** button to start the game and enjoy it! This emulator provides a basic framework for testing AI algorithms on the `gym` Atari environment. Later, we will replace the `keyboard` function with our AI player.

Data preparation

Careful readers may notice that a suffix, v0, follows each game name, and come up with the following questions: *What is the meaning of v0? Is it allowable to replace it with v1 or v2?* Actually, this suffix has a relationship with the data preprocessing step for the screen images (observations) extracted from the Atari environment.

There are three modes for each game, for example, Breakout, BreakoutDeterministic, and BreakoutNoFrameskip, and each mode has two versions, for example, Breakout-v0 and Breakout-v4. The main difference between the three modes is the value of the frameskip parameter in the Atari environment. This parameter indicates the number of frames (steps) the one action is repeated on. This is called the **frame-skipping** technique, which allows us to play more games without significantly increasing the runtime.

For Breakout, frameskip is randomly sampled from 2 to 5. The following screenshots show the frame images returned by the `step` function when the action LEFT is submitted:

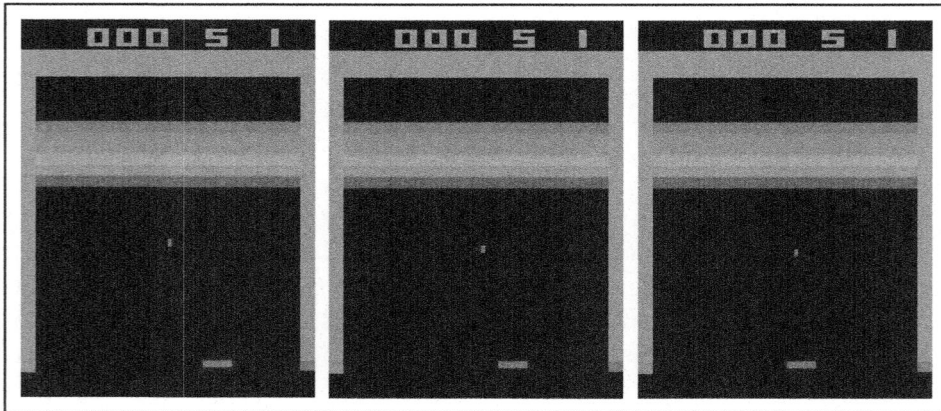

For BreakoutDeterministic, frameskip is set to 3 for the game Space Invaders, and 4 for the other games. With the same LEFT action, the `step` function returns the following:

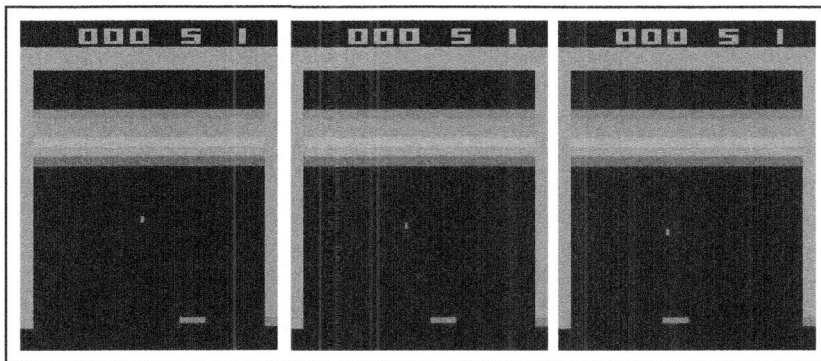

For BreakoutNoFrameskip, frameskip is always 1 for all of the games, meaning no frame-skipping. Similarly, the LEFT action is taken at each step:

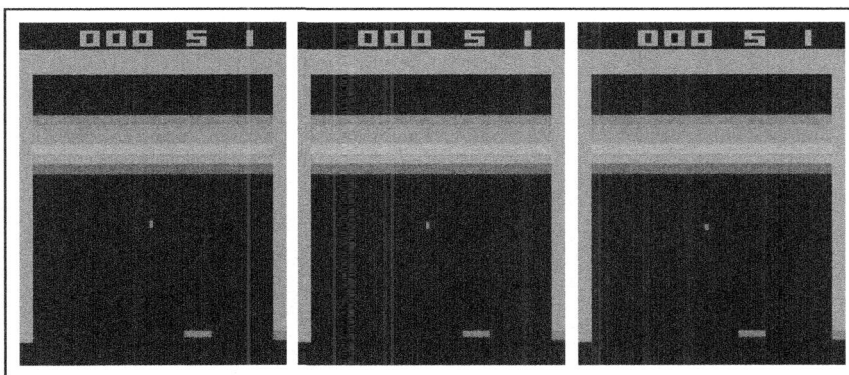

These screenshots demonstrate that although the step function is called four times with the same action, LEFT, the final positions of the paddle are quite different. Because frameskip is 4 for BreakoutDeterministic, its paddle is the closest one to the left wall. For BreakoutNoFrameskip, frameskip is set to 1 so that its paddle is farthest from the left wall. For Breakout, its paddle lies in the middle because of frameskip being sampled from [2, 5] at each step.

From this simple experiment, we can see the effect of the frameskip parameter. Its value is usually set to 4 for fast learning. Recall that there are two versions, v0 and v4, for each mode. Their main difference is the repeat_action_probability parameter. This parameter indicates the probability that a **no operation (NOOP)** action is taken, although another action is submitted. It is set to 0.25 for v0, and 0.0 for v4. Because we want a deterministic Atari environment, the v4 version is selected in this chapter.

If you have played some Atari games, you have probably noticed that the top region of the screen in a game usually contains the scoreboard, showing the current score you got and the number of lives you have. This information is not related to game playing, so that the top region can be cropped. Besides, the frame images returned by the step function are RGB images. Actually, in the Atari environment, colorful images do not provide more information than grayscale images; namely, one can play Atari games as usual with a gray screen. Therefore, it is necessary to keep only useful information by cropping frame images and converting them to grayscale.

Converting an RGB image into a grayscale image is quite easy. The value of each pixel in a grayscale image represents the light intensity, which can be calculated by this formula:

$$Y = 0.2126R + 0.7152G + 0.0722B$$

Here, R, G, and B are the red, green, and blue channels of the RGB image, respectively. Given a RGB image with shape (height, width, channel), the following Python code can be used to convert it into grayscale:

```python
def rgb_to_gray(self, im):
    return numpy.dot(im, [0.2126, 0.7152, 0.0722])
```

The following image gives an example:

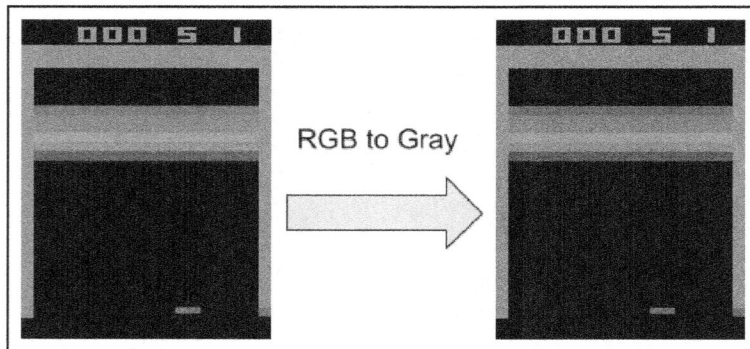

For cropping frame images, we use the `opencv-python` package or `cv2`, a Python wrapper around the original C++ OpenCV implementation. For more information, please visit the `opencv-python` website at `http://opencv-python-tutroals.readthedocs.io/en/latest/index.html`. The `opencv-python` package provides basic image transformation operations such as image scaling, translation, and rotation. In this chapter, we only need the image scaling function resize, which takes the input image, image size, and interpolation method as the input arguments, and returns the resized image.

The following code shows the image cropping operation, which involves two steps:

1. Reshaping the input image such that the width of the resulting image equals the resized width, `84`, indicated by the `resized_shape` parameter.
2. Cropping the top region of the reshaped image using `numpy` slicing:

```python
def cv2_resize_image(image, resized_shape=(84, 84),
                     method='crop', crop_offset=8):
    height, width = image.shape
    resized_height, resized_width = resized_shape
    if method == 'crop':
        h = int(round(float(height) * resized_width / width))
        resized = cv2.resize(image,
                             (resized_width, h),
                             interpolation=cv2.INTER_LINEAR)
        crop_y_cutoff = h - crop_offset - resized_height
        cropped =
resized[crop_y_cutoff:crop_y_cutoff+resized_height, :]
        return numpy.asarray(cropped, dtype=numpy.uint8)
    elif method == 'scale':
        return numpy.asarray(cv2.resize(image,
                                        (resized_width,
resized_height),
interpolation=cv2.INTER_LINEAR),
                                        dtype=numpy.uint8)
    else:
        raise ValueError('Unrecognized image resize method.')
```

For example, given a grayscale input image, the `cv2_resize_image` function returns a cropped image with size 84 × 84, as shown in the following screenshot:

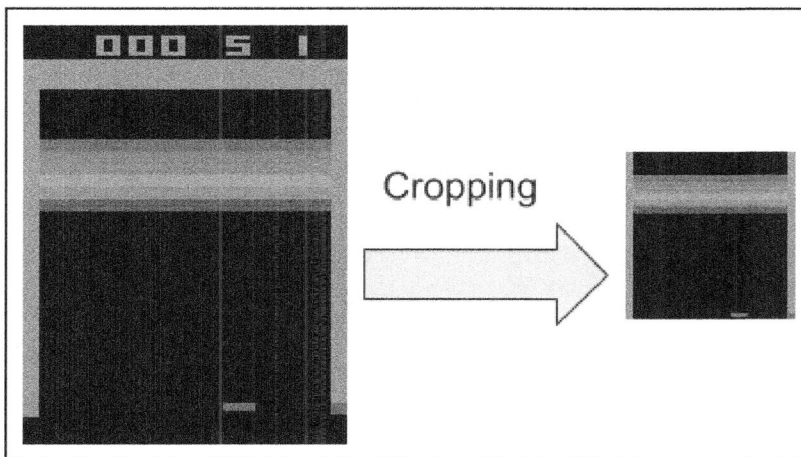

So far, we have finished the data preparation. The data is now ready to be used to train our AI player.

Deep Q-learning

Here comes the fun part—the brain design of our AI Atari player. The core algorithm is based on deep reinforcement learning or deep RL. In order to understand it better, some basic mathematical formulations are required. Deep RL is a perfect combination of deep learning and traditional reinforcement learning. Without understanding the basic concepts about reinforcement learning, it is difficult to apply deep RL correctly in real applications, for example, it is possible that someone may try to use deep RL without defining state space, reward, and transition properly.

Well, don't be afraid of the difficulty of the formulations. We only need high school-level mathematics, and will not go deep into the mathematical proofs of why traditional reinforcement learning algorithms work. The goal of this chapter is to learn the basic Q-learning algorithm, to know how to extend it into the **deep Q-learning algorithm (DQN)**, and to understand the intuition behind these algorithms. Besides, you will also learn what the advantages and disadvantages are of DQN, what exploration and exploitation are, why a replay memory is necessary, why a target network is needed, and how to design a convolutional neural network for state feature representation.

It looks quite interesting, doesn't it? We hope this chapter not only helps you to understand how to apply deep reinforcement learning to solve practical problems, but also opens a door for deep reinforcement learning research. For the readers who are familiar with convolutional neural networks, the Markov decision process, and Q-learning, skip the first section and go directly to the implementation of DQN.

Basic elements of reinforcement learning

First, let's us recall some basic elements of reinforcement learning that we discussed in the first chapter:

- **State**: The state space defines all the possible states of the environment. In Atari games, a state is a screen image or a set of several consecutive screen images observed by the player at a given time, indicating the game status of that moment.

- **Reward function**: A reward function defines the goal of a reinforcement learning problem. It maps a state or a state-action pair of the environment to a real number, indicating the desirability of that state. The reward is the score received after taking a certain action in Atari games.
- **Policy function**: A policy function defines the behavior of the player at a given time, which maps the states of the environment to actions to be taken in those states.
- **Value function**: A value function indicates which state or state-action pair is good in the long run The value of a state is the total (or discounted) amount of reward a player can expect to accumulate over the future, starting from that state.

Demonstrating basic Q-learning algorithm

To demonstrate the basic Q-learning algorithm, let's consider a simple problem. Imagine that our agent (player) lives in a grid world. One day, she was trapped in a weird maze, as shown in the following diagram:

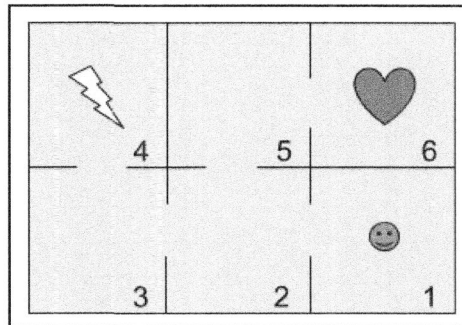

The maze contains six rooms. Our agent appears in Room 1, while she has no knowledge about the maze, that is, she doesn't know Room 6 has the sweetheart that is able to send her back home, or that Room 4 has a lightning bolt that strikes her. Therefore, she has to explore the maze carefully to escape as soon as possible. So, how do we make our lovely agent learn from experience?

Fortunately, her good friend Q-learning can help her survive. This problem can be represented as a state diagram, where each room is taken as a state and her movement from one room to another is considered as an action. The state diagram is as follows:

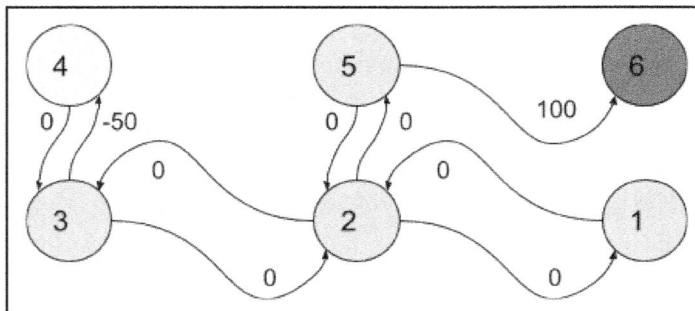

Here, an action is represented by an arrow and the number associated with an arrow is the reward of that state-action pair. For example, when our agent moves from Room 5 to Room 6, she gets 100 points because of achieving the goal. When she moves from Room 3 to Room 4, she get a negative reward because the lightning strike hurts her. This state diagram can also be represented by a matrix:

state\action	1	2	3	4	5	6
1	-	0	-	-	-	-
2	0	-	0	-	0	-
3	-	0	-	-50	-	-
4	-	-	0	-	-	-
5	-	0	-	-	-	100
6	-	-	-	-	-	-

The dash line in the matrix indicates that the action is not available in that state. For example, our agent cannot move from Room 1 to Room 6 directly because there is no door connecting them.

Let's s be a state, a be an action, $R(s, a)$ be the reward function, and $Q(s, a)$ be the value function. Recall that $Q(s, a)$ is the desirability of the state-action pair (s, a) in the long run, meaning that our agent is able to make decisions about which room she enters based on $Q(s, a)$. The Q-learning algorithm is very simple, which estimates $Q(s, a)$ for each state-action pair via the following update rule:

$$Q(s_t, a_t) = Q(s_t, a_t) + \alpha[R(s_t, a_t) + \gamma max_{a \in A(s_{t+1})} Q(s_{t+1}, a) - Q(s_t, a_t)],$$

Here, s_t is the current state, s_{t+1} is the next state after taking action a_t at s_t, $A(s_{t+1})$ is the set of the available actions at s_{t+1}, is the discount factor, and α is the learning rate. The discount factor γ lies in [0,1]. A discount factor smaller than 1 means that our agent prefers the current reward more than past rewards.

In the beginning, our agent knows nothing about the value function, so $Q(s, t)$ is initialized to 0 for all state-action pairs. She will explore from state to state until she reaches the goal. We call each exploration an episode, which consists of moving from the initial state (for example, Room 1) to the final state (for example, Room 6). The Q-learning algorithm is shown as follows:

```
Initialize Q to zero and set parameters α, γ;
Repeat for each episode:
    Randomly select an initial state s;
    While the goal state hasn't been reached:
        Select action a among all the possible actions in state s (e.g.,
using ϵ-greedy);
        Take action a and observe reward R(s,a), next state s';
        Update  Q(s,a) = Q(s,a) + α[R(s,a) + γmax_{a∈A(s')}Q(s',a) − Q(s,a)];
        Set the current state s = s';
    End while
```

A careful reader may ask a question about how to select action a in state s, for example, is action a randomly selected among all the possible actions or chosen using the policy derived from the current estimated value function, Q? What is ϵ-greedy? These questions are related to two important concepts, namely, exploration and exploitation. Exploration means trying something new to gather more information about the environment, while exploitation means making the best decision based on all the information you have. For example, trying a new restaurant is exploration and going to your favorite restaurant is exploitation. In our maze problem, the exploration is that our agent tries to enter a new room she hasn't visited before, while the exploitation is that she chooses her favorite room based on the information she gathered from the environment.

Both exploration and exploitation are necessary in reinforcement learning. Without exploration, our agent is not able to get new knowledge about the environment, so she will make bad decisions again and again. Without exploitation, the information she got from exploration becomes meaningless since she doesn't learn from it to better make a decision. Therefore, a balance or a trade-off between exploration and exploitation is indispensable. $\epsilon-$greedy is the simplest way to make such a trade-off:

With probability	Randomly select an action among all the possible actions
With probability $1 - \epsilon$	Select the best action based on Q, that is, pick so that $Q(s, a)$ is the largest among all the possible actions in state s

To further understand how Q-learning works, let's go through several steps by hand. For clarity, let's set the learning rate $\alpha = 1$ and discount factor $\gamma = 0.8$. The following code shows the implementation of Q-learning in Python:

```python
import random, numpy

def Q_learning_demo():
    alpha = 1.0
    gamma = 0.8
    epsilon = 0.2
    num_episodes = 100
    R = numpy.array([
        [-1,  0, -1, -1, -1, -1],
        [ 0, -1,  0, -1,  0, -1],
        [-1,  0, -1, -50, -1, -1],
        [-1, -1,  0, -1, -1, -1],
        [-1,  0, -1, -1, -1, 100],
        [-1, -1, -1, -1, -1, -1]
        ])
    # Initialize Q
    Q = numpy.zeros((6, 6))
    # Run for each episode
    for _ in range(num_episodes):
        # Randomly choose an initial state
        s = numpy.random.choice(5)
        while s != 5:
            # Get all the possible actions
            actions = [a for a in range(6) if R[s][a] != -1]
            # Epsilon-greedy
            if numpy.random.binomial(1, epsilon) == 1:
                a = random.choice(actions)
            else:
                a = actions[numpy.argmax(Q[s][actions])]
            next_state = a
            # Update Q(s,a)
```

```
            Q[s][a] += alpha * (R[s][a] + gamma * numpy.max(Q[next_state])
    - Q[s][a])
            # Go to the next state
            s = next_state
    return Q
```

After running for 100 episodes, the value function, Q, converges to the following(for the readers who are curious about why this algorithm converges, refer to *Reinforcement Learning: An Introduction* by Andrew Barto and Richard S. Sutton):

state\action	1	2	3	4	5	6
1	-	64	-	-	-	-
2	51.2	-	51.2	-	80	-
3	-	64	-	-9.04	-	-
4	-	-	51.2	-	-	-
5	-	64	-	-	-	100
6	-	-	-	-	-	-

Therefore, the resulting state diagram becomes this:

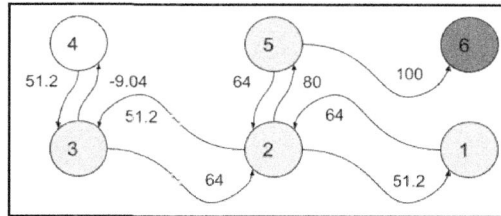

This indicates the following optimal paths to the goal state for all the other states:

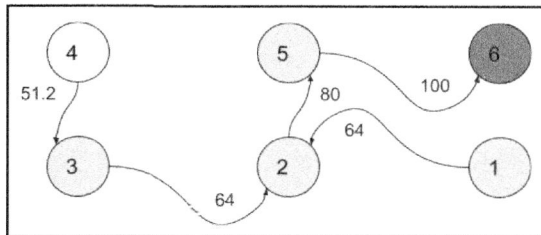

Based on this knowledge, our agent is able to go back home no matter which room she is in. More importantly, she becomes smarter and happier, achieving our goal to train a smart AI agent or player.

This simplest Q-learning algorithm can only handle discrete states and actions. For continuous states, it fails because the convergence is not guaranteed due to the existence of infinite states. How can we apply Q-learning in an infinite state space such as Atari games? The answer is replacing the tableau with neural networks to approximate the action-value function $Q(s, a)$. This is the intuition behind the *Playing Atari with deep reinforcement learning*, by Google DeepMind paper.

To extend the basic Q-learning algorithm into the deep Q-learning algorithm, there are two key questions that need to be answered:

1. What kind of neural networks can be used to extract high-level features from observed data such as screen images in the Atari environment?
2. How can we update the action-value function, $Q(s, a)$, at each training step?

For the first question, there are several possible ways of approximating the action-value function, $Q(s, a)$. One approach is that both the state and the action are used as the inputs to the neural network, which outputs the scalar estimates of their Q-value, as shown in the following diagram:

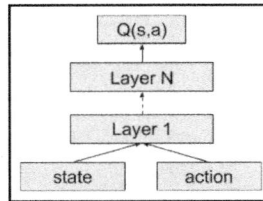

The main disadvantage of this approach is that an additional forward pass is required to compute $Q(s, a)$ as the action is taken as one of the inputs to the network, resulting in a cost that scales linearly with the number of all the possible actions. Another approach is that the state is the only input to the neural network, while there is a separate output for each possible action:

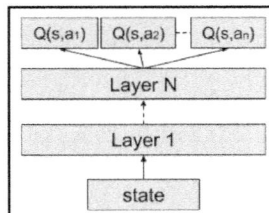

The main advantage of this approach is the ability to compute Q-values for all possible actions in a given state with only a single forward pass through the network, and the simplicity to access the Q-value for an action by picking the corresponding output head.

In the deep Q-network, the second architecture is applied. Recall that the output in the data preprocessing step is an 84×84 grayscale frame image. However, the current screen is not enough for playing Atari games because it doesn't contain the dynamic information about game status. Take Breakout as an example; if we only see one frame, we can only know the locations of the ball and the paddle, but we cannot know the direction or the velocity of the ball. Actually, the direction and the velocity are quite important for making decisions about how to move the paddle. Without them, the game is unplayable. Therefore, instead of taking only one frame image as the input, the last four frame images of a history are stacked together to produce the input to the neural network. These four frames form an $84 \times 84 \times 4$ image. Besides the input layer, the Q-network contains three convolutional layers and one fully connected layer, which is shown as follows:

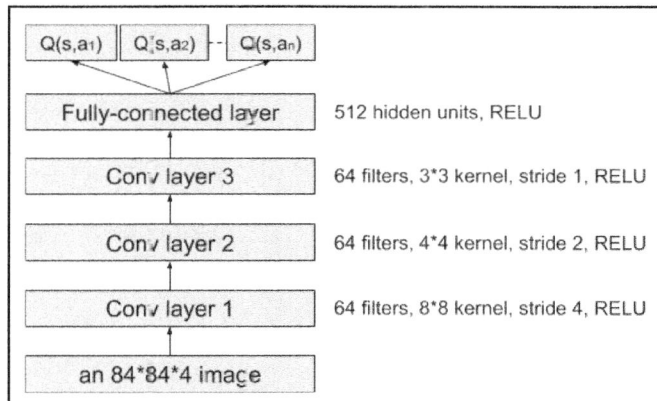

The first convolutional layer has 64 8×8 filters with stride 4, followed by a **rectifier nonlinearity (RELU)**. The second convolutional layer has 64 4×4 filters with stride 2, followed by RELU. The third convolutional layer has 64 3×3 filters with stride 2, followed by RELU. The fully connected hidden layer has 512 hidden units, again followed by RELU. The output layer is also a fully connected layer with a single output for each action.

Readers who are familiar with convolutional neural networks may ask why the first convolutional layer uses a 8×8 filter, instead of a 3×3 filter or a 5×5 filter that is widely applied in computer vision applications. The main reason of using a big filter is that Atari games usually contain very small objects such as a ball, a bullet, or a pellet. A convolutional layer with larger filters is able to zoom in on these small objects, providing benefits for learning feature representations of states. For the second and third convolutional layers, a relatively small filter is enough to capture useful features.

So far, we have discussed the architecture of the Q-network. But, how do we train this Q-network in the Atari environment with an infinite state space? Is it possible to develop an algorithm based on the basic Q-learning to train it? Fortunately, the answer is YES. Recall that the update rule for $Q(s,a)$ in basic Q-learning is as follows:

$$Q(s,a) = Q(s,a) + \alpha[R(s,a) + \gamma max_{a \in A(s')} Q(s',a) - Q(s,a)].$$

When the learning rate $\alpha = 1$, this update rule becomes as follows:

$$Q(s,a) = R(s,a) + \gamma max_{a \in A(s')} Q(s',a),$$

This is called the **Bellman equation**. Actually, the Bellman equation is the backbone of many reinforcement learning algorithms. The algorithms using the Bellman equation as an iterative update are called value iteration algorithms. In this book, we will not go into detail about value iteration or policy iteration. If you are interested in them, refer to *Reinforcement Learning: An Introduction*, by Andrew Barto and Richard S. Sutton.

The equation just shown is only suitable for a deterministic environment where the next state s' is fixed given the current state s and the action a. In a nondeterministic environment, the Bellman equation should be as follows:

$$Q(s,a) = E_{s' \sim S}[R(s,a) + \gamma max_{a \in A(s')} Q(s',a)|s,a],$$

Here, the right-hand side takes the expectation of $R(s,a) + \gamma max_{a \in A(s')} Q(s',a)$ with respect to the next state s' (for example, the distribution of s' is determined by the Atari emulator). For an infinite state space, it is common to use a function approximator such as the Q-network to estimate the action-value function $Q(s,a)$. Then, instead of iteratively updating $Q(s,a)$, the Q-network can be trained by minimizing the following loss function at the ith iteration:

$$L_i(\theta_i) = E_{s,a \sim P(s,a)}[y_i - Q(s,a;\theta_i)^2],$$

Here, $Q(s,a;)$ represents the Q-network parameterized by, $y_i = E_{s' \sim S}[R(s,a) + \gamma max_{a \in A(s')} Q(s',a; \theta_{i-1}) | s,a]$ is the target for the ith iteration, and $P(s,a)$ is a probability distribution over sequences and actions. The parameters from the previous iteration *i-1* are fixed when optimizing the loss function $L_i(\theta_i)$ over θ_i. In practice, it is impossible to exactly calculate the expectations in $L_i(\theta_i)$. Instead of optimizing $L_i(\theta_i)$ directly, we minimize the empirical loss of $L_i(\theta_i)$, which replaces the expectations by samples $\{(s,a,s'), \cdots\}$ from the probability distribution $P(s,a)$ and the Atari emulator. As with other deep learning algorithms. the empirical loss function can be optimized by stochastic gradient descent.

This algorithm doesn't need to construct an estimate of the emulator, for example, it doesn't need to know the internal game mechanism about the Atari emulator, because it only uses samples from the emulator to solve the reinforcement learning problem. This property is called **model-free**, namely, it can treat the underlying model as a black box. Another property of this algorithm is off-policy. It learns about the greedy policy $a = \arg\max_a Q(s,a; \theta)$ while following the probability distribution $P(s,a)$ that balances exploration and exploitation of the state space. As discussed previously, $P(s,a)$ can be selected as an $\epsilon-$greedy strategy.

The derivation of the deep Q-learning algorithm may be a little bit difficult for readers who are not familiar with reinforcement learning or the Markov decision process. In order to make it more understandable, let's see the following diagram:

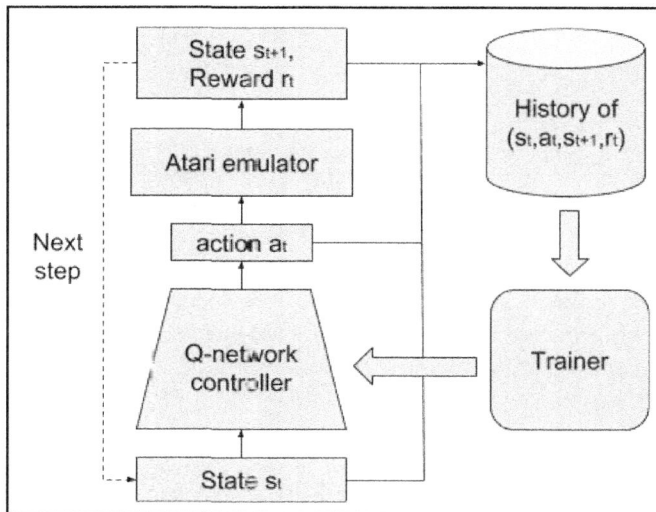

The brain of our AI player is the Q-network controller. At each time step t, she observes the screen image s_t (recall that st is an $84 \times 84 \times 4$ image that stacks the last four frames). Then, her brain analyzes this observation and comes up with an action, a_t. The Atari emulator receives this action and returns the next screen image, s_{t+1}, and the reward, r_t. The quadruplet (s_t, a_t, r_t, s_{t+1}) is stored in the memory and is taken as a sample for training the Q-network by minimizing the empirical loss function via stochastic gradient descent.

How do we draw samples from the quadruplets stored in the memory? One approach is that these samples, $\{(s_t, a_t, r_t, s_{t+1}), \cdots\}$, are drawn from our AI player's interactions with the environment, for example, samples

$\{(s_t, a_t, r_t, s_{t+1}), (s_{t+1}, a_{t+1}, r_{t+1}, s_{t+2}), \cdots, (s_{t+n}, a_{t+n}, r_{t+n}, s_{t+n+1})\}$ are used to train the Q-network. The main drawback of this approach is that the samples in one batch are strongly correlated. The strong correlation breaks the assumption that the samples for constructing the empirical loss function are independent, making the training procedure unstable and leading to bad performance:

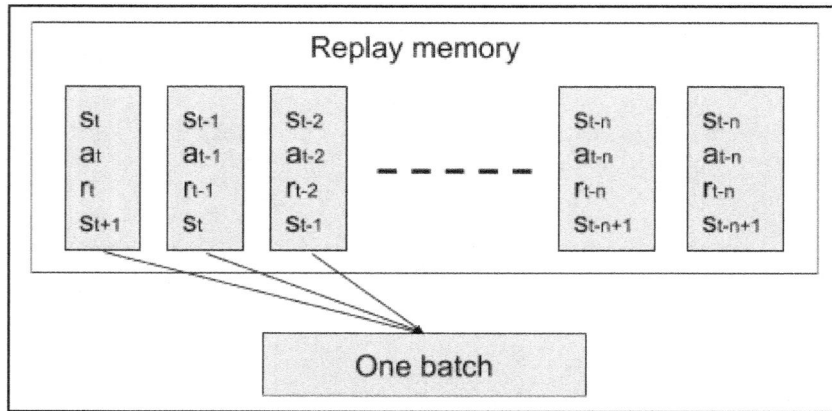

The deep Q-learning algorithm applies another approach, utilizing a technique known as experience replay. The AI player's experiences at each time step (s_t, a_t, r_t, s_{t+1}) are stored into the replay memory from which a batch of samples are randomly drawn in order to train the Q-network. Mathematically, we cannot guarantee the independence between the samples we drew. But practically, this approach can stabilize the training procedure and generate reasonable results:

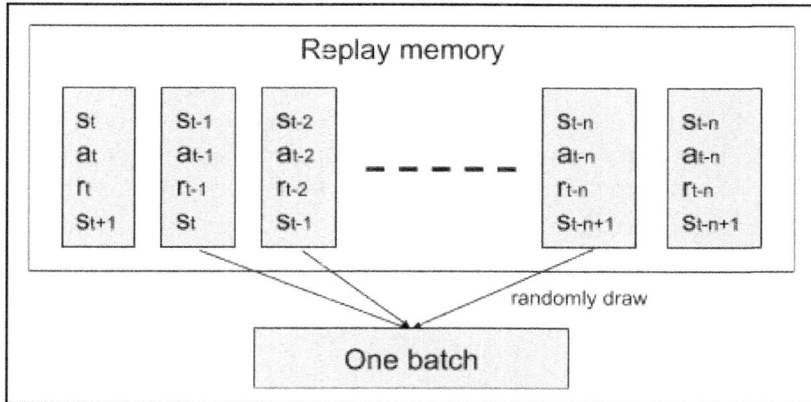

So far, we have discussed all the components in the deep Q-learning algorithm. The full algorithm is shown as follows:

```
Initialize replay memory R to capacity N;
Initialize the Q-network Q(s,a;θ) with random weights θ;
Repeat for each episode:
    Set time step t = 1;
    Receive an initial screen image x₁ and do preprocessing s₁ = f(x₁);
    While the terminal state hasn't been reached:
        Select an action at via ε-greedy, i.e., select a random action with
```
probability , otherwise select $a_t = \arg\max_a Q(s_t, a; \theta)$;
```
        Execute action at in the emulator and observe reward rt and image
```
x_{t+1} ;
```
        Set sₜ₊₁ = f(xₜ₊₁, sₜ) and store transition (sₜ, aₜ, rₜ, sₜ₊₁) into replay
```
memory R;
```
        Randomly sample a batch of transitions (sᵢ, aᵢ, rᵢ, sᵢ₊₁) from R;
        Set yᵢ = rᵢ if sᵢ₊₁ is a terminal state or
```
$y_i = r_i + \gamma \max_a Q(s_{i+1}, a; \theta)$ if s_{i+1} is a
```
non-terminal state;
        Perform a gradient descent step on
```
$\sum_i (y_i - Q(s_i, a_i; \theta))^2$;
```
    End while
```

This algorithm works well for some Atari games, for example, Breakout, Seaquest, Pong, and Qbert, but it still cannot reach human-level control. One drawback is that computing the targets y_i uses the current estimate of the action-value function Q, which makes the training step unstable, that is, an update that increases $Q(s_t, a)$ usually also increases $Q(s_{t+1}, a)$ for all and hence also increases the target y_i, possibly leading to oscillations or divergence of the policy.

To address this problem, Google DeepMind introduced the target network in their paper, *Human-level control through deep reinforcement learning*, which was published in Nature. The idea behind the target network is quite simple: a separate network is used for generating the targets y_i in the Q-learning update. More precisely, for every M Q-learning updates, the network Q is cloned to obtain a target network Q, which is used for generating the targets y_i in the following M updates to Q. Therefore, the deep Q-learning algorithm becomes as follows:

```
Initialize replay memory R to capacity N;
Initialize the Q-network Q(s,a;θ) with random weights θ;
Initialize the target network Q̂(s,a;θ̂) with weights θ̂ = θ;
Repeat for each episode:

Set time step t = 1;
    Receive an initial screen image x₁ and do preprocessing s₁ = f(x₁);
    While the terminal state hasn't been reached:
        Select an action at via ε−greedy, i.e., select a random action with
                                aₜ = arg max Q(sₜ, a; θ)
probability , otherwise select           a              ;
        Execute action at in the emulator and observe reward rₜ and image
xₜ₊₁;
        Set sₜ₊₁ = f(xₜ₊₁, sₜ) and store transition (sₜ, aₜ, rₜ, sₜ₊₁) into replay memory
R;
        Randomly sample a batch of transitions (sᵢ, aᵢ, rᵢ, sᵢ₊₁) from R;
        Set yᵢ = rᵢ if sᵢ₊₁ is a terminal state or yᵢ = rᵢ + γ max Q̂(sᵢ₊₁,a;θ̂) if sᵢ₊₁ is a
                                                             a
non-terminal state;
        Perform a gradient descent step on Σᵢ(yᵢ − Q(sᵢ,aᵢ;θ))² ;

        Set Q̂ = Q for every M steps;
    End while
```

With the target network, the AI player trained by the deep Q-learning algorithm is able to surpass the performance of most previous reinforcement learning algorithms and achieves a human-level performance across a set of 49 Atari 2600 games, for example, Star Gunner, Atlantis, Assault, and Space Invaders.

The deep Q-learning algorithm has made an important step toward general artificial intelligence. Although it performs well in the Atari 2600 games, it still has a lot of unsolved issues:

- **Slow convergence**: It requires a long time (7 days on one GPU) to reach human-level performance
- **Failing with sparse rewards**: It doesn't work for the game Montezuma's Revenge, which requires long-term planning
- **Need for a large amount of data**: This is a common issue among most reinforcement learning algorithms

In order to solve these issues, different variants of the deep Q-learning algorithm have been proposed recently, for example, double Q-learning, prioritized experience replay, bootstrapped DQN, and dueling network architectures. We will not discuss these algorithms in this book. For readers who want to learn more about DQN, please refer to the related papers.

Implementation of DQN

This chapter will show you how to implement all the components, for example, Q-network, replay memory, trainer, and Q-learning optimizer, of the deep Q-learning algorithm with Python and TensorFlow.

We will implement the QNetwork class for the Q-network that we discussed in the previous chapter, which is defined as follows:

```
class QNetwork:
    def __init__(self, input_shape=(84, 84, 4), n_outputs=4,
                 network_type='cnn', scope='q_network'):
        self.width = input_shape[0]
        self.height = input_shape[1]
        self.channel = input_shape[2]
        self.n_outputs = n_outputs
        self.network_type = network_type
        self.scope = scope
        # Frame images
        self.x = tf.placeholder(dtype=tf.float32,
                                shape=(None, self.channel,
                                       self.width, self.height))
        # Estimates of Q-value
        self.y = tf.placeholder(dtype=tf.float32, shape=(None,))
        # Selected actions
        self.a = tf.placeholder(dtype=tf.int32, shape=(None,))
```

```
with tf.variable_scope(scope):
    self.build()
    self.build_loss()
```

The constructor requires four arguments, `input_shape`, `n_outputs`, `network_type` and `scope`. `input_shape` is the size of the input image. After data preprocessing, the input is an $84 \times 84 \times 4$ image, so that the default parameter is $(84, 84, 4)$. `n_outputs` is the number of all the possible actions, for example, `n_outputs` is four in Breakout. `network_type`, indicates the type of the Q-network we want to use. Our implementation contains three different networks. Two of them are the convolutional neural networks proposed by Google DeepMind. The other one is a feed-forward neural network used for testing. `scope` is the name of the Q-network object, which can be set to `q_network` or `target_network`.

In the constructor, three input tensors are created. The `x` variable represents the input state (a batch of $84 \times 84 \times 4$ images). The `y` and `a` variables are the estimates of the action-value function and the selected actions corresponding to the input state, which are used for training the Q-network. After creating the input tensors, two functions, `build` and `build_loss`, are called to build the Q-network.

Constructing the Q-network using TensorFlow is quite easy, as shown here:

```
def build(self):
    self.net = {}
    self.net['input'] = tf.transpose(self.x, perm=(0, 2, 3, 1))
    init_b = tf.constant_initializer(0.01)
    if self.network_type == 'cnn':
        self.net['conv1'] = conv2d(self.net['input'], 32,
                                   kernel=(8, 8), stride=(4, 4),
                                   init_b=init_b, name='conv1')
        self.net['conv2'] = conv2d(self.net['input'], 64,
                                   kernel=(4, 4), stride=(2, 2),
                                   init_b=init_b, name='conv2')
        self.net['conv3'] = conv2d(self.net['input'], 64,
                                   kernel=(3, 3), stride=(1, 1),
                                   init_b=init_b, name='conv3')
        self.net['feature'] = dense(self.net['conv2'], 512,
                                    init_b=init_b, name='fc1')
    elif self.network_type == 'cnn_nips':
        self.net['conv1'] = conv2d(self.net['input'], 16,
                                   kernel=(8, 8), stride=(4, 4),
                                   init_b=init_b, name='conv1')
        self.net['conv2'] = conv2d(self.net['conv1'], 32,
                                   kernel=(4, 4), stride=(2, 2),
                                   init_b=init_b, name='conv2')
```

```
        self.net['feature'] = dense(self.net['conv2'], 256,
                            init_b=init_b, name='fc1')
    elif self.network_type == 'mlp':
        self.net['fc1'] = dense(self.net['input'], 50,
                            init_b=init_b), name='fc1')
        self.net['feature'] = dense(self.net['fc1'], 50,
                            init_b=init_b, name='fc2')
    else:
        raise NotImplementedError('Unknown network type')
    self.net['values'] = dense(self.net['feature'],
                            self.n_outputs, activation=None,
                            init_b=init_b, name='values')
    self.net['q_value'] = tf.reduce_max(self.net['values'],
                                axis=1, name='q_value')
    self.net['q_action'] = tf.argmax(self.net['values'],
                            axis=1, name='q_action',
                            output_type=tf.int32)
    self.vars = tf.get_collection(tf.GraphKeys.TRAINABLE_VARIABLES,
                            tf.get_variable_scope().name)
```

As discussed in the previous chapter, the Q-network for the Atari environment contains three convolutional layers and one hidden layer, which can be constructed when the network_type is cnn. The cnn_nips type is a simplified Q-network for Atari games, which only contains two convolutional layers and one hidden layer with less filters and hidden units. The mlp type is a feed-forward neural network with two hidden layers, which is used for debugging. The vars variable is the list of all the trainable variables in the Q-network.

Recall that the loss function is $\sum_i (y_i - Q(s_i, a_i; \theta))^2$, which can be implemented as follows:

```
def build_loss(self):
    indices = tf.transpose(tf.stack([tf.range(tf.shape(self.a)[0]),
                                self.a], axis=0))
    value = tf.gather_nd(self.net['values'], indices)
    self.loss = 0.5 * tf.reduce_mean(tf.square((value - self.y)))
    self.gradient = tf.gradients(self.loss, self.vars)
    tf.summary.scalar("loss", self.loss, collections=['q_network'])
    self.summary_op = tf.summary.merge_all('q_network')
```

The tf.gather_nd function is used to get the action-value $Q(s_i, a_i; \theta)$ given a batch of action,s ai. The variable loss represents the loss function, and gradient is the gradient of the loss function with respect to the trainable variables. summary_op is for TensorBoard visualization.

The implementation of the replay memory doesn't involve TensorFlow:

```
class ReplayMemory:
    def __init__(self, history_len=4, capacity=1000000,
                 batch_size=32, input_scale=255.0):
        self.capacity = capacity
        self.history_length = history_len
        self.batch_size = batch_size
        self.input_scale = input_scale
        self.frames = deque([])
        self.others = deque([])
```

The `ReplayMemory` class takes four input parameters, that is, `history_len`, `capacity`, `batch_size`, and `input_scale`. `history_len` is the number of frames stacked together. Typically, `history_len` is set to 4 for Atari games, forming an $84 \times 84 \times 4$ input image. `capacity` is the capacity of the replay memory, namely, the maximum number of frames that can be stored in it. `batch_size` is the size of one batch for training. `input_scale` is the normalization factor for input images, for example, it is set to 255 for RGB images. The variable frames record all the frame images and the variable others record the corresponding actions, rewards, and termination signals.

`ReplayMemory` provides a function for adding a record (frame image, action, reward, termination signal) into the memory:

```
def add(self, frame, action, r, termination):
    if len(self.frames) == self.capacity:
        self.frames.popleft()
        self.others.popleft()
    self.frames.append(frame)
    self.others.append((action, r, termination))
def add_nullops(self, init_frame):
    for _ in range(self.history_length):
        self.add(init_frame, 0, 0, 0)
```

It also provides a function for constructing an $84 \times 84 \times 4$ input image by concatenating the last four frame images of a history:

```
def phi(self, new_frame):
    assert len(self.frames) > self.history_length
    images = [new_frame] + [self.frames[-1-i] for i in
range(self.history_length-1)]
    return numpy.concatenate(images, axis=0)
```

The following function randomly draws a transition (state, action, reward, next state, termination signal) from the replay memory:

```
def sample(self):
    while True:
        index = random.randint(a=self.history_length-1,
                                b=len(self.frames)-2)
        infos = [self.others[index-i] for i in
range(self.history_length)]
        # Check if termination=1 before "index"
        flag = False
        for i in range(1, self.history_length):
            if infos[i][2] == 1:
                flag = True
                break
        if flag:
            continue
        state = self._phi(index)
        new_state = self._phi(index+1)
        action, r, termination = self.others[index]
        state = numpy.asarray(state / self.input_scale,
                              dtype=numpy.float32)
        new_state = numpy.asarray(new_state / self.input_scale,
                                  dtype=numpy.float32)
        return (state, action, r, new_state, termination)
```

Note that only the termination signal corresponding to the last frame in a state is allowed to be True. The _phi(index) function stacks the four frames together:

```
def _phi(self, index):
    images = [self.frames[index-i] for i in range(self.history_length)]
    return numpy.concatenate(images, axis=0)
```

The Optimizer class is used for training the Q-network:

```
class Optimizer:
    def __init__(self, config, feedback_size,
                 q_network, target_network, replay_memory):
        self.feedback_size = feedback_size
        self.q_network = q_network
        self.target_network = target_network
        self.replay_memory = replay_memory
        self.summary_writer = None
        self.gamma = config['gamma']
        self.num_frames = config['num_frames']
        optimizer = create_optimizer(config['optimizer'],
                                     config['learning_rate'],
                                     config['rho'],
```

```
                                        config['rmsprop_epsilon'])
        self.train_op = optimizer.apply_gradients(
                zip(self.q_network.gradient,
                self.q_network.vars))
```

It takes the Q-network, the target network, the replay memory, and the size of input images as the input arguments. In the constructor, it creates an optimizer (one of the popular optimizers such as ADAM, RMSPROP, or MOMENTUM) and then builds an operator for training.

To train the Q-network, it needs to construct a mini-batch of samples (states, actions, targets) corresponding to s_i, a_i, and y_i in the loss function $\sum_i (y_i - Q(s_i, a_i; \theta))^2$:

```
    def sample_transitions(self, sess, batch_size):
        w, h = self.feedback_size
        states = numpy.zeros((batch_size, self.num_frames, w, h),
                        dtype=numpy.float32)
        new_states = numpy.zeros((batch_size, self.num_frames, w, h),
                        dtype=numpy.float32)
        targets = numpy.zeros(batch_size, dtype=numpy.float32)
        actions = numpy.zeros(batch_size, dtype=numpy.int32)
        terminations = numpy.zeros(batch_size, dtype=numpy.int32)
        for i in range(batch_size):
            state, action, r, new_state, t = self.replay_memory.sample()
            states[i] = state
            new_states[i] = new_state
            actions[i] = action
            targets[i] = r
            terminations[i] = t

        targets += self.gamma * (1 - terminations) *
    self.target_network.get_q_value(sess, new_states)
        return states, actions, targets
```

Note that the targets y_i are computed by the target network instead of the Q-network. Given a mini-batch of states, actions, or targets, the Q-network can be easily trained by use of the following:

```
    def train_one_step(self, sess, step, batch_size):
        states, actions, targets = self.sample_transitions(sess,
    batch_size)
        feed_dict = self.q_network.get_feed_dict(states, actions, targets)
        if self.summary_writer and step % 1000 == 0:
            summary_str, _, = sess.run([self.q_network.summary_op,
                                    self.train_op],
                                feed_dict=feed_dict)
        self.summary_writer.add_summary(summary_str, step)
```

```
            self.summary_writer.flush()
        else:
            sess.run(self.train_op, feed_dict=feed_dict)
```

Besides the training procedure, for each 1000 steps, the summary is written to the log file. This summary is for monitoring the training process, helping to tune the parameters, and debugging.

Combining these modules together, we can implement the class DQN for the main deep Q-learning algorithm:

```
class DQN:
    def __init__(self, config, game, directory,
                    callback=None, summary_writer=None):
        self.game = game
        self.actions = game.get_available_actions()
        self.feedback_size = game.get_feedback_size()
        self.callback = callback
        self.summary_writer = summary_writer
        self.config = config
        self.batch_size = config['batch_size']
        self.n_episode = config['num_episode']
        self.capacity = config['capacity']
        self.epsilon_decay = config['epsilon_decay']
        self.epsilon_min = config['epsilon_min']
        self.num_frames = config['num_frames']
        self.num_nullops = config['num_nullops']
        self.time_between_two_copies = config['time_between_two_copies']
        self.input_scale = config['input_scale']
        self.update_interval = config['update_interval']
        self.directory = directory

        self._init_modules()
```

Here, `config` includes all the parameters of DQN, for example, batch size and learning rate for training. `game` is an instance of the Atari environment. In the constructor, the replay memory, Q-network, target network, and optimizer are initialized. To begin the training process, the following function can be called:

```
    def train(self, sess, saver=None):
        num_of_trials = -1
        for episode in range(self.n_episode):
            self.game.reset()
            frame = self.game.get_current_feedback()
            for _ in range(self.num_nullops):
                r, new_frame, termination = self.play(action=0)
                self.replay_memory.add(frame, 0, r, termination)
```

```
                        frame = new_frame
            for _ in range(self.config['T']):
                num_of_trials += 1
                epsilon_greedy = self.epsilon_min + \
                    max(self.epsilon_decay - num_of_trials, 0) / \
                    self.epsilon_decay * (1 - self.epsilon_min)

                if num_of_trials % self.update_interval == 0:
                    self.optimizer.train_one_step(sess,
                                                  num_of_trials,
                                                  self.batch_size)
                state = self.replay_memory.phi(frame)
                action = self.choose_action(sess, state, epsilon_greedy)
                r, new_frame, termination = self.play(action)
                self.replay_memory.add(frame, action, r, termination)
                frame = new_frame
                if num_of_trials % self.time_between_two_copies == 0:
                    self.update_target_network(sess)
                    self.save(sess, saver)
                if self.callback:
                    self.callback()
                if termination:
                    score = self.game.get_total_reward()
                    summary_str = sess.run(self.summary_op,
                                           feed_dict={self.t_score: score})
                    self.summary_writer.add_summary(summary_str,
                                                    num_of_trials)
                    self.summary_writer.flush()
                    break
```

This function is easy to understand. In each episode, it calls `replay_memory.phi` to get the current state and calls the `choose_action` function to select an action via the ϵ-greedy policy. This action is submitted into the Atari emulator by calling the `play` function, which returns the corresponding reward, next frame image, and termination signal. Then, the transition (current frame image, action, reward, termination) is stored in the replay memory. For every `update_interval` step (`update_interval` = 1 by default), the Q-network is trained with a batch of transitions randomly sampled from the replay memory. For every `time_between_two_copies` step, the target network copies the Q-network, and the weights of the Q-network are saved to the hard disk.

After the training step, the following function can be called for evaluating the AI player's performance:

```
        def evaluate(self, sess):
            for episode in range(self.n_episode):
                self.game.reset()
```

```
frame = self.game.get_current_feedback()
for _ in range(self.num_nullops):
    r, new_frame, termination = self.play(action=0)
    self.replay_memory.add(frame, 0, r, termination)
    frame = new_frame
for _ in range(self.config['T']):
    state = self.replay_memory.phi(frame)
    action = self.choose_action(sess, state, self.epsilon_min)
    r, new_frame, termination = self.play(action)
    self.replay_memory.add(frame, action, r, termination)
    frame = new_frame

    if self.callback:
        self.callback()
        if termination:
            break
```

Now, we are ready to train our first AI player for Atari games. The implementation is not hard if you understand the intuition behind the algorithm, is it? Now is the time to run the program and witness the magic!

Experiments

The full implementation of the deep Q-learning algorithm can be downloaded from GitHub (link xxx). To train our AI player for Breakout, run the following command under the `src` folder:

```
python train.py -g Breakout -d gpu
```

There are two arguments in `train.py`. One is `-g` or `--game`, indicating the name of the game one wants to test. The other one is `-d` or `--device`, which specifies the device (CPU or GPU) one wants to use to train the Q-network.

For Atari games, even with a high-end GPU, it will take 4-7 days to make our AI player achieve human-level performance. In order to test the algorithm quickly, a special game called **demo** is implemented as a lightweight benchmark. Run the demo via the following:

```
python train.py -g demo -d cpu
```

The demo game is based on the GridWorld game on the website at `https://cs.stanford.edu/people/karpathy/convnetjs/demo/rldemo.html`:

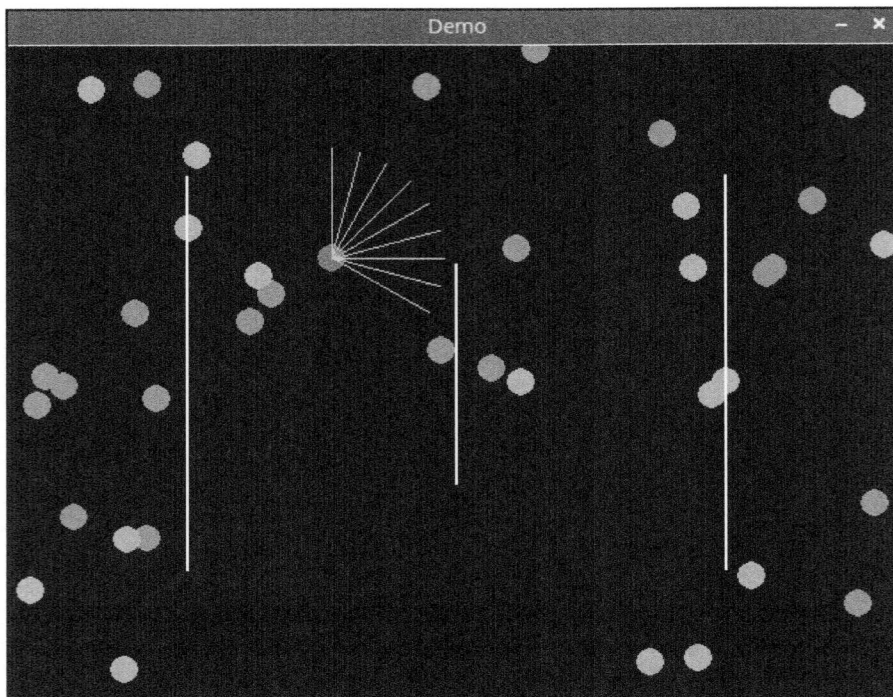

In this game, a robot in a 2D grid world has nine eyes pointing in different angles, and each eye senses three values along its direction: distance to a wall, distance to a green bean, or distance to a red bean. It navigates by using one of five actions that turn it different angles. It gets a positive reward (+1) for eating green beans while a negative reward (-1) for eating red beans. The goal is to eat green beans as much as possible in one episode.

The training will take several minutes. During the training, you can open a new terminal and type the following command to visualize the architecture of the Q-network and the training procedure:

```
tensorboard --logdir=log/demo/train
```

Here, `logdir` points to the folder where the log file of demo is stored. Once TensorBoard is running, navigate your web browser to `localhost:6006` to view the TensorBoard:

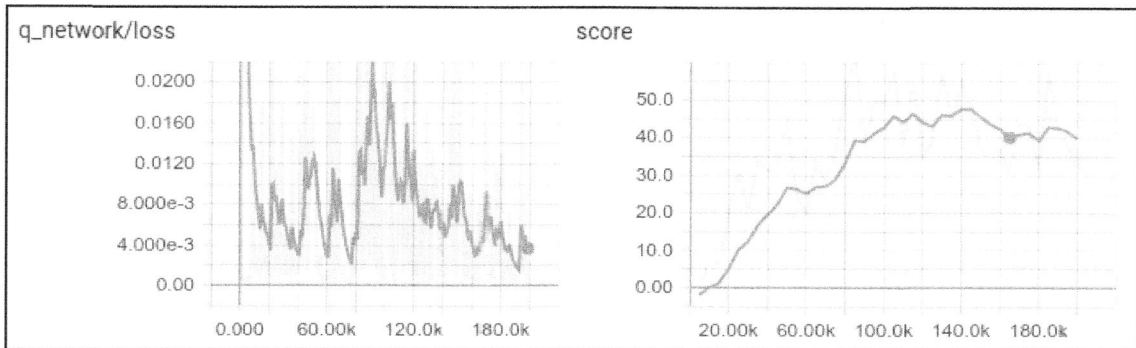

The two graphs plot the loss and the score against the training step, respectively. Clearly, after 100k training steps, the performance of the robot becomes stable, for example, the score is around 40.

You can also visualize the weights of the Q-network through TensorBoard. For more details, visit the TensorBoard guide at `https://www.tensorflow.org/programmers_guide/summaries_and_tensorboard`. This tool is quite useful for debugging and optimizing the code, especially for complicated algorithms such as DQN.

Summary

Congratulations! You just learned four important things. The first one is how to implement an Atari game emulator using gym, and how to play Atari games for relaxation and having fun. The second one is that you learned how to preprocess data in reinforcement learning tasks such as Atari games. For practical machine learning applications, you will spend a great deal of time on understanding and refining data, which affects the performance of an AI system a lot. The third one is the deep Q-learning algorithm. You learned the intuition behind it, for example, why the replay memory is necessary, why the target network is needed, where the update rule comes from, and so on. The final one is that you learned how to implement DQN using TensorFlow, and how to visualize the training process. Now, you are ready for the more advanced topics that we will discuss in the following chapters.

In the next chapter, you will learn how to simulate classic control tasks, and how to implement the state-of-the-art actor-critic algorithms for control.

4
Simulating Control Tasks

In the previous chapter, we saw the notable success of **deep Q-learning (DQN)** in training an AI agent to play Atari games. One limitation of DQN is that the action space must be discrete, namely, only a finite number of actions are available for the agent to select and the total number of actions cannot be too large. However, many practical tasks require continuous actions, which makes DQN difficult to apply. A naive remedy for DQN in this case is discretizing the continuous action space. But this remedy doesn't work due to the curse of dimensionality, meaning that DQN quickly becomes infeasible and does not generalize well.

This chapter will discuss deep reinforcement learning algorithms for control tasks with a continuous action space. Several classic control tasks, such as CartPole, Pendulum, and Acrobot, will be introduced first. You will learn how to simulate these tasks using Gym and understand the goal and the reward for each task. Then, a basic actor-critic algorithm, called the **deterministic policy gradient (DPG)**, will be represented. You will learn what the actor-critic architecture is, and why these kinds of algorithms can address continuous control tasks. Besides this, you will also learn how to implement DPG via Gym and TensorFlow. Finally, a more advanced algorithm, called the **trust region policy optimization (TRPO)**, will be introduced. You will understand why TRPO works much better than DPG and how to learn a policy by applying the conjugate gradient method.

This chapter requires some background knowledge of mathematical programming and convex/non-convex optimization. Don't be afraid-we will discuss these algorithms step by step to make sure that you fully understand the mechanism behind them. Understanding why they work, when they cannot work, and what their advantages and disadvantages are is much more important than simply knowing how to implement them with Gym and TensorFlow. After finishing this chapter, you will understand that the magic show of deep reinforcement learning is directed by mathematics and deep learning together.

The following topics will be covered in this chapter:

- Introduction to classic control tasks
- Deterministic policy gradient methods
- Trust region policy optimization for complex control tasks

Introduction to control tasks

OpenAI Gym offers classic control tasks from the classic reinforcement learning literature. These tasks include CartPole, MountainCar, Acrobot, and Pendulum. To find out more, visit the OpenAI Gym website at: `https://gym.openai.com/envs/#classic_control`. Besides this, Gym also provides more complex continuous control tasks running in the popular physics simulator MuJoCo. Here is the homepage for MuJoCo: `http://www.mujoco.org/`. MuJoCo stands for Multi-Joint Dynamics with Contact, which is a physics engine for research and development in robotics, graphics, and animation. The tasks provided by Gym are Ant, HalfCheetah, Hopper, Humanoid, InvertedPendulum, Reacher, Swimmer, and Walker2d. These names are very tricky, aren't they? For more details about these tasks, please visit the following link: `https://gym.openai.com/envs/#mujoco`.

Getting started

If you don't have a full installation of OpenAI Gym, you can install the `classic_control` and `mujoco` environment dependencies as follows:

```
pip install gym[classic_control]
pip install gym[mujoco]
```

MuJoCo is not open source, so you'll have to follow the instructions in `mujoco-py` (available at `https://github.com/openai/mujoco-py#obtaining-the-binaries-and-license-key`) to set it up. After the classic control environment is installed, try the following commands:

```
import gym
atari = gym.make('Acrobot-v1')
atari.reset()
atari.render()
```

If it runs successfully, a small window will pop up, showing the screen of the Acrobot task:

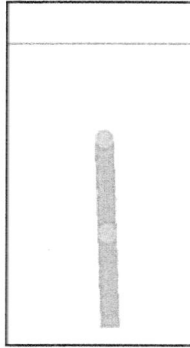

Besides Acrobot, you can replace the `Acrobot-v1` task name with `CartPole-v0`, `MountainCarContinuous-v0`, and `Pendulum-v0` to check out the other control tasks. You can run the following code to simulate these tasks and try to get a high-level understanding of their physical properties:

```python
import gym
import time

def start(task_name):
    task = gym.make(task_name)
    observation = task.reset()
    while True:
        task.render()
        action = task.env.action_space.sample()
        observation, reward, done, _ = task.step(action)
        print("Action {}, reward {}, observation {}".format(action, reward,
observation))
        if done:
            print("Game finished")
            break
        time.sleep(0.05)
    task.close()

if __name__ == "__main__":
    task_names = ['CartPole-v0', 'MountainCarContinuous-v0',
                  'Pendulum-v0', 'Acrobot-v1']
    for task_name in task_names:
        start(task_name)
```

Gym uses the same interface for all the tasks, including Atari games, classic control tasks, and MuJoCo control tasks. At each step, an action is randomly drawn from the action space by calling `task.env.action_space.sample()` and then this action is submitted to the simulator via `task.step(action)`, which tells the simulator to execute it.

The `step` function returns the observation and the reward corresponding to this action.

The classic control tasks

We will now go through the details of each control task and answer the following questions:

1. What are the control inputs and the corresponding feedbacks?
2. How is the reward function defined?
3. Is the action space continuous or discrete?

Understanding the details of these control tasks is quite important for designing proper reinforcement learning algorithms because their specifications, such as the dimension of the action space and the reward function, can affect the performance a lot.

CartPole is quite a famous control task in both the control and reinforcement learning communities. Gym implements the CartPole system described by *Barto, Sutton, and Anderson* in their paper *Neuronlike Adaptive Elements That Can Solve Difficult Learning Control Problem*, 1983. In CartPole, a pole is attached by an un-actuated joint to a cart, which moves along a frictionless track, as illustrated here:

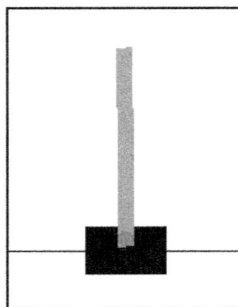

Here are the specifications of CartPole:

Goal	The goal is to prevent the pole from falling over.
Action	The action space is discrete, namely, the system is controlled by applying a force of +1 (right direction) and -1 (left direction) to the cart.
Observation	The observation is a vector with four elements, for example, [0.0316304, -0.1893631, -0.0058115, 0.27025422], which describe the positions of the pole and the cart.
Reward	A reward of +1 is provided for every timestep that the pole remains upright.
Termination	The episode ends when the pole is more than 15 degrees from vertical, or the cart moves more than 2.4 units from the center.

Because this chapter talks about solving continuous control tasks, we will later design a wrapper for CartPole to convert its discrete action space into a continuous one.

MountainCar was first described by Andrew Moore in his PhD thesis *A. Moore, Efficient Memory-Based Learning for Robot Control.* 1990, which is widely applied as the benchmark for control, **Markov decision process (MDP)**, and reinforcement learning algorithms. In MountainCar, a small car is on a one-dimensional track, moving between two mountains and trying to reach the yellow flag, as shown here:

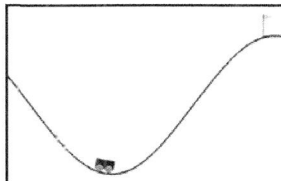

The following table provides its specifications:

Goal	The goal is to reach the top of the right mountain. However, the car's engine is not strong enough to scale the mountain in a single pass. Therefore, the only way to succeed is to drive back and forth to build up momentum.
Action	The action space is continuous. The input action is the engine force applied to the car.
Observation	The observation is a vector with two elements, for example, [-0.46786288, -0.00619457], which describe the velocity and the position of the car.
Reward	The reward is greater if you spend less energy to reach the goal.
Termination	The episode ends when the car reaches the goal flag or the maximum number of steps is reached.

The Pendulum swing-up problem is a classic problem in the control literature and is used as a benchmark for testing control algorithms. In Pendulum, a pole is attached to a pivot point, as shown here:

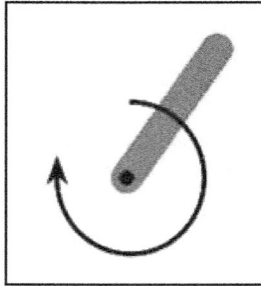

Here are the specifications of Pendulum:

Goal	The goal is to swing the pole up so it stays upright and to prevent it from falling over.
Action	The action space is continuous. The input action is the torque applied to the pole.
Observation	The observation is a vector with three elements, for example, [-0.19092327, 0.98160496, 3.36590881], which indicate the angle and angular velocity of the pole.
Reward	The reward is computed by a function with the angle, angular velocity, and the torque as the inputs.
Termination	The episode ends when the maximum number of steps is reached.

Acrobot was first described by Sutton in the paper *Generalization in Reinforcement Learning: Successful Examples Using Sparse Coarse Coding*, 1996. The Acrobot system includes two joints and two links, where the joint between the two links is actuated:

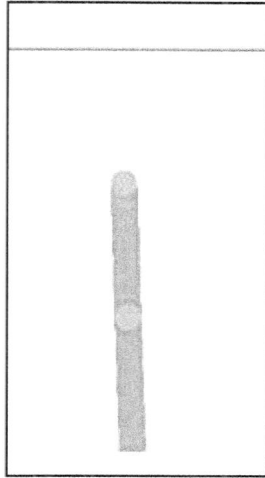

Here are the settings of Acrobot:

Goal	The goal is to swing the end of the lower link up to a given height.
Action	The action space is discrete, namely, the system is controlled by applying a torque of 0, +1 and -1 to the links.
Observation	The observation is a vector with six elements, for example, [0.9926474, 0.12104186, 0.99736744, -0.07251337, 0.47965018, -0.31494488], which describe the positions of the two links.
Reward	A reward of +1 is provided for every timestep where the lower link is at the given height or, otherwise, -1.
Termination	The episode ends when the end of the lower link is at the given height, or the maximum number of steps is reached.

Note that, in Gym, both CartPole and Acrobot have discrete action spaces, which means these two tasks can be solved by applying the deep Q-learning algorithm. Well, because this chapter considers continuous control tasks, we need to convert their action spaces into continuous ones. The following class provides a wrapper for Gym classic control tasks:

```
class Task:
    def __init__(self, name):
        assert name in ['CartPole-v0', 'MountainCar-v0',
                        'Pendulum-v0', 'Acrobot-v1']
        self.name = name
        self.task = gym.make(name)
        self.last_state = self.reset()
    def reset(self):
        state = self.task.reset()
```

```
            self.total_reward = 0
            return state
        def play_action(self, action):
            if self.name not in ['Pendulum-v0', 'MountainCarContinuous-v0']:
                action = numpy.fmax(action, 0)
                action = action / numpy.sum(action)
                action = numpy.random.choice(range(len(action)), p=action)
            else:
                low = self.task.env.action_space.low
                high = self.task.env.action_space.high
                action = numpy.fmin(numpy.fmax(action, low), high)
            state, reward, done, _ = self.task.step(action)
            self.total_reward += reward
            termination = 1 if done else 0
            return reward, state, termination
        def get_total_reward(self):
            return self.total_reward
        def get_action_dim(self):
            if self.name not in ['Pendulum-v0', 'MountainCarContinuous-v0']:
                return self.task.env.action_space.n
            else:
                return self.task.env.action_space.shape[0]
        def get_state_dim(self):
            return self.last_state.shape[0]
        def get_activation_fn(self):
            if self.name not in ['Pendulum-v0', 'MountainCarContinuous-v0']:
                return tf.nn.softmax
            else:
                return None
```

For CartPole and Acrobot, the input action should be a probability vector indicating the probability of selecting each action. In the `play_action` function, an action is randomly sampled based on this probability vector and submitted to the system.

The `get_total_reward` function returns the total reward in one episode.

The `get_action_dim` and `get_state_dim` functions return the dimension of the action space and the observation, respectively. The `get_activation_fn` function is used for the output layer in the actor network, which we will discuss later.

Deterministic policy gradient

As discussed in the previous chapter, DQN uses the Q-network to estimate the `state-action value` function, which has a separate output for each available action. Therefore, the Q-network cannot be applied, due to the continuous action space. A careful reader may remember that there is another architecture of the Q-network that takes both the state and the action as its inputs, and outputs the estimate of the corresponding Q-value. This architecture doesn't require the number of available actions to be finite, and has the capability to deal with continuous input actions:

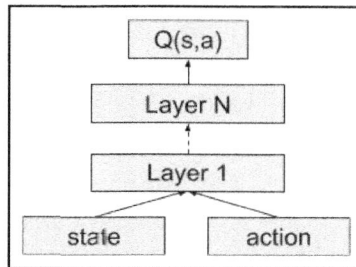

If we use this kind of network to estimate the `state-action value` function, there must be another network that defines the behavior policy of the agent, namely outputting a proper action given the observed state. In fact, this is the intuition behind actor-critic reinforcement learning algorithms. The actor-critic architecture contains two parts:

1. **Actor**: The actor defines the behavior policy of the agent. In control tasks, it outputs the control signal given the current state of the system.
2. **Critic**: The critic estimates the Q-value of the current policy. It can judge whether the policy is good or not.

Therefore, if both the actor and the critic can be trained with the feedbacks (state, reward, next state, termination signal) received from the system, as in training the Q-network in DQN, then the classic control tasks will be solved. But how do we train them?

The theory behind policy gradient

One solution is the **deep deterministic policy gradient (DDPG)** algorithm, which combines the actor-critic approach with insights from the success of DQN. This is discussed in the following papers:

- D. Silver, G. Lever, N. Heess, T. Degris, D. Wierstra and M. Riedmiller. *Deterministic policy gradient algorithms.* In ICML, 2014.
- T. P. Lillicrap, J. J. Hunt, A. Pritzel, N. Heess, T. Erez, Y. Tassa, D. Silver and D. Wierstra. *Continuous control with deep reinforcement learning.* In ICLR, 2016.

The reason why DDPG is introduced first is that it is quite similar to DQN, so you can understand the mechanism behind it much more easily after finishing the previous chapter. Recall that DQN is able to train the Q-network in a stable and robust way for the following reasons:

- The Q-network is trained with the samples randomly drawn from the replay memory to minimize the correlations between samples.
- A target network is used to estimate the target Q-value, reducing the probability that oscillation or divergence of the policy occurs. DDPG applies the same strategy, which means that DDPG is also a model-free and off-policy method.

We use the same notations as in the previous chapter for the reinforcement learning setting. At each timestep t, the agent observes state s_t, takes action a_t ,and then receives the corresponding reward r_t generated from a function $R(s_t, a_t)$. Instead of using $A(s_t)$ to represent the set of all the available actions at state s_t, here, we use $\pi(a_t|s_t)$ to denote the policy of the agent, which maps states to a probability distribution over the actions. Many approaches in reinforcement learning, such as DQN, use the Bellman equation as the backbone:

$$Q(s_t, a_t) = E_{s_{t+1} \sim S}[R(s_t, a_t) + \gamma E_{a_{t+1} \sim \pi(a_{t+1}|s_{t+1})} Q(s_{t+1}, a_{t+1})]$$

The only difference between this formulation and the one in DQN is that the policy π here is stochastic, so that the expectation of $Q(s_{t+1}, a_{t+1})$ is taken over a_{t+1}. If the target policy π is deterministic, which can be described as a function $\mu(s_t)$, then this inner expectation can be avoided:

$$Q(s_t, a_t) = E_{s_{t+1} \sim S}[R(s_t, a_t) + \gamma Q(s_{t+1}, \mu(s_{t+1}))]$$

The expectation depends only on the environment. This means that it is possible to learn the `state-action value` function Q off-policy, using transitions that are generated from other policies, as we did in DQN. The function Q, the critic, can be approximated by a neural network parameterized by θ^Q and the policy μ, the actor, can also be represented by another neural network parameterized by θ^μ (in DQN, $\mu(s_t)$ is just $^{\arg\max_a Q(s_t,a)}$). Then, the critic Q can be be trained by minimizing the following loss function:

$$L(\theta^Q) = E_{s_t \sim S, a_t \sim A}[(y_t - Q(s_t, a_t|\theta^Q))^2]$$,

Here, $y_t = R(s_t, a_t) + \gamma Q(s_{t+1}, \mu(s_{t+1})|\theta^Q)$. As in DQN, y_t can be estimated via the target network and the samples for approximating $L(\theta^Q)$ can be randomly drawn from the replay memory.

To train the actor μ, we fix the critic Q, learned by minimizing the loss function L, and try to maximize $Q(s_t, \mu(s_t|\theta^\mu))$ over θ^μ, since a larger Q-value means a better policy. This can be done by following the applying the chain rule to the expected return with respect to the actor parameters:

$$\nabla_{\theta^\mu} E_{s_t \sim S}[Q(s_t, \mu(s_t|\theta^\mu)|\theta^Q)] = E_{s_t \sim S}[\nabla_a Q(s_t, a|\theta^Q)\nabla_{\theta^\mu}\mu(s_t|\theta^\mu)]$$.

The following diagram shows the high-level architecture of DDPG:

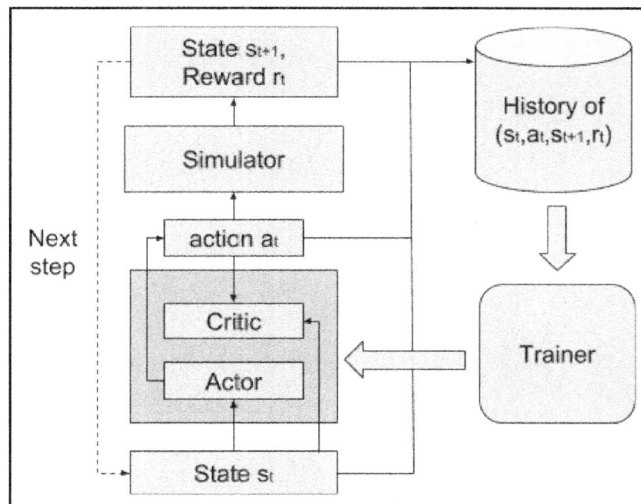

Compared to DQN, there is a small difference in updating the target network. Instead of directly copying the weights of Q to the target network after several iterations, a soft update is used:

$$\theta^{Q'} = \tau\theta^{Q} + (1 - \tau)\theta^{Q'}$$

Here, $\theta^{Q'}$ represents the weights of the target network. This update means that the target values are constrained to change slowly, greatly improving the stability of learning. This simple change moves the relatively unstable problem of learning the value function closer to the case of supervised learning.

Similar to DQN, DDPG also needs to balance exploration and exploitation during the training. Since the action generated by the policy μ is continuous, the ϵ-greedy method cannot be applied. Instead, we can construct an exploration policy μ' by adding noise sampled from a distribution P to the actor policy μ:

$$\mu'(s_t) = \mu(s_t|\theta^{\mu}) + \epsilon \text{ where } \epsilon \sim P$$

P can be chosen as σN, where N is the standard Gaussian distribution and σ decreases during each training step. Another choice is to apply an Ornstein-Uhlenbeck process to generate the exploration noise ϵ.

DPG algorithm

The following pseudo code shows the DDPG algorithm:

```
Initialize replay memory R to capacity N;
Initialize the critic network Q(s,a;θ^Q) and actor network μ(s;θ^μ) with random
weights θ^Q and θ^μ;
Initialize the target networks Q'(s,a;θ^Q') and μ'(s;θ^μ') with weights θ^Q' = θ^Q and θ^μ' = θ^μ
;
Repeat for each episode:
    Set time step t = 1;
    Initialize a random process P₁ for action exploration noise;
    Receive an initial observation state s₁;
    While the terminal state hasn't been reached:
        Select an action a_t = μ(s_t;θ^μ) + P_t according to the current policy and
exploration noise;
        Execute action a_t in the simulator and observe reward r_t and the next
state s_t+1;
        Store transition (s_t,a_t,r_t,s_t+1) into replay memory R;
        Randomly sample a batch of n transitions (s_i,a_i,r_i,s_i+1) from R;
```

Set $y_i = r_i$ if s_{i+1} is a terminal state or $y_i = r_i + \gamma Q'(s_{i+1}, \mu'(s_{i+1}; \theta^{\mu'}); \theta^{Q'})$ if s_{i+1} is a non-terminal state:
    Update critic by minimizing the loss:
$$\frac{1}{n} \sum_i (y_i - Q(s_i, a_i; \theta^Q))^2 \ ;$$
    Update the actor policy using the sampled policy gradient:
$$\frac{1}{n} \sum_i \nabla_a Q(s_t, a|\theta^Q) \nabla_{\theta^\mu} \mu(s_t|\theta^\mu) \ ;$$
    Update the target networks:
$$\theta^{Q'} = \tau\theta^Q + (1-\tau)\theta^{Q'} ,$$
$$\theta^{\mu'} = \tau\theta^\mu + (1-\tau)\theta^{\mu'} ;$$
End while

There is a natural extension of DDPG by replacing the feedforward neural networks used for approximating the actor and the critic with recurrent neural networks. This extension is called the **recurrent deterministic policy gradient** algorithm (**RDPG**) and is discussed in the f paper N. Heess, J. J. Hunt, T. P. Lillicrap and D. Silver. *Memory-based control with recurrent neural networks*. 2015.

The recurrent critic and actor are trained using **backpropagation through time (BPTT)**. For readers who are interested in it, the paper can be downloaded from https://arxiv.org/abs/1512.04455.

Implementation of DDPG

This section will show you how to implement the actor-critic architecture using TensorFlow. The code structure is almost the same as the DQN implementation that was shown in the previous chapter.

The ActorNetwork is a simple MLP that takes the observation state as its input:

```
class ActorNetwork:
    def __init__(self, input_state, output_dim, hidden_layers,
activation=tf.nn.relu):
        self.x = input_state
        self.output_dim = output_dim
        self.hidden_layers = hidden_layers
        self.activation = activation
        with tf.variable_scope('actor_network'):
            self.output = self._build()
            self.vars = tf.get_collection(tf.GraphKeys.TRAINABLE_VARIABLES,
                                    tf.get_variable_scope().name)
    def _build(self):
        layer = self.x
```

```
        init_b = tf.constant_initializer(0.01)
        for i, num_unit in enumerate(self.hidden_layers):
            layer = dense(layer, num_unit, init_b=init_b,
name='hidden_layer_{}'.format(i))
        output = dense(layer, self.output_dim, activation=self.activation,
init_b=init_b, name='output')
        return output
```

The constructor requires four arguments: `input_state`, `output_dim`, `hidden_layers`, and `activation`. `input_state` is a tensor for the observation state. `output_dim` is the dimension of the action space. `hidden_layers` specifies the number of the hidden layers and the number of units for each layer. `activation` indicates the activation function for the output layer.

The `CriticNetwork` is also a MLP, which is enough for the classic control tasks:

```
class CriticNetwork:
    def __init__(self, input_state, input_action, hidden_layers):
        assert len(hidden_layers) >= 2
        self.input_state = input_state
        self.input_action = input_action
        self.hidden_layers = hidden_layers
        with tf.variable_scope('critic_network'):
            self.output = self._build()
            self.vars = tf.get_collection(tf.GraphKeys.TRAINABLE_VARIABLES,
                                          tf.get_variable_scope().name)
    def _build(self):
        layer = self.input_state
        init_b = tf.constant_initializer(0.01)
        for i, num_unit in enumerate(self.hidden_layers):
            if i != 1:
                layer = dense(layer, num_unit, init_b=init_b,
name='hidden_layer_{}'.format(i))
            else:
                layer = tf.concat([layer, self.input_action], axis=1,
name='concat_action')
                layer = dense(layer, num_unit, init_b=init_b,
name='hidden_layer_{}'.format(i))
        output = dense(layer, 1, activation=None, init_b=init_b,
name='output')
        return tf.reshape(output, shape=(-1,))
```

The network takes the state and the action as its inputs. It first maps the state into a hidden feature representation and then concatenates this representation with the action, followed by several hidden layers. The output layer generates the Q-value that corresponds to the inputs.

The actor-critic network combines the actor network and the critic network together:

```python
class ActorCriticNet:
    def __init__(self, input_dim, action_dim,
                    critic_layers, actor_layers, actor_activation,
                    scope='ac_network'):
        self.input_dim = input_dim
        self.action_dim = action_dim
        self.scope = scope
        self.x = tf.placeholder(shape=(None, input_dim), dtype=tf.float32,
name='x')
        self.y = tf.placeholder(shape=(None,), dtype=tf.float32, name='y')
        with tf.variable_scope(scope):
            self.actor_network = ActorNetwork(self.x, action_dim,
                                        hidden_layers=actor_layers,
                                        activation=actor_activation)
            self.critic_network = CriticNetwork(self.x,
self.actor_network.get_output_layer(),
hidden_layers=critic_layers)
            self.vars = tf.get_collection(tf.GraphKeys.TRAINABLE_VARIABLES,
                                        tf.get_variable_scope().name)
            self._build()
    def _build(self):
        value = self.critic_network.get_output_layer()
        actor_loss = -tf.reduce_mean(value)
        self.actor_vars = self.actor_network.get_params()
        self.actor_grad = tf.gradients(actor_loss, self.actor_vars)
        tf.summary.scalar("actor_loss", actor_loss, collections=['actor'])
        self.actor_summary = tf.summary.merge_all('actor')
        critic_loss = 0.5 * tf.reduce_mean(tf.square((value - self.y)))
        self.critic_vars = self.critic_network.get_params()
        self.critic_grad = tf.gradients(critic_loss, self.critic_vars)
        tf.summary.scalar("critic_loss", critic_loss,
collections=['critic'])
        self.critic_summary = tf.summary.merge_all('critic')
```

The constructor requires six arguments, as follows: `input_dim` and `action_dim` are the dimensions of the state space and the action space, respectively. `critic_layers` and `actor_layers` specify the hidden layers of the critic network and the actor network. `actor_activation` indicates the activation function for the output layer of the actor network. `scope` is the scope name used for the `scope` TensorFlow variable.

The constructor first creates an instance of the `self.actor_network` actor network with an input of `self.x`, where `self.x` represents the current state. It then creates an instance of the critic network using the following as the inputs: `self.actor_network.get_output_layer()` as the output of the actor network and `self.x` as the current state. Given these two networks, the constructor calls `self._build()` to build the loss functions for the actor and critic that we discussed previously. The actor loss is `-tf.reduce_mean(value)`, where `value` is the Q-value computed by the critic network. The critic loss is `0.5 * tf.reduce_mean(tf.square((value - self.y)))`, where `self.y` is a tensor for the predicted target value computed by the target network.

The class `ActorCriticNet` provides the functions for calculating the action and the Q-value given the current state, that is, `get_action` and `get_value`. It also provides `get_action_value`, which computes the `state-action value` function given the current state and the action taken by the agent:

```
class ActorCriticNet:
    def get_action(self, sess, state):
        return self.actor_network.get_action(sess, state)
    def get_value(self, sess, state):
        return self.critic_network.get_value(sess, state)
    def get_action_value(self, sess, state, action):
        return self.critic_network.get_action_value(sess, state, action)
    def get_actor_feed_dict(self, state):
        return {self.x: state}
    def get_critic_feed_dict(self, state, action, target):
        return {self.x: state, self.y: target,
                self.critic_network.input_action: action}
    def get_clone_op(self, network, tau=0.9):
        update_ops = []
        new_vars = {v.name.replace(network.scope, ''): v for v in
network.vars}
        for v in self.vars:
            u = (1 - tau) * v + tau * new_vars[v.name.replace(self.scope,
'')]
            update_ops.append(tf.assign(v, u))
        return update_ops
```

Because DPG has almost the same architecture as DQN, the implementations of the replay memory and the optimizer are not shown in this chapter. For more details, you can refer to the previous chapter or visit our GitHub repository (`https://github.com/PacktPublishing/Python-Reinforcement-Learning-Projects`). By combining these modules together, we can implement the DPG class for the deterministic policy gradient algorithm:

```
class DPG:
    def __init__(self, config, task, directory, callback=None,
summary_writer=None):
        self.task = task
        self.directory = directory
        self.callback = callback
        self.summary_writer = summary_writer
        self.config = config
        self.batch_size = config['batch_size']
        self.n_episode = config['num_episode']
        self.capacity = config['capacity']
        self.history_len = config['history_len']
        self.epsilon_decay = config['epsilon_decay']
        self.epsilon_min = config['epsilon_min']
        self.time_between_two_copies = config['time_between_two_copies']
        self.update_interval = config['update_interval']
        self.tau = config['tau']
        self.action_dim = task.get_action_dim()
        self.state_dim = task.get_state_dim() * self.history_len
        self.critic_layers = [50, 50]
        self.actor_layers = [50, 50]
        self.actor_activation = task.get_activation_fn()
        self._init_modules()
```

Here, `config` includes all the parameters of DPG, for example, batch size and learning rate for training. The `task` is an instance of a certain classic control task. In the constructor, the replay memory, Q-network, target network, and optimizer are initialized by calling the `_init_modules` function:

```
    def _init_modules(self):
        # Replay memory
        self.replay_memory = ReplayMemory(history_len=self.history_len,
                                          capacity=self.capacity)
        # Actor critic network
        self.ac_network = ActorCriticNet(input_dim=self.state_dim,
                                         action_dim=self.action_dim,
                                         critic_layers=self.critic_layers,
                                         actor_layers=self.actor_layers,
actor_activation=self.actor_activation,
                                         scope='ac_network')
```

```
        # Target network
        self.target_network = ActorCriticNet(input_dim=self.state_dim,
                                        action_dim=self.action_dim,
critic_layers=self.critic_layers,
actor_layers=self.actor_layers,
actor_activation=self.actor_activation,
                                        scope='target_network')
        # Optimizer
        self.optimizer = Optimizer(config=self.config,
                                ac_network=self.ac_network,
                                target_network=self.target_network,
                                replay_memory=self.replay_memory)
        # Ops for updating target network
        self.clone_op = self.target_network.get_clone_op(self.ac_network,
tau=self.tau)
        # For tensorboard
        self.t_score = tf.placeholder(dtype=tf.float32, shape=[],
name='new_score')
        tf.summary.scalar("score", self.t_score, collections=['dpg'])
        self.summary_op = tf.summary.merge_all('dpg')
    def choose_action(self, sess, state, epsilon=0.1):
        x = numpy.asarray(numpy.expand_dims(state, axis=0),
dtype=numpy.float32)
        action = self.ac_network.get_action(sess, x)[0]
        return action + epsilon * numpy.random.randn(len(action))
    def play(self, action):
        r, new_state, termination = self.task.play_action(action)
        return r, new_state, termination

    def update_target_network(self, sess):
        sess.run(self.clone_op)
```

The choose_action function selects an action based on the current estimate of the actor-critic network and the observed state.

> Note that a Gaussian noise controlled by epsilon is added for exploration.

The play function submits an action into the simulator and returns the feedback from the simulator. The update_target_network function updates the target network from the current actor-critic network.

To begin the training process, the following function can be called:

```
def train(self, sess, saver=None):
    num_of_trials = -1
    for episode in range(self.n_episode):
        frame = self.task.reset()
        for _ in range(self.history_len+1):
            self.replay_memory.add(frame, 0, 0, 0)
        for _ in range(self.config['T']):
            num_of_trials += 1
            epsilon = self.epsilon_min + \
                    max(self.epsilon_decay - num_of_trials, 0) / \
                    self.epsilon_decay * (1 - self.epsilon_min)
            if num_of_trials % self.update_interval == 0:
                self.optimizer.train_one_step(sess, num_of_trials,
self.batch_size)
            state = self.replay_memory.phi(frame)
            action = self.choose_action(sess, state, epsilon)
            r, new_frame, termination = self.play(action)
            self.replay_memory.add(frame, action, r, termination)
            frame = new_frame
            if num_of_trials % self.time_between_two_copies == 0:
                self.update_target_network(sess)
                self.save(sess, saver)
            if self.callback:
                self.callback()
            if termination:
                score = self.task.get_total_reward()
                summary_str = sess.run(self.summary_op,
feed_dict={self.t_score: score})
                self.summary_writer.add_summary(summary_str,
num_of_trials)
                self.summary_writer.flush()
                break
```

In each episode, it calls `replay_memory.phi` to get the current state and calls the `choose_action` function to select an action based on the current state. This action is submitted into the simulator by calling the `play` function, which returns the corresponding reward, next state, and termination signal. Then, the `(current state, action, reward, termination)` transition is stored into the replay memory. For every `update_interval` step (`update_interval = 1`, by default), the actor-critic network is trained with a batch of transitions that are randomly sampled from the replay memory. For every `time_between_two_copies` step, the target network is updated and the weights of the Q-network are saved to the hard disk.

After the training step, the following function can be called for evaluating the performance of our trained agent:

```
def evaluate(self, sess):
    for episode in range(self.n_episode):
        frame = self.task.reset()
        for _ in range(self.history_len+1):
            self.replay_memory.add(frame, 0, 0, 0)
        for _ in range(self.config['T']):
            print("episode {}, total reward {}".format(episode,
self.task.get_total_reward()))
            state = self.replay_memory.phi(frame)
            action = self.choose_action(sess, state, self.epsilon_min)
            r, new_frame, termination = self.play(action)
            self.replay_memory.add(frame, action, r, termination)
            frame = new_frame

            if self.callback:
                self.callback()
                if termination:
                    break
```

Experiments

The full implementation of DPG can be downloaded from our GitHub (https://github. com/PacktPublishing/Python-Reinforcement-Learning-Projects). To train an agent for CartPole, run the following command under the src folder:

```
python train.py -t CartPole-v0 -d cpu
```

There are two arguments in train.py. One is -t, or --task, indicating the name of the classic control task you want to test. The other one is -d, or --device, which specifies the device (CPU or GPU) that you want to use to train the actor-critic network. Since the dimensions of the state spaces of these classic control tasks are relatively low compared to the Atari environment, using the CPU to train the agent is fast enough. It should only take several minutes to finish.

During the training, you can open a new Terminal and type the following command to visualize both the architecture of the actor-critic network and the training procedure:

```
tensorboard --logdir=log/CartPole-v0/train
```

Here, `lcgdir` points to the folder where the `CartPole-v0` log file is stored. Once TensorBoard is running, navigate your web browser to `localhost:6006` to view the TensorBoard:

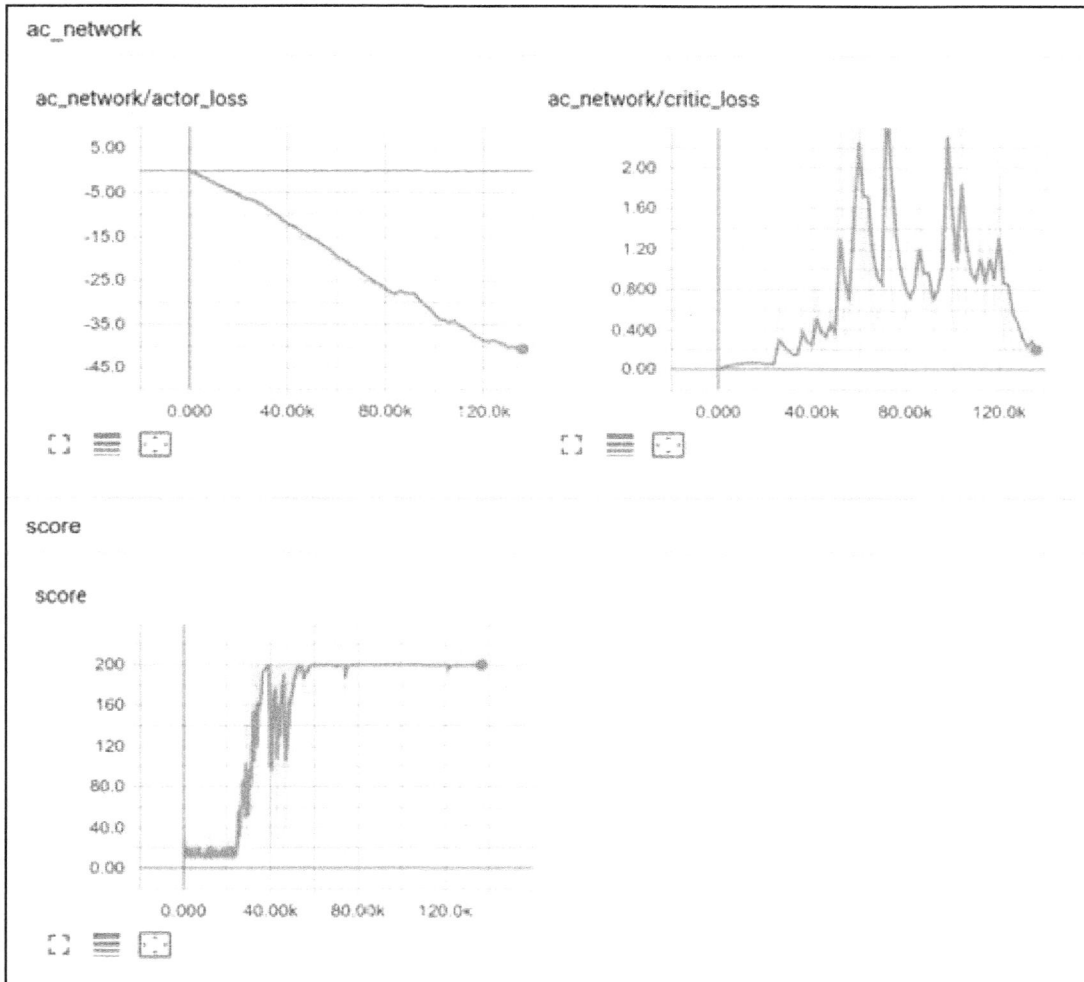

The top two graphs show the changes of the actor loss and the critic loss against the training step. For classical control tasks, the actor loss usually decreases consistently, while the critic loss has a large fluctuation. After 60,000 training steps, the score becomes stable, achieving 200, the highest score that can be reached in the CartPole simulator.

Using a similar command, you can also train an agent for the `Pendulum` task:

```
python train.py -t Pendulum-v0 -d cpu
```

Then, check the training procedure via `Tensorboard`:

```
tensorboard --logdir=log/Pendulum-v0/train
```

The following screenshot shows the changes of the score during training:

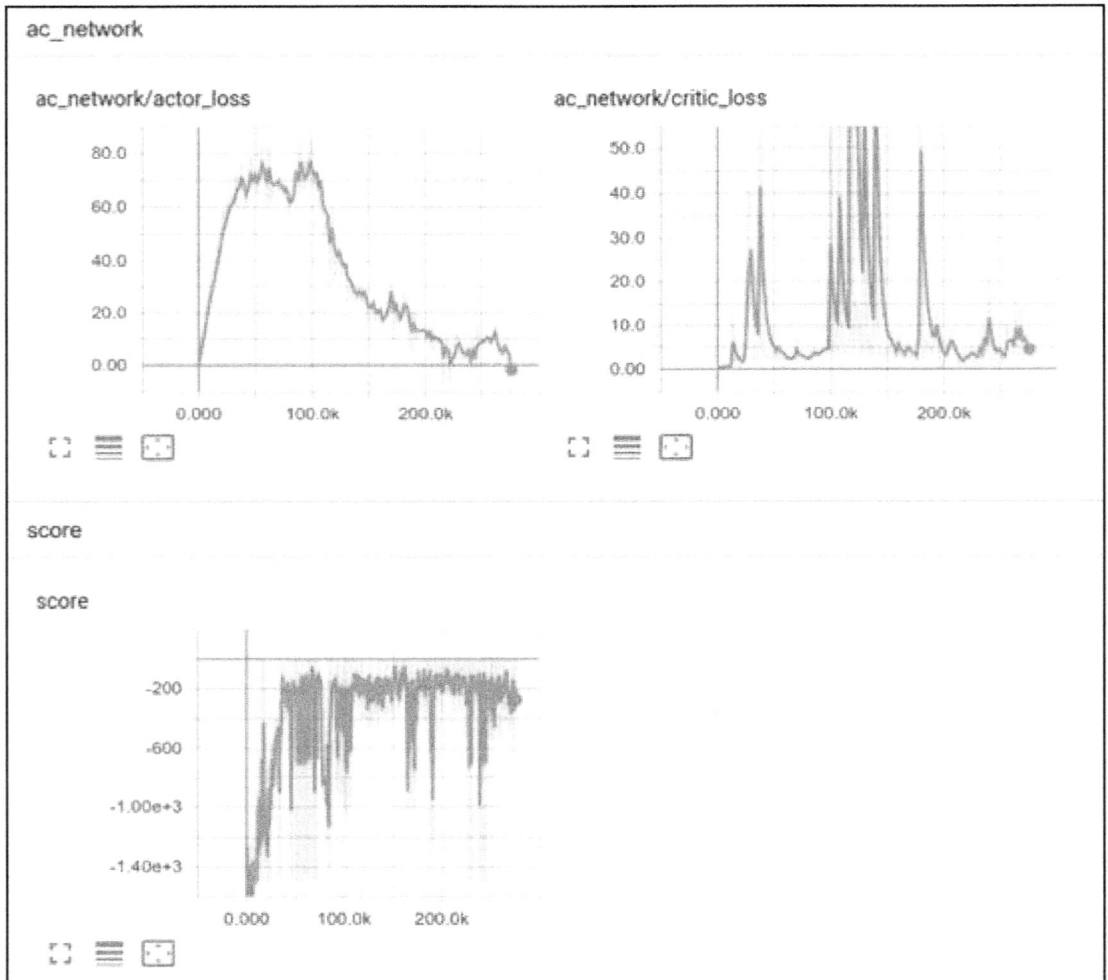

Changes in score during training

A careful reader may notice that the score of Pendulum fluctuates widely compared to the score of CartPole. There are two reasons that are causing this problem:

- In Pendulum, the starting position of the pole is not deterministic, namely, it may be different for two episodes
- The train procedure in DPG may not be always stable, especially for complicated tasks, such as MuJoCo control tasks

The MuJoCo control tasks, for example, Ant, HalfCheetah, Hopper, Humanoid, InvertedPendulum, Reacher, Swimmer, and Walker2d provided by Gym, have high-dimensional state and action space, which makes DPG fail. If you are curious about what happens when running DPG with the `Hopper-v0` task, you can try the following:

```
python train.py -t Hopper-v0 -d cpu
```

After several minutes, you will see that DPG cannot teach Hopper how to walk. The main reason why DPG fails in this case is that the simple actor and critic updates discussed here become unstable with high-dimensional inputs.

Trust region policy optimization

The **trust region policy optimization (TRPO)** algorithm was proposed to solve complex continuous control tasks in the following paper: Schulman, S. Levine, P. Moritz, M. Jordan and P. Abbeel. *Trust Region Policy Optimization*. In ICML, 2015.

To understand why TRPO works requires some mathematical background. The main idea is that it is better to guarantee that the new policy, π_{new}, optimized by one training step, not only monotonically decreases the optimization loss function (and thus improves the policy), but also does not deviate from the previous policy π_{old} much, which means that there should be a constraint on the difference between π_{new} and π_{old}, for example, $C(\pi_{new}, \pi_{old}) \leq \delta$ for a certain constraint function $C(\cdot)$ constant δ.

Theory behind TRPO

Let's see the mechanism behind TRPO. If you feel that this part is hard to understand, you can skip it and go directly to how to run TRPO to solve MuJoCo control tasks. Consider an infinite-horizon discounted Markov decision process denoted by $(S, a, P, c, \rho_0, \gamma)$, where S is a finite set of states, A is a finite set of actions, P is the transition probability distribution, C is the cost function, ρ_0 is the distribution of the initial state, and γ is the discount factor. Let π be a stochastic policy that we want to learn by minimizing the following expected discounted cost:

$$\eta(\pi) = E_{s_0, a_0, \cdots} \left[\sum_{t=0}^{\infty} \gamma^t c(s_t) \right]$$

Here, this is $s_0 \sim \rho_0$, $a_t \sim \pi(a_t | s_t)$ and $s_{t+1} \sim P(s | s_t, a_t)$. The definitions of the `state-action value` function Q_π, the value function V_π, and the advantage function A_π under policy π are as follows:

$$Q_\pi(s_t, a_t) = E_{s_{t+1}, a_{t+1}, \cdots} \left[\sum_{l=0}^{\infty} \gamma^l c(s_{t+l}) \right]$$

$$V_\pi(s_t) = E_{a_t, s_{t+1}, \cdots} \left[\sum_{l=0}^{\infty} \gamma^l c(s_{t+l}) \right]$$

$$A_\pi(s, a) = Q_\pi(s, a) - V_\pi(s)$$

Here, this is $a_t \sim \pi(a_t | s_t)$ and $s_{t+1} \sim P(s | s_t, a_t)$.

Our goal is to improve policy π (by reducing the expected discounted cost) during each training step. In order to design an algorithm monotonically improving π, let's consider the following equation:

$$\eta(\tilde{\pi}) = \eta(\pi) + E_{s_0, a_0, \cdots} \left[\sum_{t=0}^{\infty} \gamma^t A_\pi(s_t, a_t) \right]$$

Here, this is $s_0 \sim p_0$, $a_t \sim \tilde{\pi}(a_t | s_t)$ and $s_{t+1} \sim P(s | s_t, a_t)$. This equation holds for any policy $\tilde{\pi}$. For the readers who are interested in the proof of this equation, refer to the appendix in the TRPO paper or the paper *Approximately optimal approximate reinforcement learning*, written by Kakade and Langford. To simplify this equation, let ρ_π be the discounted visitation frequencies:

$$\rho_\pi(s) = P(s_0 = s) + \gamma P(s_1 = s) + \gamma^2 P(s_2 = s) + \cdots$$

By rearranging the preceding equation to sum over states instead of timesteps, it becomes the following:

$$\eta(\tilde{\pi}) = \eta(\pi) + \sum_s \rho_{\tilde{\pi}}(s) \sum_a \tilde{\pi}(a | s) A_\pi(s, a)$$

From this equation, we can see that any policy update $\pi \to \tilde{\pi}$ that has a non-positive expected advantage at every state s, that is, $\sum_a \tilde{\pi}(a|s) A_\pi(s,a) \leq 0$, is guaranteed to reduce the cost η. Therefore, for discrete action space such as the Atari environment, the deterministic policy $\tilde{\pi}(s) = \arg\min_a A_\pi(s, a)$, selected in DQN, guarantees to improves the policy if there is at least one state-action pair with a negative advantage value and nonzero state visitation probability. However, in practical problems, especially when the policy is approximated by a neural network, there will be some state for which the expected advantage is positive, due to approximation errors. Besides this, the dependency of $\rho_{\tilde{\pi}}(s)$ on $\tilde{\pi}$ makes this equation hard to optimize, so TRPO considers optimizing the following function by replacing $\rho_{\tilde{\pi}}$ with ρ_π:

$$L_\pi(\tilde{\pi}) = \eta(\pi) - \sum_s \rho_\pi(s) \sum_a \tilde{\pi}(a | s) A_\pi(s, a)$$

Kakade and Langford showed that if we have a parameterized policy, π_θ, which is a differentiable function of the parameter θ, then for any parameter θ_0:

$$L_{\pi_{\theta_0}} = \eta(\pi_{\theta_0})$$

$$\nabla_\theta L_{\pi_{\theta_0}}(\pi_\theta)|_{\theta=\theta_0} = \nabla_\theta \eta(\pi_\theta)|_{\theta=\theta_0}$$

This means that improving L will also improve η with a sufficient small update on π_θ. Based on this idea, Kakade and Langford proposed a policy updating scheme called the conservative policy iteration:

$$\pi_{new}(a | s) = (1 - \alpha)\pi_{old}(a | s) + \alpha\pi'(a | s)$$

Here, π_{old} is the current policy, π_{old} is the new policy, and π' is obtained by solving $\pi' = \arg\min_{\pi'} L_{\pi_{old}}(\pi')$. They proved the following bound for this update:

$$\eta(\pi_{new}) \leq L_{\pi_{old}}(\pi_{new}) + \frac{2\epsilon\gamma}{(1-\gamma)^2}\alpha^2,$$
where $\epsilon = \max_s |E_{a\sim\pi'(a|s)}[A_\pi(s,a)]|$

Note that this bound only applies to mixture policies generated by the preceding update. In TRPO, the authors extended this bound to general stochastic policies, rather than just mixture policies. The main idea is to replace mixture weight α with a distance measure between π_{new} and π_{old}. An interesting pick of the distance measure is the total variation divergence. Taking two discrete distributions P and q as an example, the total variation divergence is defined as follows:

$$D_{TV}(p,q) = \frac{1}{2}\sum_i |p_i - q_i|$$

For policies π_{new} and π_{old}, let $D_{TV}^{\max}(\pi_{old}, \pi_{new})$ be the maximum total variation divergence over all the states:

$$D_{TV}^{\max}(\pi_{old}, \pi_{new}) = \max_s D_{TV}(\pi_{old}(\cdot|s), \pi_{new}(\cdot|s))$$

With $\alpha = D_{TV}^{\max}(\pi_{old}, \pi_{new})$ and $\epsilon = \max_s |E_{a\sim\pi'(a|s)}[A_\pi(s,a)]|$, it can be shown that:

$$\eta(\pi_{new}) \leq L_{\pi_{old}}(\pi_{new}) + CD_{TV}^{\max}(\pi_{old}, \pi_{new})^2,$$
where $C = \frac{2\epsilon\gamma}{(1-\gamma)^2}$.

Actually, the total variation divergence can be upper bounded by the KL divergence, namely, $D_{TV}^{\max}(\pi_{old}, \pi_{new})^2 \leq D_{KL}^{\max}(\pi_{old}, \pi_{new})$, which means that:

$$\eta(\pi_{new}) \leq L_{\pi_{old}}(\pi_{new}) + CD_{KL}^{\max}(\pi_{old}, \pi_{new}),$$
where $C = \frac{2\epsilon\gamma}{(1-\gamma)^2}$.

TRPO algorithm

Based on the preceding policy improvement bound, the following algorithm is develcped:

```
Initialize policy π0;
Repeat for each step i = 1, 2, ··· :
    Compute all advantage values Aπi(s, a);
    Solve the following optimization problem:
    πi+1 = arg minπ Lπi(π) + CDKL^max(πi, π);
Until convergence
```

In each step, this algorithm minimizes the upper bound of $\eta(\pi)$, so that:

$$\eta(\pi_{i+1}) \leq L_{\pi_i}(\pi_{i+1}) - CD_{KL}^{\max}(\pi_{i+1}, \pi_i) \leq L_{\pi_i}(\pi_i) + CD_{KL}^{\max}(\pi_i, \pi_i) = \eta(\pi_i)$$

The last equation follows from that $L_\pi(\pi) = \eta(\pi)$ for any policy π. This implies that this algorithm is guaranteed to generate a sequence of monotonically improving policies.

In practice, since the exact value of ϵ in C is hard to calculate, and it is difficult to control the step size of each update using the penalty term, TRPO replaces the penalty term with the constraint that KL divergence is bounded by a constant δ:

$$\text{minimize}_\pi L_{\pi_{old}}(\pi), \text{ subject to } D_{KL}^{\max}(\pi_{old}, \pi) \leq \delta$$

But this problem is still impractical to solve due to the large number of constraints. Therefore, TRPO uses a heuristic approximation that considers the average KL divergence:

$$\bar{D}_{KL}(\pi_{\theta_{old}}, \pi_\theta) = E_{s \sim \rho}[D_{KL}(\pi_{\theta_{old}}(\cdot|s), \pi_\theta(\cdot|s))]$$

This leads to the following optimization problem:

$$\text{minimize}_\pi \, L_{\pi_{old}}(\pi), \text{ subject to } \bar{D}_{KL}(\pi_{old}, \pi) \leq \delta$$

In other words, by expanding $L_{\pi_{old}}$, we need to solve the following:

$$\text{minimize}_\pi \sum_s \rho_{\pi_{old}}(s) \sum_a \pi(a|s) A_{\pi_{old}}(s, a), \text{ subject to } \bar{D}_{KL}(\pi_{old}, \pi) \leq \delta$$

Now, the question is: how do we optimize this problem? A straightforward idea is to sample several trajectories by simulating the policy π_{old} for some number of steps and then approximate the objective function of this problem using these trajectories. Since the advantage function $A_\pi(s, a) = Q_\pi(s, a) - V_\pi(s)$, we replace $A_{\pi_{old}}$ with by the Q-value $Q_{\pi_{old}}$ in the objective function, which only changes the objective by a constant. Besides, note the following:

$$\sum_a \pi(a|s) A_{\pi_{old}}(s, a) = E_{a \sim \pi_{old}(a|s)} \left[\frac{\pi(a|s)}{\pi_{old}(a|s)} A_{\pi_{old}}(s, a) \right]$$

Therefore, given a trajectory $T = \{(s_0, a_0), \cdots, (s_m, a_m)\}$ generated under policy π_{old}, we will optimize as follows:

$$\text{minimize}_\pi \frac{1}{m} \sum_{(s,a) \in T} \pi(a|s) A_{\pi_{old}}(s, a), \text{ subject to } \frac{1}{m} \sum_{(s,a) \in T} D_{KL}(\pi_{old}(\cdot|s), \pi(\cdot|s)) \leq \delta$$

For the MuJoCo control tasks, both the policy π and the `state-action value` function $Q(s, a)$ are approximated by neural networks. In order to optimize this problem, the KL divergence constraint can be approximated by the Fisher information matrix. This problem can then be solved via the conjugate gradient algorithm. For more details, you can download the source code of TRPO from GitHub and check `optimizer.py`, which implements the conjugate gradient algorithm using TensorFlow.

Experiments on MuJoCo tasks

The Swimmer task is a good example to test TRPO. This task involves a 3-link swimming robot in a viscous fluid, where the goal is to make it swim forward as fast as possible by actuating the two joints (http://gym.openai.com/envs/Swimmer-v2/). The following screenshot shows how Swimmer looks in the MuJoCo simulator:

To train an agent for Swimmer, run the following command under the src folder:

```
CUDA_VISIBLE_DEVICES= python train.py -t Swimmer
```

There are two arguments in train.py One is -t, or --task, indicating the name of the MuJoCo or classic control task you want to test. Since the state spaces of these control tasks have relatively low dimensions compared to the Atari environment, it is enough to use CPU alone to train the agent by setting CUDA_VISIBLE_DEVICES to empty, which will take between 30 minutes and two hours.

During the training, you can open a new Terminal and type the following command to visualize the training procedure:

```
tensorboard --logdir=log/Swimmer
```

Here, `logdir` points to the folder where the `Swimmer` log file is stored. Once TensorBoard is running, navigate your web browser to `localhost:6006` to view the TensorBoard:

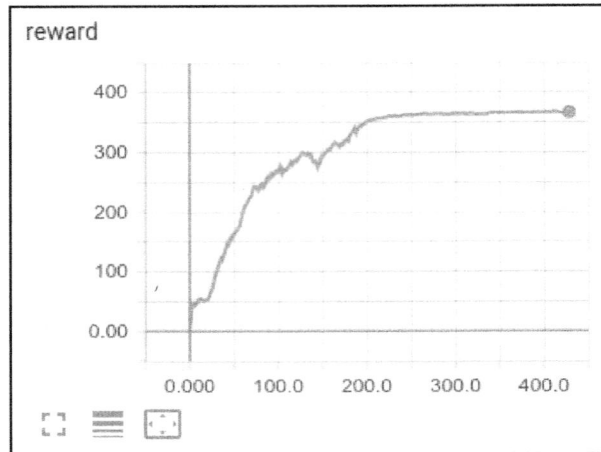

Clearly, after 200 episodes, the total reward achieved in each episode becomes stable, namely, around 366. To check how `Swimmer` moves after the training, run the following command:

```
CUDA_VISIBLE_DEVICES= python test.py -t Swimmer
```

You will see a funny-looking `Swimmer` object walking on the floor.

Summary

This chapter introduced the classical control tasks and the MuJoCo control tasks provided by Gym. You have learned the goals and specifications of these tasks and how to implement a simulator for them. The most important parts of this chapter were the deterministic DPG and the TRPO for continuous control tasks. You learned the theory behind them, which explains why they work well in these tasks. You also learned how to implement DPG and TRPO using TensorFlow, and how to visualize the training procedure.

In the next chapter, we will learn about how to apply reinforcement learning algorithms to more complex tasks, for example, playing Minecraft. We will introduce the **Asynchronous Actor-Critic (A3C)** algorithm, which is much faster than DQN at complex tasks, and has been widely applied as a framework in many deep reinforcement learning algorithms.

Building Virtual Worlds in Minecraft

5

In the two previous chapters, we discussed the **deep Q-learning (DQN)** algorithm for playing Atari games and the **Trust Region Policy Optimization (TRPO)** algorithm for continuous control tasks. We saw the big success of these algorithms in solving complex problems when compared to traditional reinforcement learning algorithms without the use of deep neural networks to approximate the value function or the policy function. Their main disadvantage, especially for DQN, is that the training step converges too slowly; for example, training an agent to play Atari games takes about one week. For more complex games, even one week's training is insufficient.

This chapter will introduce a more complicated example, Minecraft, which is a popular online video game created by Swedish game developer Markus Persson and later developed by Mojang. You will learn how to launch a Minecraft environment using OpenAI Gym and play different missions. In order to build an AI player to accomplish these missions, you will learn the **asynchronous advantage actor-critic (A3C)** algorithm, which is a lightweight framework for deep reinforcement learning that uses asynchronous gradient descent for optimization of deep neural network controllers. A3C is a widely applied deep reinforcement learning algorithm for different kinds of tasks, training for half the time on a single multi-core CPU instead of a GPU. For Atari games such as Breakout, A3C achieves human-level performance after 3 hours' training, which is much faster than DQN, which requires 3 days' training. You will learn how to implement A3C using Python and TensorFlow. This chapter does not require as much of a mathematical background as the previous chapter—just have fun!

The following topics will be covered in this chapter:

- Introduction to the Minecraft environment
- Data preparation for training an AI bot in the Minecraft environment
- The asynchronous advantage actor-critic framework
- Implementation of the A3C framework

Introduction to the Minecraft environment

The original OpenAI Gym does not contain the Minecraft environment. We need to install a Minecraft environment bundle, available at `https://github.com/tambetm/gym-minecraft`. This bundle is built based on Microsoft's Malmö, which is a platform for AI experimentation and research built on top of Minecraft.

Before installing the `gym-minecraft` package, Malmö should first be downloaded from `https://github.com/Microsoft/malmo`. We can download the latest pre-built version from `https://github.com/Microsoft/malmo/releases`. After unzipping the package, go to the `Minecraft` folder and run `launchClient.bat` on Windows, or `launchClient.sh` on Linux/MacOS, to launch a Minecraft environment. If it is successfully launched, we can now install `gym-minecraft` via the following scripts:

```
python3 -m pip install gym
python3 -m pip install pygame

git clone https://github.com/tambetm/minecraft-py.git
cd minecraft-py
python setup.py install

git clone https://github.com/tambetm/gym-minecraft.git
cd gym-minecraft
python setup.py install
```

Then, we can run the following code to test whether `gym-minecraft` has been successfully installed or not:

```
import logging
import minecraft_py
logging.basicConfig(level=logging.DEBUG)

proc, _ = minecraft_py.start()
minecraft_py.stop(proc)
```

The `gym-minecraft` package provides 15 different missions, including `MinecraftDefaultWorld1-v0` and `MinecraftBasic-v0`. For example, in `MinecraftBasic-v0`, the agent can move around in a small chamber with a box placed in the corner, and the goal is to reach the position of this box. The following screenshots show several missions available in `gym-minecraft`:

The `gym-minecraft` package has the same interface as other Gym environments, such as Atari and classic control tasks. You can run the following code to test different Minecraft missions and try to get a high-level understanding of their properties, for example, goal, reward, and observation:

```
import gym
import gym_minecraft
import minecraft_py

def start_game():
    env = gym.make('MinecraftBasic-v0')
    env.init(start_minecraft=True)
    env.reset()
    done = False
    while not done:
        env.render(mode='human')
        action = env.action_space.sample()
        obs, reward, done, info = env.step(action)
    env.close()

if __name__ == "__main__":
    start_game()
```

At each step, an action is randomly drawn from the action space by calling `env.action_space.sample()`, and then this action is submitted to the system by calling the `env.step(action)` function, which returns the observation and the reward corresponding to this action. You can also try other missions by replacing `MinecraftBasic-v0` with other names, for example, `MinecraftMaze1-v0` and `MinecraftObstacles-v0`.

Data preparation

In the Atari environment, recall that there are three modes for each Atari game, for example, Breakout, BreakoutDeterministic, and BreakoutNoFrameskip, and each mode has two versions, for example, Breakout-v0 and Breakout-v4. The main difference between the three modes is the frameskip parameter that indicates the number of frames (steps) the one action is repeated on. This is called the **frame-skipping** technique, which allows us to play more games without significantly increasing the runtime.

However, in the Minecraft environment, there is only one mode where the frameskip parameter is equal to one. Therefore, in order to apply the frame-skipping technique, we need to explicitly repeat a certain action frameskip multiple times during one timestep. Besides this, the frame images returned by the `step` function are RGB images. Similar to the Atari environment, the observed frame images are converted to grayscale and then resized to 84x84. The following code provides the wrapper for `gym-minecraft`, which contains all the data preprocessing steps:

```
import gym
import gym_minecraft
import minecraft_py
import numpy, time
from utils import cv2_resize_image

class Game:

    def __init__(self, name='MinecraftBasic-v0', discrete_movement=False):
        self.env = gym.make(name)
        if discrete_movement:
            self.env.init(start_minecraft=True,
allowDiscreteMovement=["move", "turn"])
        else:
            self.env.init(start_minecraft=True,
allowContinuousMovement=["move", "turn"])
        self.actions = list(range(self.env.action_space.n))
        frame = self.env.reset()
        self.frame_skip = 4
        self.total_reward = 0
        self.crop_size = 84
        self.buffer_size = 8
        self.buffer_index = 0
        self.buffer = [self.crop(self.rgb_to_gray(frame)) for _ in
range(self.buffer_size)]
        self.last_frame = frame
    def rgb_to_gray(self, im):
        return numpy.dot(im, [0.2126, 0.7152, 0.0722])
    def reset(self):
```

```
        frame = self.env.reset()
        self.total_reward = 0
        self.buffer_index = 0
        self.buffer = [self.crop(self.rgb_to_gray(frame)) for _ in
range(self.buffer_size)]
        self.last_frame = frame
    def add_frame_to_buffer(self, frame):
        self.buffer_index = self.buffer_index % self.buffer_size
        self.buffer[self.buffer_index] = frame
        self.buffer_index += 1
    def get_available_actions(self):
        return list(range(len(self.actions)))
    def get_feedback_size(self):
        return (self.crop_size. self.crop_size)
    def crop(self, frame):
        feedback = cv2_resize_image(frame,
                                    resized_shape=(self.crop_size,
self.crop_size),
                                    method='scale', crop_offset=0)
        return feedback
    def get_current_feedback(self, num_frames=4):
        assert num_frames < self.buffer_size, "Frame buffer is not large
enough."
        index = self.buffer_index - 1
        frames = [numpy.expand_dims(self.buffer[index - k], axis=0) for k
in range(num_frames)]
        if num_frames > 1:
            return numpy.concatenate(frames, axis=0)
        else:
            return frames[0]
    def play_action(self, action, num_frames=4):
        reward = 0
        termination = 0
        for i in range(self.frame_skip):
            a = self.actions[action]
            frame, r, done, _ = self.env.step(a)
            reward += r
            if i == self.frame_skip - 2:
                self.last_frame = frame
            if done:
                termination = 1
self.add_frame_to_buffer(self.crop(numpy.maximum(self.rgb_to_gray(frame),
self.rgb_to_gray(self.last_frame))))
        r = numpy.clip(reward, -1, 1)
        self.total_reward += reward
        return r, self.get_current_feedback(num_frames), termination
```

In the constructor, the available actions for Minecraft are restricted to `move` and `turn` (not considering other actions, such as the camera controls). Converting an RGB image into a grayscale image is quite easy. Given an RGB image with shape (height, width, channel), the `rgb_to_gray` function is used to convert an image to grayscale. For cropping and reshaping frame images, we use the `opencv-python` or `cv2` packages, which contain a Python wrapper around the original C++ OpenCV implementation, that is, the `crop` function reshapes an image into an 84x84 matrix. Unlike the Atari environment, where `crop_offset` is set to 8 to remove the scoreboard from the screen, here, we set `crop_offset` to 0 and just reshape the frame images.

The `play_action` function submits the input action to the Minecraft environment and returns the corresponding reward, observation, and termination signal. The default frameskip parameter is set to 4, meaning that one action is repeated four times for each `play_action` call. The `get_current_feedback` function returns the observation that stacks the last four frame images together, since only considering the current frame image is not enough for playing Minecraft because it doesn't contain dynamic information about the game status.

This wrapper has the same interface as the wrappers for the Atari environment and classic control tasks. Therefore, you can try to run DQN or TRPO with the Minecraft environment without changing anything. If you have one idle GPU, it is better to run DQN first before trying the A3C algorithm that we will discuss next.

Asynchronous advantage actor-critic algorithm

In the previous chapters, we discussed the DQN for playing Atari games and the use of the DPG and TRPO algorithms for continuous control tasks. Recall that DQN has the following architecture:

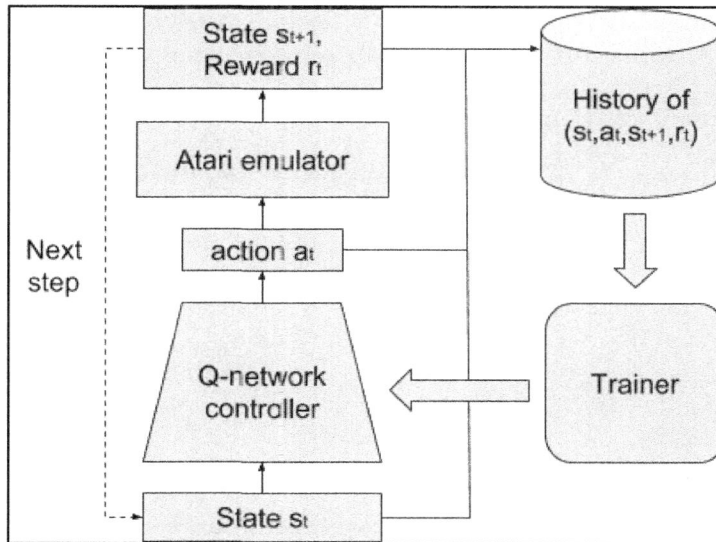

At each timestep t, the agent observes the frame image s_t and selects an action a_t based on the current learned policy. The emulator (the Minecraft environment) executes this action and returns the next frame image s_{t+1} and the corresponding reward r_t. The quadruplet (s_t, a_t, r_t, s_{t+1}) is then stored in the experience memory and is taken as a sample for training the Q-network by minimizing the empirical loss function via stochastic gradient descent.

Deep reinforcement learning algorithms based on experience replay have achieved unprecedented success in playing Atari games. However, experience replay has several disadvantages:

- It uses more memory and computation per real interaction
- It requires off-policy learning algorithms that can update from data generated by an older policy

In order to reduce memory consumption and accelerate the training of an AI agent, Mnih et al. proposed an A3C framework for deep reinforcement learning that dramatically reduces the training time without performance loss. This work, *Asynchronous Methods for Deep Reinforcement Learning*, was published in ICML, 2016.

Instead of experience replay, A3C asynchronously executes multiple agents in parallel on multiple instances of the environment, such as the Atari or Minecraft environments. Since the parallel agents experience a variety of different states, this parallelism breaks the correlation between the training samples and stabilizes the training procedure, which means that the experience memory can be removed. This simple idea enables a much larger spectrum of fundamental on-policy reinforcement learning algorithms, such as Sarsa and actor-critic methods, as well as off-policy reinforcement learning algorithms, such as Q-learning, to be applied robustly and effectively using deep neural networks.

Another advantage is that A3C is able to run on a standard multi-core CPU without relying on GPUs or massively distributed architectures, and requires far less training time than GPU-based algorithms, such as DQN, when applied to Atari games. A3C is good for a beginner in deep reinforcement learning since you can apply it to Atari games on a standard PC with multiple cores. For example, for Breakout, it takes only two-three hours to achieve a score of 300 when executing eight agents in parallel.

In this chapter, we will use the same notations as before. At each timestep t, the agent observes state s_t, takes action a_t, and then receives the corresponding reward r_t generated from a function $R(s_t, a_t)$. We use $\pi(a_t|s_t)$ to denote the policy of the agent, which maps states to a probability distribution over the actions. The Bellman equation is as follows:

$$Q(s_t, a_t) = E_{s_{t+1} \sim S}[R(s_t, a_t) + \gamma E_{a_{t+1} \sim \pi(a_{t+1}|s_{t+1})} Q(s_{t+1}, a_{t+1})]$$

The state-action value function Q can be approximated by a neural network parameterized by θ^Q, and the policy π can also be represented by another neural network parameterized by θ^π. Then, Q can be be trained by minimizing the following loss function:

$$L(\theta^Q) = E_{s_t, a_t}[(y_t - Q(s_t, a_t | \theta^Q))^2]$$

y_t is the approximated state-action value function at step t. In one-step Q-learning such as DQN, $\pi(a_t | s_t)$ equals $\overset{\arg\max Q'(s_t, a)}{a}$, so that the following is true:

$$y_t = R(s_t, a_t) + \gamma \max_a Q(s_{t+1}, a) | \theta^Q)$$

One drawback of using one-step Q-learning is that obtaining a reward $R(s_t, a_t)$ only directly affects the value of the state action pair (s_t, a_t) that led to the reward. This can make the learning process slow since many updates are required to propagate a reward to the relevant preceding states and actions. One way of propagating rewards faster is by using n-step returns. In n-step Q-learning, y_t can be set to this:

$$R(s_t, a_t) + \gamma R(s_{t+1}, a_{t+1}) + \gamma^2 R(s_{t+2}, a_{t+2}) + \cdots + \gamma^{n-1} R(s_{t+n-1}, a_{t+n-1}) + \gamma^n \max_a Q(s_{t+n}, a) | \theta^Q)$$

As opposed to value-based methods, a policy-based method, such as TRPO, directly optimizes the policy network π. Besides TRPO, a much simpler method is REINFORCE, which updates the policy parameter θ^π in the direction $\nabla_{\theta^\pi} \log \pi(a_t | s_t; \theta^\pi) A(s_t, a_t)$, where $A(a_t, s_t) = Q(s_t, a_t) - V(s_t)$ is the the advantage of action a_t in state s_t. This method is an actor-critic approach due to the fact that it is required to estimate the value function $V(s_t)$ and the policy $\pi(a_t | s_t)$.

The asynchronous reinforcement learning framework can be applied in the approaches already discussed here. The main idea is that we run multiple agents in parallel with their own instances of the environment, for example, multiple players play the same game using their own games consoles. These agents are likely to be exploring different parts of the environment. The parameters θ^Q and θ^π are shared among all agents. Each agent updates the policy and the value function asynchronously without considering read–write conflicts. Although it seems weird that there is no synchronization in updating the policy, this asynchronous method not only removes the communication costs of sending gradients and parameters, but also guarantees the convergence. For more details, please refer to the following paper: *A lock-free approach to parallelizing stochastic gradient descent*, Recht et al. This chapter focuses on A3C, namely, we apply the asynchronous reinforcement learning framework in REINFORCE. The following diagram shows the A3C architecture:

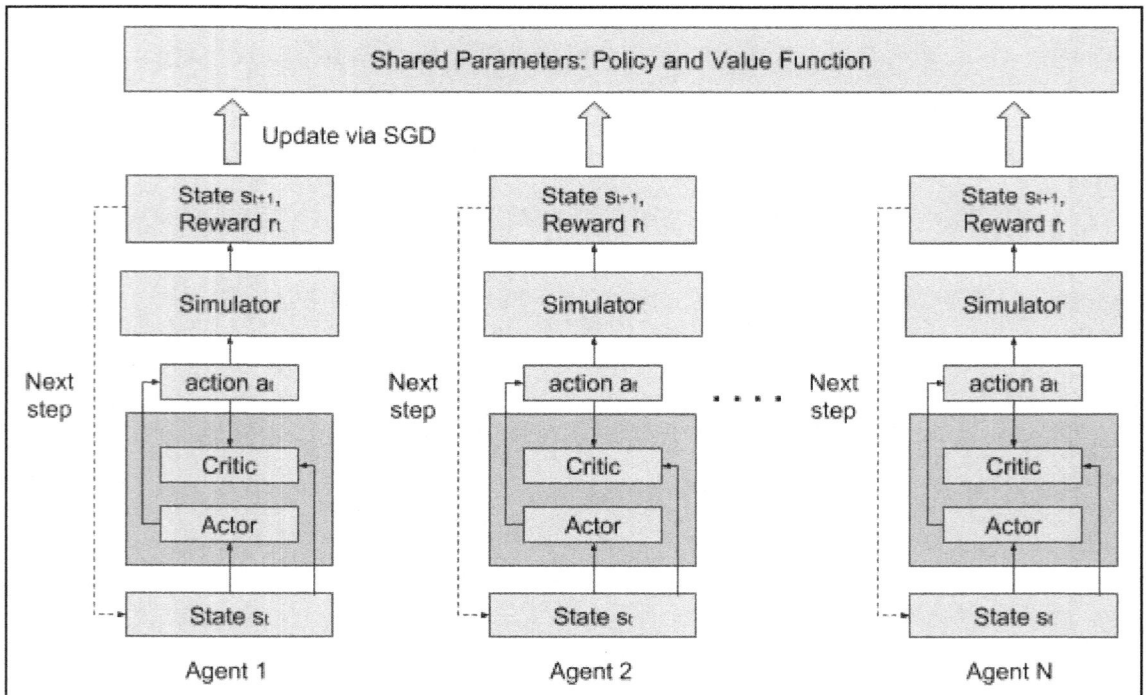

For A3C, the policy $\pi(a_t|s_t;\theta^\pi)$ and the value function $V(s_t;\theta^V)$ are approximated by two neural networks. A3C updates the policy parameter θ^π in the direction $\nabla_{\theta^\pi}\log\pi(a_t|s_t;\theta^\pi)A(s_t,a_t)$, where $A(s_t,a_t)$ is fixed, which is estimated by the following:

$$A(s_t,a_t) = \sum_{i=0}^{k-1}\gamma^i R(s_{t+1},a_{t+i}) + \gamma^k V(s_{t+k}) - V(s_t)$$

A3C updates the value function parameter θ^V by minimizing the loss:

$$(V(s_t;\theta^V)) - (\sum_{i=0}^{k-1}\gamma^i R(s_{t+1},a_{t+i}) + \gamma^k V(s_{t+k})))$$

$V(s_{t+k})$ is computed via the previous estimate. To encourage exploration during training, the entropy of the policy π is also added to the policy update, acting as a regularization term. Then, the gradient for the policy update becomes the following:

$$\nabla_{\theta^\pi}\log\pi(a_t|s_t;\theta^\pi)A(s_t,a_t) + \beta\nabla_{\theta^\pi}H(\pi(s_t;\theta^\pi))$$

The following pseudo code shows the A3C algorithm for each agent (thread):

```
Initialize thread step counter t = 1;
Initialize global shared parameters θ^V and θ^π;
Repeat for each episode:
    Reset gradients dθ^V = 0 and dθ^π = 0;
    Synchronize thread-specific parameters θ_a^V = θ^V and θ_a^π = θ^π;
    Set the start time step t_start = t;
    Receive an observation state s_t;
    While s_t is not the terminal state and t - t_start < t_max:
        Select an action a_t according to π(s_t; θ_a^π);
        Execute action a_t in the simulator and observe reward r_t and the
next state s_{t+1};
        Set t = t + 1;
    End While
    Set R = 0 if s_t is the terminal state or R = V(s_t; θ_a^V) otherwise;
    For i ∈ {t - 1, ···, t_start} do
        Update R = r_i + γR;
        Accumulate gradients wrt θ_a^π:
dθ^π = dθ^π + ∇_{θ_a^π} log π(a_i|s_i; θ_a^π)(R - V(s_i; θ_a^V)) + β∇_{θ_a^π}H(π(s_i; θ_a^π));
        Accumulate gradients wrt θ_a^V:    dθ^V = dθ^V + ∇_{θ_a^V}(R - V(s_i; θ_a^V))^2;
    End For
    Perform asynchronous update of θ^V using dθ^V and of θ^π using dθ^π.
```

A3C uses ADAM or RMSProp to perform an asynchronous update of the parameters. For different environments, it is hard to tell which method leads to better performance. We can use RMSProp for the Atari and Minecraft environments.

Implementation of A3C

We will now look at how to implement A3C using Python and TensorFlow. Here, the policy network and value network share the same feature representation. We implement two kinds of policies: one is based on the CNN architecture used in DQN, and the other is based on LSTM.

We implement the `FFPolicy` class for the policy based on CNN:

```
class FFPolicy:
    def __init__(self, input_shape=(84, 84, 4), n_outputs=4,
network_type='cnn'):
        self.width = input_shape[0]
        self.height = input_shape[1]
        self.channel = input_shape[2]
        self.n_outputs = n_outputs
        self.network_type = network_type
        self.entropy_beta = 0.01
        self.x = tf.placeholder(dtype=tf.float32,
                                shape=(None, self.channel, self.width,
self.height))
        self.build_model()
```

The constructor requires three arguments:

1. `input_shape`
2. `n_outputs`
3. `network_type`

`input_shape` is the size of the input image. After data preprocessing, the input is an 84x84x4 image, so the default parameter is (84, 84, 4). `n_outputs` is the number of all the available actions. `network_type` indicates the type of the feature representation we want to use. Our implementation contains two different networks. One is the CNN architecture used in DQN. The other is a feedforward neural network used for testing.

1. In the constructor, the x variable represents the input state (a batch of 84x84x4 images). After creating the input tensors, the `build_model` function is called to build the policy and value network. Here is the `build_model`:

```
def build_model(self):
    self.net = {}
    self.net['input'] = tf.transpose(self.x, perm=(0, 2, 3, 1))
    if self.network_type == 'cnn':
        self.net['conv1'] = conv2d(self.net['input'], 16, kernel=(8,
8), stride=(4, 4), name='conv1')
        self.net['conv2'] = conv2d(self.net['conv1'], 32, kernel=(4,
4), stride=(2, 2), name='conv2')
        self.net['feature'] = linear(self.net['conv2'], 256,
name='fc1')
    else:
        self.net['fc1'] = linear(self.net['input'], 50, init_b =
tf.constant_initializer(0.0), name='fc1')
        self.net['feature'] = linear(self.net['fc1'], 50, init_b =
tf.constant_initializer(0.0), name='fc2')
    self.net['value'] = tf.reshape(linear(self.net['feature'], 1,
activation=None, name='value',
                                          init_b =
tf.constant_initializer(0.0)),
                                   shape=(-1,))
    self.net['logits'] = linear(self.net['feature'], self.n_outputs,
activation=None, name='logits',
                                  init_b = tf.constant_initializer(0.0))
    self.net['policy'] = tf.nn.softmax(self.net['logits'],
name='policy')
    self.net['log_policy'] = tf.nn.log_softmax(self.net['logits'],
name='log_policy')
    self.vars = tf.get_collection(tf.GraphKeys.TRAINABLE_VARIABLES,
tf.get_variable_scope().name)
```

The CNN architecture contains two convolutional layers and one hidden layer, while the feedforward architecture contains two hidden layers. As discussed previously, the policy network and the value network share the same feature representation.

2. The loss function for updating the network parameters can be constructed via the following function:

```
def build_gradient_op(self, clip_grad=None):

    self.action = tf.placeholder(dtype=tf.float32, shape=(None,
self.n_outputs), name='action')
    self.reward = tf.placeholder(dtype=tf.float32, shape=(None,),
name='reward')
    self.advantage = tf.placeholder(dtype=tf.float32, shape=(None,),
name='advantage')

    value = self.net['value']
    policy = self.net['policy']
    log_policy = self.net['log_policy']
    entropy = -tf.reduce_sum(policy * log_policy, axis=1)
    p_loss = -tf.reduce_sum(tf.reduce_sum(log_policy * self.action,
axis=1) * self.advantage + self.entropy_beta * entropy)
    v_loss = 0.5 * tf.reduce_sum((value - self.reward) ** 2)
    total_loss = p_loss + v_loss
    self.gradients = tf.gradients(total_loss, self.vars)
    if clip_grad is not None:
        self.gradients, _ = tf.clip_by_global_norm(self.gradients,
clip_grad)
    tf.summary.scalar("policy_loss", p_loss,
collections=['policy_network'])
    tf.summary.scalar("value_loss", v_loss,
collections=['policy_network'])
    tf.summary.scalar("entropy", tf.reduce_mean(entropy),
collections=['policy_network'])
    self.summary_op = tf.summary.merge_all('policy_network')
    return self.gradients
```

3. This function creates three input tensors:
    1. `action`
    2. `reward`
    3. `advantage`

4. The `action` variable represents the selected actions a_t. The `reward` variable is the discounted cumulative reward R in the preceding A3C algorithm. The `advantage` variable is the advantage function computed by $R - V(s_t)$. In this implementation, the losses of the policy and the value function are combined together, since the feature representation layers are shared.

5. Therefore, instead of updating the `policy` parameter and the `value` parameter separately, our implementation updates these parameters simultaneously. This function also creates `summary_op` for TensorBoard visualization.

The implementation of the LSTM policy is quite similar to the feedforward policy. The main difference is the `build_model` function:

```
def build_model(self):
    self.net = {}
    self.net['input'] = tf.transpose(self.x, perm=(0, 2, 3, 1))
    if self.network_type == 'cnn':
        self.net['conv1'] = conv2d(self.net['input'], 16, kernel=(8,
8), stride=(4, 4), name='conv1')
        self.net['conv2'] = conv2d(self.net['conv1'], 32, kernel=(4,
4), stride=(2, 2), name='conv2')
        self.net['feature'] = linear(self.net['conv2'], 256,
name='fc1')
    else:
        self.net['fc1'] = linear(self.net['input'], 50, init_b =
tf.constant_initializer(0.0), name='fc1')
        self.net['feature'] = linear(self.net['fc1'], 50, init_b =
tf.constant_initializer(0.0), name='fc2')
    num_units = self.net['feature'].get_shape().as_list()[-1]
    self.lstm = tf.contrib.rnn.BasicLSTMCell(num_units=num_units,
forget_bias=0.0, state_is_tuple=True)
    self.init_state = self.lstm.zero_state(batch_size=1,
dtype=tf.float32)
    step_size = tf.shape(self.x)[:1]
    feature = tf.expand_dims(self.net['feature'], axis=0)
    lstm_outputs, lstm_state = tf.nn.dynamic_rnn(self.lstm, feature,
initial_state=self.init_state,
sequence_length=step_size,
                                                time_major=False)
    outputs = tf.reshape(lstm_outputs, shape=(-1, num_units))
    self.final_state = lstm_state
    self.net['value'] = tf.reshape(linear(outputs, 1, activation=None,
name='value',
                                            init_b =
tf.constant_initializer(0.0),
                                    shape=(-1,))
    self.net['logits'] = linear(outputs, self.n_outputs,
```

```
activation=None, name='logits',
                                    init_b = tf.constant_initializer(0.0))
        self.net['policy'] = tf.nn.softmax(self.net['logits'],
name='policy')
        self.net['log_policy'] = tf.nn.log_softmax(self.net['logits'],
name='log_policy')
        self.vars = tf.get_collection(tf.GraphKeys.TRAINABLE_VARIABLES,
tf.get_variable_scope().name)
```

In this function, a LSTM layer follows the feature representation layers. In TensorFlow, you can easily create a LSTM layer by constructing `BasicLSTMCell` and then calling `tf.nn.dynamic_rnn` to get the layer outputs. `tf.nn.dynamic_rnn` returns the output for each time step and the final cell state.

We now implement the main A3C algorithm—the `A3C` class:

```
class A3C:
    def __init__(self, system, directory, param, agent_index=0,
callback=None):
        self.system = system
        self.actions = system.get_available_actions()
        self.directory = directory
        self.callback = callback
        self.feedback_size = system.get_feedback_size()
        self.agent_index = agent_index
        self.set_params(param)
        self.init_network()
```

The `system` parameter is the emulator, either the Atari environment or Minecraft environment. `directory` indicates the folder for the saved model and logs. `param` includes all the training parameters of A3C, for example, the batch size and learning rate. `agent_index` is the label for one agent. The constructor calls `init_network` to initialize the policy network and the value network. Here is the implementation of `init_network`:

```
    def init_network(self):
        input_shape = self.feedback_size + (self.num_frames,)
        worker_device =
"/job:worker/task:{}/cpu:0".format(self.agent_index)
        with tf.device(tf.train.replica_device_setter(1,
worker_device=worker_device)):
            with tf.variable_scope("global"):
                if self.use_lstm is False:
                    self.shared_network = FFPolicy(input_shape,
len(self.actions), self.network_type)
                else:
                    self.shared_network = LSTMPolicy(input_shape,
len(self.actions), self.network_type)
```

```
                self.global_step = tf.get_variable("global_step", shape=[],
initializer=tf.constant_initializer(0, dtype=tf.int32),
                                                        trainable=False,
dtype=tf.int32)
                self.best_score = tf.get_variable("best_score", shape=[],
initializer=tf.constant_initializer(-1e2, dtype=tf.float32),
                                                        trainable=False,
dtype=tf.float32)
        with tf.device(worker_device):
            with tf.variable_scope('local'):
                if self.use_lstm is False:
                    self.network = FFPolicy(input_shape, len(self.actions),
self.network_type)
                else:
                    self.network = LSTMPolicy(input_shape,
len(self.actions), self.network_type)
                # Sync params
                self.update_local_ops =
update_target_graph(self.shared_network.vars, self.network.vars)
                # Learning rate
                self.lr = tf.get_variable(name='lr', shape=[],
initializer=tf.constant_initializer(self.learning_rate),
                                            trainable=False,
dtype=tf.float32)
                self.t_lr = tf.placeholder(dtype=tf.float32, shape=[],
name='new_lr')
                self.assign_lr_op = tf.assign(self.lr, self.t_lr)
                # Best score
                self.t_score = tf.placeholder(dtype=tf.float32, shape=[],
name='new_score')
                self.assign_best_score_op = tf.assign(self.best_score,
self.t_score)
                # Build gradient_op
                self.increase_step = self.global_step.assign_add(1)
                gradients = self.network.build_gradient_op(clip_grad=40.0)
                # Additional summaries
                tf.summary.scalar("learning_rate", self.lr,
collections=['a3c'])
                tf.summary.scalar("score", self.t_score,
collections=['a3c'])
                tf.summary.scalar("best_score", self.best_score,
collections=['a3c'])
                self.summary_op = tf.summary.merge_all('a3c')
        if self.shared_optimizer:
            with tf.device(tf.train.replica_device_setter(1,
worker_device=worker_device)):
                with tf.variable_scope("global"):
                    optimizer = create_optimizer(self.update_method,
```

```
                 self.lr, self.rho, self.rmsprop_epsilon)
                              self.train_op =
        optimizer.apply_gradients(zip(gradients, self.shared_network.vars))
              else:
                  with tf.device(worker_device):
                      with tf.variable_scope('local'):
                          optimizer = create_optimizer(self.update_method,
                 self.lr, self.rho, self.rmsprop_epsilon)
                              self.train_op =
        optimizer.apply_gradients(zip(gradients, self.shared_network.vars))
```

The tricky part in this function is how to implement the global shared parameters. In TensorFlow, we can do this with the `tf.train.replica_device_setter` function. We first create a `global` device shared among all the agents. Within this device, the global shared network is created. Then, we create a local device and a local network for each agent. To synchronize the global and local parameters, `update_local_ops` is created by calling the `update_target_graph` function:

```
def update_target_graph(from_vars, to_vars):
    op_holder = []
    for from_var, to_var in zip(from_vars, to_vars):
        op_holder.append(to_var.assign(from_var))
    return op_holder
```

Then, the `gradients` op is constructed by calling `build_gradient_op`, which is used to compute the gradient update for each agent. With `gradients`, an optimizer is built via the `create_optimizer` function that is used for updating the global shared parameters. The `create_optimizer` function is used as follows:

```
def create_optimizer(method, learning_rate, rho, epsilon):
    if method == 'rmsprop':
        opt = tf.train.RMSPropOptimizer(learning_rate=learning_rate,
                                        decay=rho,
                                        epsilon=epsilon)
    elif method == 'adam':
        opt = tf.train.AdamOptimizer(learning_rate=learning_rate,
                                     beta1=rho)
    else:
        raise
    return opt
```

The main function in A3C is `run`, which starts and trains the agent:

```
def run(self, sess, saver=None):
    num_of_trials = -1
    for episode in range(self.num_episodes):
        self.system.reset()
```

```
            cell = self.network.run_initial_state(sess)
            state = self.system.get_current_feedback(self.num_frames)
            state = numpy.asarray(state / self.input_scale,
dtype=numpy.float32)
            replay_memory = []
            for _ in range(self.T):
                num_of_trials += 1
                global_step = sess.run(self.increase_step)
                if len(replay_memory) == 0:
                    init_cell = cell
                    sess.run(self.update_local_ops)
                action, value, cell = self.choose_action(sess, state, cell)
                r, new_state, termination = self.play(action)
                new_state = numpy.asarray(new_state / self.input_scale,
dtype=numpy.float32)
                replay = (state, action, r, new_state, value, termination)
                replay_memory.append(replay)
                state = new_state

                if len(replay_memory) == self.async_update_interval or
termination:
                    states, actions, rewards, advantages =
self.n_step_q_learning(sess, replay_memory, cell)
                    self.train(sess, states, actions, rewards, advantages,
init_cell, num_of_trials)
                    replay_memory = []

                if global_step % 40000 == 0:
                    self.save(sess, saver)
                if self.callback:
                    self.callback()
                if termination:
                    score = self.system.get_total_reward()
                    summary_str = sess.run(self.summary_op,
feed_dict={self.t_score: score})
                    self.summary_writer.add_summary(summary_str,
global_step)
                    self.summary_writer.flush()
                    break

            if global_step - self.eval_counter > self.eval_frequency:
                self.evaluate(sess, n_episode=10, saver=saver)
                self.eval_counter = global_step
```

At each timestep, it calls `choose_action` to select an action according to the current policy, and executes this action by calling `play`. Then, the received reward, the new state, and the termination signal, as well as the current state and the selected action, are stored in the `replay_memory`, which records the trajectory that the agent visited. Given this trajectory, it then calls `n_step_q_learning` to estimate the cumulative reward and the `advantage` function:

```
def n_step_q_learning(self, sess, replay_memory, cell):
    batch_size = len(replay_memory)
    w, h = self.system.get_feedback_size()
    states = numpy.zeros((batch_size, self.num_frames, w, h),
dtype=numpy.float32)
    rewards = numpy.zeros(batch_size, dtype=numpy.float32)
    advantages = numpy.zeros(batch_size, dtype=numpy.float32)
    actions = numpy.zeros((batch_size, len(self.actions)),
dtype=numpy.float32)
    for i in reversed(range(batch_size)):
        state, action, r, new_state, value, termination =
replay_memory[i]
        states[i] = state
        actions[i][action] = 1
        if termination != 0:
            rewards[i] = r
        else:
            if i == batch_size - 1:
                rewards[i] = r + self.gamma * self.Q_value(sess,
new_state, cell)
            else:
                rewards[i] = r + self.gamma * rewards[i+1]
        advantages[i] = rewards[i] - value
    return states, actions, rewards, advantages
```

It then updates the global shared parameters by calling `train`:

```
    def train(self, sess, states, actions, rewards, advantages, init_cell,
iter_num):
        lr = self.anneal_lr(iter_num)
        feed_dict = self.network.get_feed_dict(states, actions, rewards,
advantages, init_cell)
        sess.run(self.assign_lr_op, feed_dict={self.t_lr: lr})
        step = int((iter_num - self.async_update_interval + 1) /
self.async_update_interval)
        if self.summary_writer and step % 10 == 0:
            summary_str, _, step = sess.run([self.network.summary_op,
self.train_op, self.global_step],
                                        feed_dict=feed_dict)
            self.summary_writer.add_summary(summary_str, step)
```

```
            self.summary_writer.flush()
        else:
            sess.run(self.train_op, feed_dict=feed_dict)
```

Note that the model will be saved on the disk after 40,000 updates, and an evaluation procedure starts after `self.eval_frequency` updates.

To launch one agent, we can run the following codes written in the `worker.py` file:

```python
import numpy, time, random
import argparse, os, sys, signal
import tensorflow as tf
from a3c import A3C
from cluster import cluster_spec
from environment import new_environment

def set_random_seed(seed):
    random.seed(seed)
    numpy.random.seed(seed)

def delete_dir(path):
    if tf.gfile.Exists(path):
        tf.gfile.DeleteRecursively(path)
    tf.gfile.MakeDirs(path)
    return path

def shutdown(signal, frame):
    print('Received signal {}: exiting'.format(signal))
    sys.exit(128 + signal)

def train(args, server):
    os.environ['OMP_NUM_THREADS'] = '1'
    set_random_seed(args.task * 17)
    log_dir = os.path.join(args.log_dir, '{}/train'.format(args.env))
    if not tf.gfile.Exists(log_dir):
        tf.gfile.MakeDirs(log_dir)

    game, parameter = new_environment(args.env)
    a3c = A3C(game, log_dir, parameter.get(), agent_index=args.task,
callback=None)

    global_vars = [v for v in tf.global_variables() if not
v.name.startswith("local")]
    ready_op = tf.report_uninitialized_variables(global_vars)
    config = tf.ConfigProto(device_filters=["/job:ps",
"/job:worker/task:{}/cpu:0".format(args.task)])

    with tf.Session(target=server.target, config=config) as sess:
```

```
        saver = tf.train.Saver()
        path = os.path.join(log_dir, 'log_%d' % args.task)
        writer = tf.summary.FileWriter(delete_dir(path), sess.graph_def)
        a3c.set_summary_writer(writer)
        if args.task == 0:
            sess.run(tf.global_variables_initializer())
        else:
            while len(sess.run(ready_op)) > 0:
                print("Waiting for task 0 initializing the global
variables.")
                time.sleep(1)
        a3c.run(sess, saver)

def main():
    parser = argparse.ArgumentParser(description=None)
    parser.add_argument('-t', '--task', default=0, type=int, help='Task
index')
    parser.add_argument('-j', '--job_name', default="worker", type=str,
help='worker or ps')
    parser.add_argument('-w', '--num_workers', default=1, type=int,
help='Number of workers')
    parser.add_argument('-l', '--log_dir', default="save", type=str,
help='Log directory path')
    parser.add_argument('-e', '--env', default="demo", type=str,
help='Environment')
    args = parser.parse_args()
    spec = cluster_spec(args.num_workers, 1)
    cluster = tf.train.ClusterSpec(spec)

    signal.signal(signal.SIGHUP, shutdown)
    signal.signal(signal.SIGINT, shutdown)
    signal.signal(signal.SIGTERM, shutdown)
    if args.job_name == "worker":
        server = tf.train.Server(cluster,
                                 job_name="worker",
                                 task_index=args.task,
config=tf.ConfigProto(intra_op_parallelism_threads=0,
inter_op_parallelism_threads=0)) # Use default op_parallelism_threads
        train(args, server)
    else:
        server = tf.train.Server(cluster,
                                 job_name="ps",
                                 task_index=args.task,
config=tf.ConfigProto(device_filters=["/job:ps"]))
        # server.join()
        while True:
            time.sleep(1000)
```

```
if __name__ == "__main__":
    main()
```

The main function will create a new agent and begin the training procedure if the `job_name` parameter is `worker`. Otherwise, it will start the TensorFlow parameter server for the global shared parameters. Notice that before launching multiple agents, we need to start the parameter server first. In the `train` function, an environment is created by calling `new_environment` and then an agent is built for this environment. After the agent is successfully created, the global shared parameters are initialized and the train procedure starts by calling `a3c.run(sess, saver)`.

Because manually launching 8 or 16 agents is quite inconvenient, this can be done automatically by the following script:

```
import argparse, os, sys, cluster
from six.moves import shlex_quote

parser = argparse.ArgumentParser(description="Run commands")
parser.add_argument('-w', '--num_workers', default=1, type=int,
                    help="Number of workers")
parser.add_argument('-e', '--env', type=str, default="demo",
                    help="Environment")
parser.add_argument('-l', '--log_dir', type=str, default="save",
                    help="Log directory path")

def new_cmd(session, name, cmd, logdir, shell):
    if isinstance(cmd, (list, tuple)):
        cmd = " ".join(shlex_quote(str(v)) for v in cmd)
    return name, "tmux send-keys -t {}:{} {} Enter".format(session, name,
shlex_quote(cmd))

def create_commands(session, num_workers, logdir, env, shell='bash'):

    base_cmd = ['CUDA_VISIBLE_DEVICES=',
                sys.executable,
                'worker.py',
                '--log_dir', logdir,
                '--num_workers', str(num_workers),
                '--env', env]

    cmds_map = [new_cmd(session, "ps", base_cmd + ["--job_name", "ps"],
logdir, shell)]
    for i in range(num_workers):
        cmd = base_cmd + ["--job_name", "worker", "--task", str(i)]
        cmds_map.append(new_cmd(session, "w-%d" % i, cmd, logdir, shell))
    cmds_map.append(new_cmd(session, "htop", ["htop"], logdir, shell))
    windows = [v[0] for v in cmds_map]
```

```
    notes = ["Use `tmux attach -t {}` to watch process
output".format(session),
            "Use `tmux kill-session -t {}` to kill the
job".format(session),
            "Use `ssh -L PORT:SERVER_IP:SERVER_PORT username@server_ip` to
remote Tensorboard"]

    cmds = ["kill $(lsof -i:{}-{} -t) > /dev/null
2>&1".format(cluster.PORT, num_workers+cluster.PORT),
            "tmux kill-session -t {}".format(session),
            "tmux new-session -s {} -n {} -d {}".format(session,
windows[0], shell)]
    for w in windows[1:]:
        cmds.append("tmux new-window -t {} -n {} {}".format(session, w,
shell))
    cmds.append("sleep 1")

    for _, cmd in cmds_map:
        cmds.append(cmd)
    return cmds, notes

def main():
    args = parser.parse_args()
    cmds, notes = create_commands("a3c", args.num_workers, args.log_dir,
args.env)

    print("Executing the following commands:")
    print("\n".join(cmds))
    os.environ["TMUX"] = ""
    os.system("\n".join(cmds))
    print("Notes:")
    print('\n'.join(notes))
if __name__ == "__main__":
    main()
```

This script creates the bash commands used to create the parameter server and a set of agents. To handle the consoles of all the agents, we use TMUX (more information is available at `https://github.com/tmux/tmux/wiki`). TMUX is a terminal multiplexer that allows us to switch easily between several programs in one terminal, detach them, and reattach them to a different terminal. TMUX is quite a convenient tool for checking the training status of A3C. Note that since A3C runs on CPUs, we set `CUDA_VISIBLE_DEVICES` to empty.

A3C is much more sensitive to the training parameters than DQN. Random seed, initial weights, learning rate, batch size, discount factor, and even hyperparameters for RMSProp can affect the performance a lot. After testing it on different Atari games, we select the following hyperparameters listed in the `Parameter` class:

```
class Parameter:
    def __init__(self, lr=7e-4, directory=None):
        self.directory = directory
        self.learning_rate = lr
        self.gamma = 0.99
        self.num_history_frames = 4
        self.iteration_num = 100000
        self.async_update_interval = 5
        self.rho = 0.99
        self.rmsprop_epsilon = 1e-1
        self.update_method = 'rmsprop'
        self.clip_delta = 0
        self.max_iter_num = 10 ** 8
        self.network_type = 'cnn'
        self.input_scale = 255.0
```

Here, `gamma` is the discount factor, `num_history_frames` is the parameter frameskip, `async_update_interval` is the batch size for the training update, and `rho` and `rmsprop_epsilon` are the internal hyperparameters for RMSProp. This set of hyperparameters can be used for both Atari and Minecraft.

Experiments

The full implementation of the A3C algorithm can be downloaded from our GitHub repository (`https://github.com/PacktPublishing/Python-Reinforcement-Learning-Projects`). There are three environments in our implementation we can test. The first one is the special game, `demo`, introduced in `Chapter 3`, *Playing Atari Games*. For this game, A3C only needs to launch two agents to achieve good performance. Run the following command in the `src` folder:

```
python3 train.py -w 2 -e demo
```

The first argument, `-w`, or `--num_workers`, indicates the number of launched agents. The second argument, `-e`, or `--env`, specifies the environment, for example, `demo`. The other two environments are Atari and Minecraft. For Atari games, A3C requires at least 8 agents running in parallel. Typically, launching 16 agents can achieve better performance:

```
python3 train.py -w 8 -e Breakout
```

For Breakout, A3C takes about 2-3 hours to achieve a score of 300. If you have a decent PC with more than 8 cores, it is better to test it with 16 agents. To test Minecraft, run the following command:

```
python3 train.py -w 8 -e MinecraftBasic-v0
```

The Gym Minecraft environment provides more than 10 missions. To try other missions, just replace `MinecraftBasic-v0` with other mission names.

After running one of the preceding commands, type the following to monitor the training procedure:

```
tmux attach -t a3c
```

To switch between console windows, press *Ctrl + b* and then press *0-9*. Window 0 is the parameter server. Windows 1-8 show the training stats of the 8 agents (if there are 8 launched agents). The last window runs htop. To detach TMUX, press *Ctrl* and then press *b*.

The `tensorboard` logs are saved in the `save/<environment_name>/train/log_<agent_index>` folder. To visualize the training procedure using TensorBoard, run the following command under this folder:

```
tensorboard --logdir=.
```

Summary

This chapter introduced the Gym Minecraft environment, available at `https://github.com/tambetm/gym-minecraft`. You have learned how to launch a Minecraft mission and how to implement an emulator for it. The most important part of this chapter was the asynchronous reinforcement learning framework. You learned what the shortcomings of DQN are, and why DQN is difficult to apply in complex tasks. Then, you learned how to apply the asynchronous reinforcement learning framework in the actor-critic method REINFORCE, which led us to the A3C algorithm. Finally, you learned how to implement A3C using Tensorflow and how to handle multiple terminals using TMUX. The tricky part in the implementation is that of the global shared parameters. This is related to creating a cluster of TensorFlow servers. For the readers who want to learn more about this, visit `https://www.tensorflow.org/deploy/distributed`.

In the following chapters, you will learn more about how to apply reinforcement learning algorithms in other tasks, for example, the board game Go, and generating deep image classifiers. This will help you to get a deep understanding about reinforcement learning and help you solve real-world problems.

Learning to Play Go

6

When considering the capabilities of AI, we often compare its performance for a particular task with what humans can achieve. AI agents are now able to surpass human-level competency in more complex tasks. In this chapter, we will build an agent that learns how to play what is considered the most complex board game of all time: Go. We will become familiar with the latest deep reinforcement learning algorithms that achieve superhuman performances, namely AlphaGo, and AlphaGo Zero, both of which were developed by Google's DeepMind. We will also learn about Monte Carlo tree search, a popular tree-searching algorithm that is an integral component of turn-based game agents.

This chapter will cover the following topics:

- Introduction to Go and relevant research in AI
- Overview of AlphaGo and AlphaGo Zero
- The Monte Carlo tree search algorithm
- Implementation of AlphaGo Zero

A brief introduction to Go

Go is a board game that was first recorded in China two millennia ago. Similar to other common board games, such as chess, shogi, and Othello, Go involves two players alternately placing black and white stones on a 19x19 board with the objective of capturing as much territory as possible by surrounding a larger total area of the board. One can capture their opponent's pieces by surrounding the opponent's pieces with their own pieces. Captured stones are removed from the board, thereby creating a void in which the opponent can no longer place stones unless the territory is captured back.

A game ends when both players refuse to place a stone or either player resigns. Upon the termination of a game, the winner is decided by counting each player's territory and the number of captured stones.

Go and other board games

Researchers have already created AI programs that outperform the best human players in board games such as chess and backgammon. In 1992, researchers from IBM developed TD-Gammon, which used classic reinforcement learning algorithms and an artificial neural network to play backgammon at the level of a top player. In 1997, Deep Blue, a chess-playing program developed by IBM and Carnegie Mellon University, defeated then world champion Garry Kasparov in a six-game face off. This was the first time that a computer program defeated the world champion in chess.

Developing Go playing agents is not a new topic, and hence one may wonder what took so long for researchers to replicate such successes in Go. The answer is simple—Go, despite its simple rules, is a far more complex game than chess. Imagine representing a board game as a tree, where each node is a snapshot of the board (which we also refer to as the **board state**) and its child nodes are possible moves the opponent can make. The height of the tree is essentially the number of moves a game lasts. A typical chess game lasts 80 moves, whereas a game in Go lasts 150; almost twice as long. Moreover, while the average number of possible moves in a chess turn is 35, a Go player has 250 possible plays per move. Based on these numbers, Go has 10^{761} total possible games, compared to 10^{120} games in chess. It is impossible to enumerate every possible state in Go in a computer, and the sheer complexity of the game has made it difficult for researchers to develop an agent that can play the game at a world-class level.

Go and AI research

In 2015, researchers from Google's DeepMind published a paper in Nature that detailed a novel reinforcement learning agent for Go called **AlphaGo**. In October of that year, AlphaGo beat Fan Hui, the European champion, 5-0. In 2016, AlphaGo challenged Lee Sedol, who, with 18 world championship titles, is considered one of the greatest players in modern history. AlphaGo won 4-1, marking a watershed moment in deep learning research and the game's history. In the following year, DeepMind published an updated version of AlphaGo, AlphaGo Zero, which defeated its predecessor 100 times in 100 games. In just a matter of days of training, AlphaGo and AlphaGo Zero were able to learn and surpass the wisdom that mankind has accumulated over the thousands of years of the game's existence.

The following sections will discuss how AlphaGo and AlphaGo Zero work, including the algorithms and techniques that they use to learn and play the game. This will be followed by an implementation of AlphaGo Zero. Our exploration begins with Monte Carlo tree search, an algorithm that is integral to both AlphaGo and AlphaGo Zero for making decisions on where to place stones.

Monte Carlo tree search

In games such as Go and chess, players have perfect information, meaning they have access to the full game state (the board and the positions of the pieces). Moreover, there lacks an element of chance that can affect the game state; only the players' decisions can affect the board. Such games are also referred to as perfect-information games. In perfect-information games, it is theoretically possible to enumerate all possible game states. As discussed earlier, this would look such as a tree, where each child node (a game state) is a possible outcome of the parent. In two-player games, alternating levels of this tree represent moves produced by the two competitors. Finding the best possible move for a given state is simply a matter of traversing the tree and finding which sequence of moves leads to a win. We can also store the value, or the expected outcome or reward (a win or a loss) of a given state, at each node.

However, constructing a perfect tree is impractical in practice for games such as Go. So how can an agent learn how to play the game without such knowledge? The **Monte Carlo tree-search (MCTS)** algorithm provides an efficient approximation of this complete tree. In a nutshell, MCTS involves playing a game iteratively, keeping statistics on states that were visited, and learning which moves are more favorable/likely to lead to a win. The goal of MCTS is to build a tree that approximates the aforementioned perfect tree as much as possible. Each move in a game corresponds to an iteration of the MCTS algorithm. There are four main steps in the algorithm: Selection, Expansion, Simulation, and Update (also known as **backpropagation**). We will briefly detail each procedure.

Selection

The first step of MCTS involves playing the game intelligently. That means the algorithm has enough experience to determine the next move given a state. One method for determining the next move is called **Upper Confidence Bound 1 Applied to Trees (UCT)**. In short, this formula rates moves based on the following:

- The mean reward of games where a given move was made
- How often the move was selected

Each node's rating can be expressed as follows:

$$\bar{r}_i + c\sqrt{\frac{2\ln(n)}{n_i}}$$

Where:

- $\bar{r}_i$: Is the mean reward for choosing move i (for example, the win-rate)
- n_i: Is the number of times the algorithm selected move i
- n: Is the total number of moves made after the current state (including move i)
- c: Is an exploration parameter

The following diagram shows an example of selecting the next node. In each node, the left number represents the node's rating, and the right number represents the number of times the node was visited. The color of the node indicates which player's turn it is:

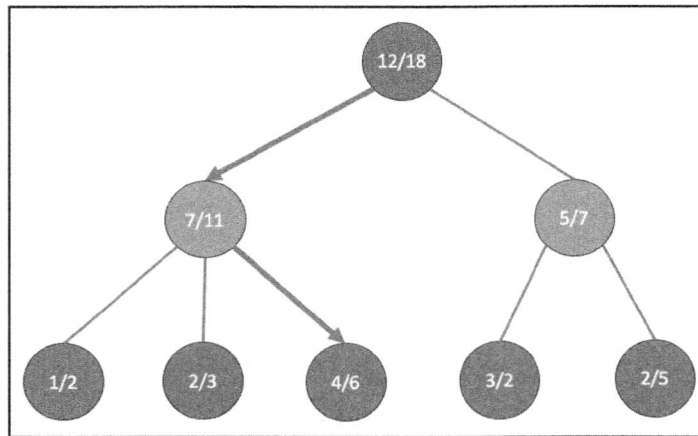

Figure 1: Selection in MCTS

In selection, the algorithm chooses the move that has the highest value for the preceding expression. The keen reader may notice that, while moves with a high mean reward, $\bar{r}_i$, are rated highly, so too are moves with fewer numbers of visits, n_i. Why is this so? In MCTS, we not only want the algorithm to choose moves that most likely result in wins but also to try less-often-selected moves. This is commonly referred to as the balance between exploitation and exploration. If the algorithm solely resorted to exploitation, the resulting tree would be very narrow and ill-experienced. Encouraging exploration allows the algorithm to learn from a broader set of experiences and simulations. In the preceding example, we simply select the node with a rating of **7** and subsequently the node with a rating of **4**.

Expansion

We apply selection to decide moves until the algorithm can no longer apply UCT to rate the next set of moves. In particular, we can no longer apply UCT when not all of the child nodes of a given state have records (number of visits, mean reward). This is when the second phase of MCTS, expansion, occurs. Here, we simply look at all possible new moves (unvisited child nodes) of a given state and randomly choose one. We then update the tree to record this new child node. The following diagram illustrates this:

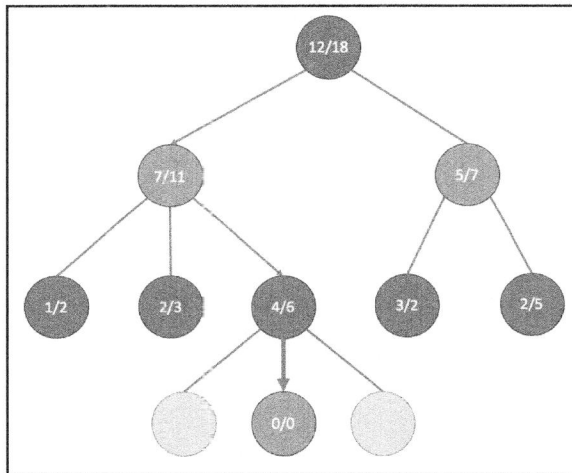

Figure 2: Expansion

You may be wondering from the preceding diagram why we initialize the visit count as zero rather than one. The visit count of this new node as well as the statistics of the nodes we have traversed so far will be incremented during the update step, which is the final step of an MCTS iteration.

Simulation

After expansion, the rest of the game is played by randomly choosing subsequent moves. This is also commonly referred to as the **playout** or **rollout**. Depending on the game, some heuristics may be applied to choose the next move. For example, in DeepBlue, simulations rely on handcrafted heuristics to select the next move intelligently rather than randomly. This is also called **heavy rollouts**. While such rollouts provide more realistic games, they are often computationally expensive, which can slow down the learning of the MCTS tree:

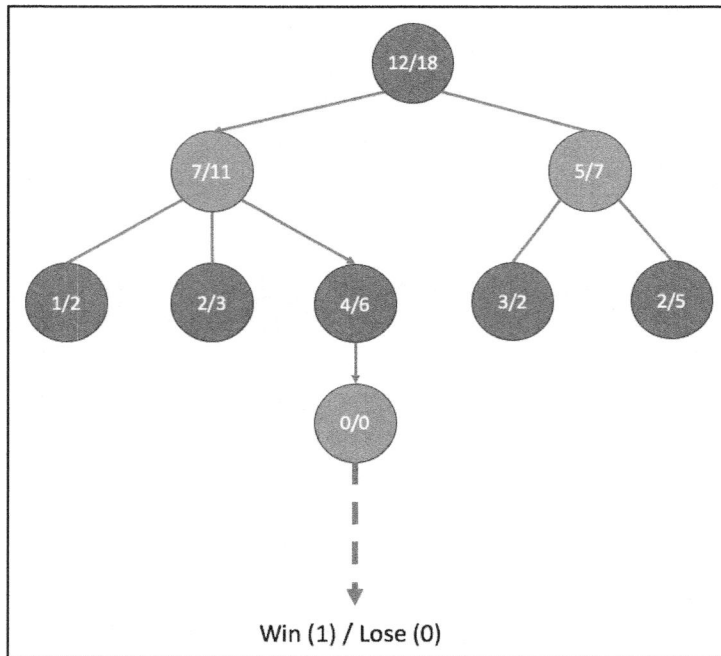

Figure 3: Simulation

In our preceding toy example, we expand a node and play until the very end of the game (represented by the dotted line), which results in either a win or loss. Simulation yields a reward, which in this case is either **1** or **0**.

Update

Finally, the update step happens when the algorithm reaches a terminal state, or when either player wins or the game culminates in a draw. For each node/state of the board that was visited during this iteration, the algorithm updates the mean reward and increments the visit count of that state. This is also called **backpropagation**:

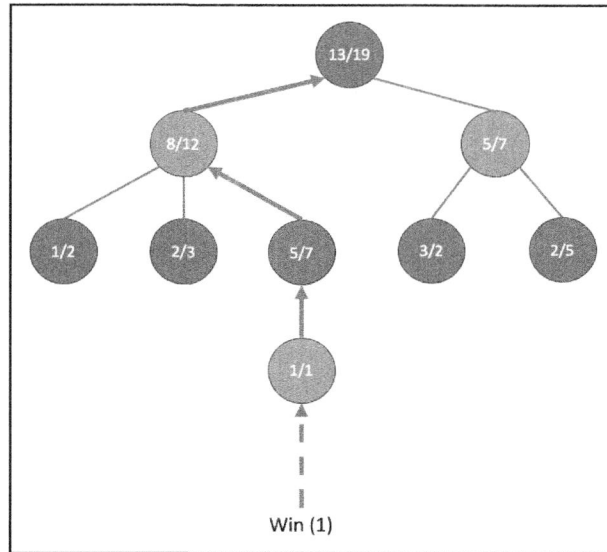

Figure 4: Update

In the preceding diagram, since we reached a terminal state that returned **1** (a win), we increment the visit count and reward accordingly for each node along the path from the root node accordingly.

That concludes the four steps that occur in one MCTS iteration. As the name Monte Carlo suggests, we conduct this search multiple times before we decide the next move to take. The number of iterations is configurable, and often depends on time/resources available. Over time, the tree learns a structure that approximates a perfect tree and can be used to guide agents to make decisions.

AlphaGo and AlphaGo Zero, DeepMind's revolutionary Go playing agents, rely on MCTS to select moves. In the next section, we will explore the two algorithms to understand how they combine neural networks and MCTS to play Go at a superhuman level of proficiency.

AlphaGo

AlphaGo's main innovation is how it combines deep learning and Monte Carlo tree search to play Go. The AlphaGo architecture consists of four neural networks: a small supervised learning policy network, a large supervised-learning policy network, a reinforcement learning policy network, and a value network. We train all four of these networks plus the MCTS tree. The following sections will cover each training step.

Supervised learning policy networks

The first step in training AlphaGo involves training policy networks on games played by two professionals (in board games such as chess and Go, it is common to keep records of historical games, the board state, and the moves made by each player at every turn). The main idea is to make AlphaGo learn and understand how human experts play Go. More formally, given a board state, s, and set of actions, a, we would like a policy network, $\pi(a|s)$, to predict the next move the human makes. The data consists of pairs (s,a) of sampled from over 30,000,000 historical games from the KGS Go server. The input to the network consists of the board state as well as metadata. AlphaGo has two supervised learning policy networks of varying sizes. The large network is a 13-layer convolutional neural network with ReLU activation functions in the hidden layers, while the smaller one is a single-layer softmax network.

Why do we train two similar networks? The larger policy network initializes the weights of the reinforcement learning policy network, which gets further refined through an RL approach called **policy gradients**. The smaller network is used during the simulation step of MCTS. Remember, while most simulations in MCTS rely on the randomized selection of moves, one can also utilize light or heavy heuristics to have more intelligent simulations. The smaller network, which lacks the accuracy of the larger supervised network yet yields much faster inference, provides light heuristics for rollout.

Reinforcement learning policy networks

Once the larger supervised learning policy network is trained, we further improve the model by having the RL policy network play against a previous version of itself. The weights of the network are updated using a method called **policy gradients**, which is a variant of gradient descent for vanilla neural networks. Formally speaking, the gradient update rule for the weights of our RL policy network can be expressed as follows:

$$\Delta w \propto \frac{\partial \log p_{rl}(a_t|s_t)}{w} z_t$$

Here, w are the weights of the RL policy network, p_{rl}, and z_t is the expected reward at timestep t. The reward is simply the outcome of the game, where a win results in +1 and a loss results in -1. Herein lies the main difference between the supervised learning policy network and the reinforcement learning policy network. For the former network, the objective is to maximize the likelihood of choosing a particular action given a state, or, in other words, to simply mimic the moves of the historical games. Since there is no reward function involved, it does not care about the eventual outcome of the game.

On the other hand, the reinforcement learning policy network incorporates the final outcome when updating the weights. More specifically, it is trying to maximize the log likelihood of the moves that contribute to higher rewards (that is, winning moves). This is because we are multiplying the gradient of the log-likelihood with the reward (either +1 or -1), which essentially determines the direction in which to move the weights. The weights of a poor move will be moved in the opposite direction, for we will likely be multiplying the gradients with -1. To summarize, the network not only tries to figure out the most likely move, but also one that helps it win. According to DeepMind's paper, the reinforcement learning policy network won the vast majority (80%~85%) of its games against its supervised counterpart and other Go playing programs, such as Pachi.

Value network

The last step of the pipeline involves training a value network to evaluate the board state, or in other words, to determine how favorable a particular board state is for winning the game. Formally speaking, given a particular policy, π, and state, s_t, we would like to predict the expected reward, z. The network is trained by minimizing the **mean-squared error** (MSE) between the predicted value, $v(s_t)$, and the final outcome:

$$\Delta w \propto \frac{\partial v(s_t)}{\partial w}(z - v(s_t))$$

Where w are the parameters of the network. In practice, the network is trained on 30,000,000 state-reward pairs, each coming from a distinct game. The dataset is constructed in this way because the board states from the same game can be highly correlated, potentially leading to overfitting.

Combining neural networks and MCTS

In AlphaGo, the policy and value networks are combined with MCTS to provide a look-ahead search when selecting actions in a game. Previously, we discussed how MCTS keeps track of the mean reward and number of visits made to each node. In AlphaGo, we have a few more values to keep track of:

- $Q(s_t, a)$: Which is the mean action value of choosing a particular action
- $P(s_t, a)$: The probability of taking an action for a given board state given by the larger supervised learning policy network
- $V(s_{leaf})$: The value evaluation of a state that is not explored yet (a leaf node)
- $N(s_t, a)$: The number of times a particular action was chosen given a state

During a single simulation of our tree search, the algorithm selects an action, a_t, for a given state, s_t, at a particular timestep, t, according to the following formula:

$$a_t = argmax_a Q(s_t, a) + u(s_t, a)$$

Where

$$u(s_t, a) = \frac{P(s_t, a)}{1 + N(s_t, a)}$$

Hence $u(s_t, a)$ is a value that favors moves determined to be more likely by the larger policy network, but also supports exploration by penalizing those that have been visited more frequently.

During expansion, when we don't have the preceding statistics for a given board state and move, we use the value network and the simulation to evaluate the leaf node. In particular, we take a weighted sum of the expected value given by the value network and outcome of the rollout:

$$V(s_{leaf}) = (1 - \lambda)v(s_{leaf}) + \lambda z_{leaf}$$

Where $v(s_{leaf})$ is the evaluation of the value network, z_{leaf} is the eventual reward of the search, and λ is the weighting term that is often referred to as the mixing z_{leaf} parameter. is obtained after rollout, where the simulations are conducted using the smaller and faster supervised learning policy network. Having fast rollouts is important, especially in situations where decisions are time-boxed, hence the need for the smaller policy network.

Finally, during the update step of MCTS, visit counts for each node are updated. Moreover, the action values are recalculated by taking the mean reward of all simulations that included a given node:

$$Q(s_t, a) = \frac{W(s_t, a)}{N(s_t, a)}$$

Where $W(s_t, a)$ is the total reward across the $N(s_t, a)$ times MCTS took action a at node s_t. After the MCTS search, the model chooses the most frequently-visited move when actually playing the game.

And that concludes a rudimentary overview of AlphaGo. While an in-depth exposition of the architecture and methodology is beyond the scope of this book, this hopefully serves as an introductory guide to what makes AlphaGo work.

AlphaGo Zero

We will cover AlphaGo Zero, the upgraded version of its predecessor before we finally get into some coding. The main features of AlphaGo Zero address some of the drawbacks of AlphaGo, including its dependency on a large corpus of games played by human experts.

The main differences between AlphaGo Zero and AlphaGo are the following:

- AlphaGo Zero is trained solely with self-play reinforcement learning, meaning it does not rely on any human-generated data or supervision that is used to train AlphaGo
- Policy and value networks are represented as one network with two heads rather than two separate ones
- The input to the network is the board itself as an image, such as a 2D grid; the network does not rely on heuristics and instead uses the raw board state itself
- In addition to finding the best move, Monte Carlo tree search is also used for policy iteration and evaluation; moreover, AlphaGo Zero does not conduct rollouts during a search

Training AlphaGo Zero

Since we don't use human-generated data for training or supervision, how does AlphaGo Zero learn at all? The novel reinforcement learning algorithm developed by DeepMind involves using MCTS as a teacher for the neural network, which represents both policy and value functions.

In particular, the outputs of MCTS are 1) probabilities, π, for each selecting move during the simulation, and 2) the final outcome of the game, z. The neural network, f, takes in a board state, s, and also outputs a tuple of (p, v), where p is a vector of move probabilities and v is the value of s. Given these outputs, we want to train our network such that the network's policy, p, moves closer to the policy, π, that is produced by MCTS, and the network's value, v, moves closer to the eventual outcome, z, of the search. Note that in MCTS, the algorithm does not conduct rollouts, but instead relies on f for expansion and simulating the whole game until termination. Hence by the end of MCTS, the algorithm improves the policy from p to π and is able to act as a teacher for f. The loss function for the network consists of two parts: one is the cross-entropy between p and π, and the other is the mean-squared error between v and z. This joint loss function looks as follows:

$$L = (z - v)^2 - \pi^T \log(p) + \lambda ||\theta||^2$$

Where θ is network parameters and λ is a parameter for L2-regularization.

Comparison with AlphaGo

According to DeepMind's paper, AlphaGo Zero was able to outperform AlphaGo in 36 hours, whereas the latter took months to train. In a head-to-head competition with the version of AlphaGo that defeated Lee Sedol, AlphaGo Zero won 100 games out of 100. What's significant about these results is that, even without initial human supervision, a Go playing program can reach superhuman-level proficiency more efficiently and is able to discover much of the knowledge and wisdom that humanity spent thousands of years and millions of games cultivating.

In the following sections, we will finally implement this powerful algorithm. Additional technical details of AlphaGo Zero will be covered as we go through the code.

Implementing AlphaGo Zero

At last, we will implement AlphaGo Zero in this section. In addition to achieving better performance than AlphaGo, it is in fact relatively easier to implement. This is because, as discussed, AlphaGo Zero only relies on selfplay data for learning, and thus relieves us from the burden of searching for large amounts of historical data. Moreover, we only need to implement one neural network that serves as both the policy and value function. The following implementation makes some further simplifications—for example, we assume that the Go board size is 9 instead of 19. This is to allow for faster training.

The directory structure of our implementation looks such as the following:

```
alphago_zero/
|-- __init__.py
|-- config.py
|-- constants.py
|-- controller.py
|-- features.py
|-- go.py
|-- mcts.py
|-- alphagozero_agent.py
|-- network.py
|-- preprocessing.py
|-- train.py
`-- utils.py
```

We will especially pay attention to network.py and mcts.py, which contain the implementations for the dual network and the MCTS algorithm. Moreover, alphagozero_agent.py contains the implementation for combining the dual network and MCTS to create a Go playing agent.

Policy and value networks

Let's get started with implementing the dual network, which we will call PolicyValueNetwork. First, we will create a few modules that contain configurations and constants that our PolicyValueNetwork will use.

preprocessing.py

The `preprocessing.py` module mainly deals with reading from and writing to `TFRecords` files, which is TensorFlow's native data-representation file format. When training AlphaGo Zero, we store MCTS self-play results and moves. As discussed, these then become the ground truths from which `PolicyValueNetwork` learns. `TFRecords` provides a convenient way to save historical moves and results from MCTS. When reading these from disk, `preprocessing.py` turns `TFRecords` into `tf.train.Example`, an in-memory representation of data that can be directly fed into `tf.estimator.Estimator`.

> 💡 **TIP** `tf_records` usually have filenames that end with `*.tfrecord.zz`.

The following function reads from a `TFRecords` file. We first turn a given list of `TFRecords` into `tf.data.TFRecordDataset`, an intermediate representation before we turn them into `tf.train.Example`:

```python
def process_tf_records(list_tf_records, shuffle_records=True,
buffer_size=GLOBAL_PARAMETER_STORE.SHUFFLE_BUFFER_SIZE,
                     batch_size=GLOBAL_PARAMETER_STORE.TRAIN_BATCH_SIZE):

    if shuffle_records:
        random.shuffle(list_tf_records)

    list_dataset = tf.data.Dataset.from_tensor_slices(list_tf_records)

    tensors_dataset = list_dataset.interleave(map_func=lambda x:
tf.data.TFRecordDataset(x, compression_type='ZLIB'),
cycle_length=GLOBAL_PARAMETER_STORE.CYCLE_LENGTH,
block_length=GLOBAL_PARAMETER_STORE.BLOCK_LENGTH)
    tensors_dataset =
tensors_dataset.repeat(1).shuffle(buffer_siz=buffer_size).batch(batch_size)

    return tensors_dataset
```

The next step involves parsing this dataset so that we can feed the values into `PolicyValueNetwork`. There are three values we care about: the input, which we call either x or `board_state` throughout the implementation, the policy, `pi`, and the outcome, z, both of which are outputted by the MCTS algorithm:

```python
def parse_batch_tf_example(example_batch):
    features = {
        'x': tf.FixedLenFeature([], tf.string),
```

```
        'pi': tf.FixedLenFeature([], tf.string),
        'z': tf.FixedLenFeature([], tf.float32),
    }
    parsed_tensors = tf.parse_example(example_batch, features)

    # Get the board state
    x = tf.cast(tf.decode_raw(parsed_tensors['x'], tf.uint8), tf.float32)
    x = tf.reshape(x, [GLOBAL_PARAMETER_STORE.TRAIN_BATCH_SIZE,
GOPARAMETERS.N,
                       GOPARAMETERS.N, FEATUREPARAMETERS.NUM_CHANNELS])

    # Get the policy target, which is the distribution of possible moves
    # Each target is a vector of length of board * length of board + 1
    distribution_of_moves = tf.decode_raw(parsed_tensors['pi'], tf.float32)
    distribution_of_moves = tf.reshape(distribution_of_moves,
[GLOBAL_PARAMETER_STORE.TRAIN_BATCH_SIZE, GOPARAMETERS.N * GOPARAMETERS.N +
1])

    # Get the result of the game
    # The result is simply a scalar
    result_of_game = parsed_tensors['z']
    result_of_game.set_shape([GLOBAL_PARAMETER_STORE.TRAIN_BATCH_SIZE])

    return (x, {'pi_label': distribution_of_moves, 'z_label':
result_of_game})
```

The preceding two functions are combined in the following function to construct the input tensors to be fed into the network:

```
def get_input_tensors(list_tf_records,
buffer_size=GLOBAL_PARAMETER_STORE.SHUFFLE_BUFFER_SIZE):
    logger.info("Getting input data and tensors")
    dataset = process_tf_records(list_tf_records=list_tf_records,
                                 buffer_size=buffer_size)
    dataset = dataset.filter(lambda input_tensor:
tf.equal(tf.shape(input_tensor)[0],
GLOBAL_PARAMETER_STORE.TRAIN_BATCH_SIZE))
    dataset = dataset.map(parse_batch_tf_example)
    logger.info("Finished parsing")
    return dataset.make_one_shot_iterator().get_next()
```

Finally, the following functions are used to write self-play results to disk:

```
def create_dataset_from_selfplay(data_extracts):
    return (create_tf_train_example(extract_features(board_state), pi,
result)
            for board_state, pi, result in data_extracts)
```

```python
def shuffle_tf_examples(batch_size, records_to_shuffle):
    tf_dataset = process_tf_records(records_to_shuffle,
batch_size=batch_size)
    iterator = tf_dataset.make_one_shot_iterator()
    next_dataset_batch = iterator.get_next()
    sess = tf.Session()
    while True:
        try:
            result = sess.run(next_dataset_batch)
            yield list(result)
        except tf.errors.OutOfRangeError:
            break


def create_tf_train_example(board_state, pi, result):
    board_state_as_tf_feature =
tf.train.Feature(bytes_list=tf.train.BytesList(value=[board_state.tostring(
)]))
    pi_as_tf_feature =
tf.train.Feature(bytes_list=tf.train.BytesList(value=[pi.tostring()]))
    value_as_tf_feature =
tf.train.Feature(float_list=tf.train.FloatList(value=[result]))

    tf_example = tf.train.Example(features=tf.train.Features(feature={
        'x': board_state_as_tf_feature,
        'pi': pi_as_tf_feature,
        'z': value_as_tf_feature
    }))

    return tf_example

def write_tf_examples(record_path, tf_examples, serialize=True):
    with tf.python_io.TFRecordWriter(record_path, options=TF_RECORD_CONFIG)
as tf_record_writer:
        for tf_example in tf_examples:
            if serialize:
                tf_record_writer.write(tf_example.SerializeToString())
            else:
                tf_record_writer.write(tf_example)
```

Some of these functions will be used later when we generate training data from self-play results.

features.py

This module contains helper code for turning Go board representations into proper TensorFlow tensors, which can be provided to `PolicyValueNetwork`. The main function, `extract_features`, takes `board_state`, which is our representation of a Go board, and turns it into a tensor of the `[batch_size, N, N, 17]` shape, where N is the shape of the board (which is by default 9), and 17 is the number of feature channels, representing the past moves as well as the color to play:

```python
import numpy as np

from config import GOPARAMETERS

def stone_features(board_state):
    # 16 planes, where every other plane represents the stones of a
particular color
    # which means we track the stones of the last 8 moves.
    features = np.zeros([16, GOPARAMETERS.N, GOPARAMETERS.N],
dtype=np.uint8)

    num_deltas_avail = board_state.board_deltas.shape[0]
    cumulative_deltas = np.cumsum(board_state.board_deltas, axis=0)
    last_eight = np.tile(board_state.board, [8, 1, 1])
    last_eight[1:num_deltas_avail + 1] -= cumulative_deltas
    last_eight[num_deltas_avail +1:] =
last_eight[num_deltas_avail].reshape(1, GOPARAMETERS.N, GOPARAMETERS.N)

    features[::2] = last_eight == board_state.to_play
    features[1::2] = last_eight == -board_state.to_play
    return np.rollaxis(features, 0, 3)

def color_to_play_feature(board_state):
    # 1 plane representing which color is to play
    # The plane is filled with 1's if the color to play is black; 0's
otherwise
    if board_state.to_play == GOPARAMETERS.BLACK:
        return np.ones([GOPARAMETERS.N, GOPARAMETERS.N, 1], dtype=np.uint8)
    else:
        return np.zeros([GOPARAMETERS.N, GOPARAMETERS.N, 1],
dtype=np.uint8)

def extract_features(board_state):
    stone_feat = stone_features(board_state=board_state)
    turn_feat = color_to_play_feature(board_state=board_state)
    all_features = np.concatenate([stone_feat, turn_feat], axis=2)
    return all_features
```

The `extract_features` function will be used by both the `preprocessing.py` and `network.py` modules to construct the feature tensors to be either written to a `TFRecord` file or fed into a neural network.

network.py

This file contains our implementation of `PolicyValueNetwork`. In short, we construct a `tf.estimator.Estimator` that is trained using board states, policies, and self-play outcomes produced by MCTS self-play. The network has two heads: one acting as a value function, and the other acting as a policy network.

First, we define some layers that will be used by `PolicyValueNetwork`:

```python
import functools
import logging
import os.path

import tensorflow as tf

import features
import preprocessing
import utils
from config import GLOBAL_PARAMETER_STORE, GOPARAMETERS
from constants import *

logger = logging.getLogger(__name__)
logger.setLevel(logging.INFO)

def create_partial_bn_layer(params):
    return functools.partial(tf.layers.batch_normalization,
        momentum=params["momentum"],
        epsilon=params["epsilon"],
        fused=params["fused"],
        center=params["center"],
        scale=params["scale"],
        training=params["training"]
    )

def create_partial_res_layer(inputs, partial_bn_layer,
partial_conv2d_layer):
    output_1 = partial_bn_layer(partial_conv2d_layer(inputs))
    output_2 = tf.nn.relu(output_1)
    output_3 = partial_bn_layer(partial_conv2d_layer(output_2))
    output_4 = tf.nn.relu(tf.add(inputs, output_3))
    return output_4
```

```
def softmax_cross_entropy_loss(logits, labels):
 return
tf.reduce_mean(tf.nn.softmax_cross_entropy_with_logits(logits=logits,
labels=labels['pi_label']))

def mean_squared_loss(output_value, labels):
 return tf.reduce_mean(tf.square(output_value - labels['z_label']))

def get_losses(logits, output_value, labels):
 ce_loss = softmax_cross_entropy_loss(logits, labels)
 mse_loss = mean_squared_loss(output_value, labels)
 return ce_loss, mse_loss

def create_metric_ops(labels, output_policy, loss_policy, loss_value,
loss_l2, loss_total):
 return {'accuracy': tf.metrics.accuracy(labels=labels['pi_label'],
predictions=output_policy, name='accuracy'),
 'loss_policy': tf.metrics.mean(loss_policy),
 'loss_value': tf.metrics.mean(loss_value),
 'loss_l2': tf.metrics.mean(loss_l2),
 'loss_total': tf.metrics.mean(loss_total)}
```

Next, we have a function that is used to create `tf.estimator.Estimator`. While
TensorFlow provides several prebuilt estimators, such as `tf.estimator.DNNClassifier`,
our architecture is rather unique, which is why we need to build our own `Estimator`. This
can be done by creating `tf.estimator.EstimatorSpec`, a skeleton class where we can
define things such as the output tensors, network architecture, the loss functions, and the
evaluation metrics:

```
def generate_network_specifications(features, labels, mode, params,
config=None):
 batch_norm_params = {"epsilon": 1e-5, "fused": True, "center": True,
"scale": True, "momentum": 0.997,
 "training": mode==tf.estimator.ModeKeys.TRAIN
 }
```

Our `generate_network_specifications` function takes several input:

- `features`: The tensor representation of the Go board (with the `[batch_size, 9, 9, 17]` shape)
- `labels`: Our `pi` and `z` tensors
- `mode`: Here, we can specify whether our network is being instantiated in train or test mode
- `params`: Additional parameters to specify the network structure (for example, convolutional filter size)

We then implement the shared portion of the network, the policy output head, the value output head, and then the loss functions:

```
with tf.name_scope("shared_layers"):
    partial_bn_layer = create_partial_bn_layer(batch_norm_params)
    partial_conv2d_layer = functools.partial(tf.layers.conv2d,
        filters=params[HYPERPARAMS.NUM_FILTERS], kernel_size=[3, 3],
padding="same")
    partial_res_layer = functools.partial(create_partial_res_layer,
batch_norm=partial_bn_layer,
                                        conv2d=partial_conv2d_layer)

    output_shared =
tf.nn.relu(partial_bn_layer(partial_conv2d_layer(features)))

    for i in range(params[HYPERPARAMS.NUMSHAREDLAYERS]):
        output_shared = partial_res_layer(output_shared)

# Implement the policy network
with tf.name_scope("policy_network"):
    conv_p_output =
tf.nn.relu(partial_bn_layer(partial_conv2d_layer(output_shared, filters=2,
kernel_size=[1, 1]),
center=False, scale=False))
    logits = tf.layers.dense(tf.reshape(conv_p_output, [-1, GOPARAMETERS.N
* GOPARAMETERS.N * 2]),
                            units=GOPARAMETERS.N * GOPARAMETERS.N + 1)
    output_policy = tf.nn.softmax(logits,
                                name='policy_output')

# Implement the value network
with tf.name_scope("value_network"):
    conv_v_output =
tf.nn.relu(partial_bn_layer(partial_conv2d_layer(output_shared, filters=1,
kernel_size=[1, 1]),
        center=False, scale=False))
    fc_v_output = tf.nn.relu(tf.layers.dense(
        tf.reshape(conv_v_output, [-1, GOPARAMETERS.N * GOPARAMETERS.N]),
        params[HYPERPARAMS.FC_WIDTH]))
    fc_v_output = tf.layers.dense(fc_v_output, 1)
    fc_v_output = tf.reshape(fc_v_output, [-1])
    output_value = tf.nn.tanh(fc_v_output, name='value_output')

# Implement the loss functions
with tf.name_scope("loss_functions"):
    loss_policy, loss_value = get_losses(logits=logits,
                                        output_value=output_value,
                                        labels=labels)
```

```
loss_12 = params[HYPERPARAMS.BETA] * tf.add_n([tf.nn.l2_loss(v)
    for v in tf.trainable_variables() if not 'bias' in v.name])
loss_total = loss_policy + loss_value + loss_12
```

We then specify the optimization algorithm. Here, we use `tf.train.MomentumOptimizer`. We also adjust the learning rate during training; because we can't directly alter the learning rate once we create `Estimator`, we turn the learning rate update into a TensorFlow operation as well. We also log several metrics to TensorBoard:

```
# Steps and operations for training
global_step = tf.train.get_or_create_global_step()

learning_rate = tf.train.piecewise_constant(global_step,
GLOBAL_PARAMETER_STORE.BOUNDARIES,
GLOBAL_PARAMETER_STORE.LEARNING_RATE)

update_ops = tf.get_collection(tf.GraphKeys.UPDATE_OPS)

with tf.control_dependencies(update_ops):
    train_op = tf.train.MomentumOptimizer(learning_rate,
                params[HYPERPARAMS.MOMENTUM]).minimize(loss_total,
global_step=global_step)

metric_ops = create_metric_ops(labels=labels,
                                output_policy=output_policy,
                                loss_policy=loss_policy,
                                loss_value=loss_value,
                                loss_12=loss_12,
                                loss_total=loss_total)

for metric_name, metric_op in metric_ops.items():
    tf.summary.scalar(metric_name, metric_op[1])
```

Finally, we create a `tf.estmator.EstimatorSpec` object and return it. There are several parameters we need to specify when creating one:

- `mode`: Train or test, as specified earlier.
- `predictions`: A dictionary that maps a string (name) to the output operation of the network. Note that we can specify multiple output operations.
- `loss`: The loss function operation.
- `train_op`: The optimization operation.
- `eval_metrics_op`: Operations that are run to store several metrics, such as loss, accuracy, and variable weight values.

For the `predictions` argument, we provide outputs of both the policy and value networks:

```
return tf.estimator.EstimatorSpec(
    mode=mode,
    predictions={
        'policy_output': output_policy,
        'value_output': output_value,
    },
    loss=loss_total,
    train_op=train_op,
    eval_metric_ops=metric_ops,
)
```

In the very first step of training AlphaGo Zero, we must initialize a model with random weights. The following function implements this:

```
def initialize_random_model(estimator_dir, **kwargs):
    sess = tf.Session(graph=tf.Graph())
    params = utils.parse_parameters(**kwargs)
    initial_model_path = os.path.join(estimator_dir,
PATHS.INITIAL_CHECKPOINT_NAME)

    # Create the first model, where all we do is initialize random weights
and immediately write them to disk
    with sess.graph.as_default():
        features, labels = get_inference_input()
        generate_network_specifications(features, labels,
tf.estimator.ModeKeys.PREDICT, params)
        sess.run(tf.global_variables_initializer())
        tf.train.Saver().save(sess, initial_model_path)
```

We use the following function to create the `tf.estimator.Estimator` object based on a given set of parameters:

```
def get_estimator(estimator_dir, **kwargs):
    params = utils.parse_parameters(**kwargs)
    return tf.estimator.Estimator(generate_network_specifications,
model_dir=estimator_dir, params=params)
```

`tf.estimator.Estimator` expects a function that provides `tf.estimator.EstimatorSpec`, which is our `generate_network_specifications` function. Here, `estimator_dir` refers to a directory in which our network stores checkpoints. By providing this parameter, our `tf.estimator.Estimator` object can load weights from a previous iteration of training.

We also implement functions for training and validating a model:

```
def train(estimator_dir, tf_records, model_version, **kwargs):
    """
    Main training function for the PolicyValueNetwork
    Args:
        estimator_dir (str): Path to the estimator directory
        tf_records (list): A list of TFRecords from which we parse the
training examples
        model_version (int): The version of the model
    """
    model = get_estimator(estimator_dir, **kwargs)
    logger.info("Training model version: {}".format(model_version))
    max_steps = model_version *
GLOBAL_PARAMETER_STORE.EXAMPLES_PER_GENERATION // \
                GLOBAL_PARAMETER_STORE.TRAIN_BATCH_SIZE
    model.train(input_fn=lambda:
preprocessing.get_input_tensors(list_tf_records=tf_records),
                max_steps=max_steps)
    logger.info("Trained model version: {}".format(model_version))


def validate(estimator_dir, tf_records, checkpoint_path=None, **kwargs):
    model = get_estimator(estimator_dir, **kwargs)
    if checkpoint_path is None:
        checkpoint_path = model.latest_checkpoint()
    model.evaluate(input_fn=lambda: preprocessing.get_input_tensors(
        list_tf_records=tf_records,
        buffer_size=GLOBAL_PARAMETER_STORE.VALIDATION_BUFFER_SIZE),
            steps=GLOBAL_PARAMETER_STORE.VALIDATION_NUMBER_OF_STEPS,
            checkpoint_path=checkpoint_path)
```

The `tf.estimator.Estimator.train` function expects a function that provides the training data in batches (`input_fn`). `input_data` uses our `get_input_tensors` function from the `preprocessing.py` module to parse `TFRecords` data and turn them into input tensors. The `tf.estimator.Estimator.evaluate` function expects the same input function.

We finally encapsulate our estimator into our `PolicyValueNetwork`. This class uses the path to a network (`model_path`) and loads its weights. It uses the network to predict the value and most probable next moves of a given board state:

```
class PolicyValueNetwork():

    def __init__(self, model_path, **kwargs):
        self.model_path = model_path
        self.params = utils.parse_parameters(**kwargs)
```

```
                self.build_network()

        def build_session(self):
            config = tf.ConfigProto()
            config.gpu_options.allow_growth = True
            return tf.Session(graph=tf.Graph(), config=config)

        def build_network(self):
            self.sess = self.build_session()

            with self.sess.graph.as_default():
                features, labels = get_inference_input()
                model_spec = generate_network_specifications(features, labels,
tf.estimator.ModeKeys.PREDICT, self.params)
                self.inference_input = features
                self.inference_output = model_spec.predictions
                if self.model_path is not None:
                    self.load_network_weights(self.model_path)
                else:
                    self.sess.run(tf.global_variables_initializer())

        def load_network_weights(self, save_file):
            tf.train.Saver().restore(self.sess, save_file)
```

The `model_path` argument passed to the constructor is the directory of a particular version of the model. When this is `None`, we initialize random weights. The following functions are used to predict the probabilities of the next action and the value of a given board state:

```
def predict_on_single_board_state(self, position):
    probs, values = self.predict_on_multiple_board_states([position])
    prob = probs[0]
    value = values[0]
    return prob, value

def predict_on_multiple_board_states(self, positions):
    symmetries, processed =
utils.shuffle_feature_symmetries(list(map(features.extract_features,
positions)))
    network_outputs = self.sess.run(self.inference_output,
feed_dict={self.inference_input: processed})
    action_probs, value_pred = network_outputs['policy_output'],
network_outputs['value_output']
    action_probs = utils.invert_policy_symmetries(symmetries, action_probs)
    return action_probs, value_pred
```

Do check the GitHub repository for the full implementation of the module.

Monte Carlo tree search

The second component of our AlphaGo Zero agent is the MCTS algorithm. In our `mcts.py` module, we implement an `MCTreeSearchNode` class, which represents each node in an MCTS tree during a search. This is then used by the agent implemented in `alphagozero_agent.py` to perform MCTS using `PolicyValueNetwork`, which we implemented just now.

mcts.py

`mcts.py` contains our implementation of Monte Carlo tree search. Our first class is `RootNode`, which is meant to represent the root node of the MCTS tree at the start of a simulation. By definition, the root node does not have a parent. Having a separate class for the root node is not absolutely necessary, but it does keep the code cleaner:

```
import collections
import math

import numpy as np

import utils
from config import MCTSPARAMETERS, GOPARAMETERS


class RootNode(object):

    def __init__(self):
        self.parent_node = None
        self.child_visit_counts = collections.defaultdict(float)
        self.child_cumulative_rewards = collections.defaultdict(float)
```

Next, we implement the `MCTreeSearchNode` class. This class has several attributes, the most important ones being the following:

- `parent_node`: The parent node
- `previous_move`: The previous move that led to this node's board state

- `board_state`: The current board state
- `is_visited`: Whether the leaves (child nodes) are expanded or not; this is `False` when the node is initialized
- `child_visit_counts`: A `numpy.ndarray` representing the visit counts of each child node
- `child_cumulative_rewards`: A `numpy.ndarray` representing the cumulative reward of each child node
- `children_moves`: A dictionary of children moves

We also have parameters such as `loss_counter`, `original_prior`, and `child_prior`. These are related to advanced MCTS techniques that AlphaGo Zero implements, such as paralleling the search process as well as adding noise to the search. For the sake of brevity, we won't cover these techniques, so you can ignore them for now.

Here's the `__init__` function of `MCTreeSearchNode`:

```
class MCTreeSearchNode(object):

    def __init__(self, board_state, previous_move=None, parent_node=None):
        """
        A node of a MCTS tree. It is primarily responsible with keeping
track of its children's scores
        and other statistics such as visit count. It also makes decisions
about where to move next.

        board_state (go.BoardState): The Go board
        fmove (int): A number which represents the coordinate of the move
that led to this board state. None if pass
        parent (MCTreeSearchNode): The parent node
        """
        if parent_node is None:
            parent_node = RootNode()
        self.parent_node = parent_node
        self.previous_move = previous_move
        self.board_state = board_state
        self.is_visited = False
        self.loss_counter = 0
        self.illegal_moves = 1000 * (1 -
self.board_state.enumerate_possible_moves())
        self.child_visit_counts = np.zeros([GOPARAMETERS.N * GOPARAMETERS.N
+ 1], dtype=np.float32)
        self.child_cumulative_rewards = np.zeros([GOPARAMETERS.N *
GOPARAMETERS.N + 1], dtype=np.float32)
        self.original_prior = np.zeros([GOPARAMETERS.N * GOPARAMETERS.N +
1], dtype=np.float32)
```

```
        self.child_prior = np.zeros([GOPARAMETERS.N * GOPARAMETERS.N + 1],
dtype=np.float32)
        self.children_moves = {}
```

Each node keeps track of the mean reward and action value of every child node. We set these as properties:

```
@property
def child_action_score(self):
    return self.child_mean_rewards * self.board_state.to_play +
self.child_node_scores - self.illegal_moves

@property
def child_mean_rewards(self):
    return self.child_cumulative_rewards / (1 + self.child_visit_counts)

@property
def child_node_scores(self):
    # This scores each child according to the UCT scoring system
    return (MCTSPARAMETERS.c_PUCT * math.sqrt(1 + self.node_visit_count) *
self.child_prior /
            (1 + self.child_visit_counts))
```

And of course, we keep track of the action value, visit count, and cumulative reward of the node itself. Remember, child_mean_rewards is the mean reward, child_visit_counts is the number of times a child node was visited, and child_cumulative_rewards is the total reward of a node. We implement getters and setters for each attribute by adding the @property and @*.setter decorators:

```
@property
def node_mean_reward(self):
    return self.node_cumulative_reward / (1 + self.node_visit_count)

@property
def node_visit_count(self):
    return self.parent_node.child_visit_counts[self.previous_move]

@node_visit_count.setter
def node_visit_count(self, value):
    self.parent_node.child_visit_counts[self.previous_move] = value

@property
def node_cumulative_reward(self):
    return self.parent_node.child_cumulative_rewards[self.previous_move]

@node_cumulative_reward.setter
def node_cumulative_reward(self, value):
```

```
            self.parent_node.child_cumulative_rewards[self.previous_move] = value

    @property
    def mean_reward_perspective(self):
        return self.node_mean_reward * self.board_state.to_play
```

During the selection step of MCTS, the algorithm chooses the child node with the greatest action value. This can be easily done by calling np.argmax on the matrix of child action scores:

```
def choose_next_child_node(self):
    current = self
    pass_move = GOPARAMETERS.N * GOPARAMETERS.N
    while True:
        current.node_visit_count += 1
        # We stop searching when we reach a new leaf node
        if not current.is_visited:
            break
        if (current.board_state.recent
            and current.board_state.recent[-1].move is None
                and current.child_visit_counts[pass_move] == 0):
            current = current.record_child_node(pass_move)
            continue

        best_move = np.argmax(current.child_action_score)
        current = current.record_child_node(best_move)
    return current

def record_child_node(self, next_coordinate):
    if next_coordinate not in self.children_moves:
        new_board_state = self.board_state.play_move(
            utils.from_flat(next_coordinate))
        self.children_moves[next_coordinate] = MCTreeSearchNode(
            new_board_state, previous_move=next_coordinate,
parent_node=self)
    return self.children_moves[next_coordinate]
```

As discussed in our section about AlphaGo Zero, `PolicyValueNetwork` is used to conduct simulations in an MCTS iteration. Again, the output of the network are the probabilities and the predicted value of the node, which we then reflect in the MCTS tree itself. In particular, the predicted value is propagated throughout the tree via the `back_propagate_result` function:

```
def incorporate_results(self, move_probabilities, result, start_node):
    if self.is_visited:
        self.revert_visits(start_node=start_node)
        return
    self.is_visited = True
    self.original_prior = self.child_prior = move_probabilities
    self.child_cumulative_rewards = np.ones([GOPARAMETERS.N *
GOPARAMETERS.N + 1], dtype=np.float32) * result
    self.back_propagate_result(result, start_node=start_node)

def back_propagate_result(self, result, start_node):
    """
    This function back propagates the result of a match all the way to
where the search started from

    Args:
        result (int): the result of the search (1: black, -1: white won)
        start_node (MCTreeSearchNode): the node to back propagate until
    """
    # Keep track of the cumulative reward in this node
    self.node_cumulative_reward += result

    if self.parent_node is None or self is start_node:
        return

    self.parent_node.back_propagate_result(result, start_node)
```

Refer to the GitHub repository for a full implementation of our `MCTreeSearchNode` class and its functions.

Combining PolicyValueNetwork and MCTS

We combine our `PolicyValueNetwork` and MCTS implementations in `alphagozero_agent.py`. This module implements `AlphaGoZeroAgent`, which is the main AlphaGo Zero that conducts MCTS search and inference using `PolicyValueNetwork` to play games.

alphagozero_agent.py

Finally, we implement the agent that acts as the interface between the Go games and the algorithms. The main class we will implement is called `AlphaGoZeroAgent`. Again, this class combines `PolicyValueNetwork` with our MCTS module, as is done in AlphaGo Zero, to select moves and simulate games. Note that any missing modules (for example, `go.py`, which implements the game of Go itself) can be found in the main GitHub repository:

```python
import logging
import os
import random
import time

import numpy as np

import go
import utils
from config import GLOBAL_PARAMETER_STORE, GOPARAMETERS
from mcts import MCTreeSearchNode
from utils import make_sgf

logger = logging.getLogger(__name__)

class AlphaGoZeroAgent:

    def __init__(self, network, player_v_player=False,
workers=GLOBAL_PARAMETER_STORE.SIMULTANEOUS_LEAVES):
        self.network = network
        self.player_v_player = player_v_player
        self.workers = workers
        self.mean_reward_store = []
        self.game_description_store = []
        self.child_probability_store = []
        self.root = None
        self.result = 0
        self.logging_buffer = None
        self.conduct_exploration = True
        if self.player_v_player:
            self.conduct_exploration = True
        else:
            self.conduct_exploration = False
```

We start a Go game by initializing our agent and the game itself. This is done via the `initialize_game` method, which initializes `MCTreeSearchNode` and buffers that keep track of move probabilities and action values outputted by the network:

```
def initialize_game(self, board_state=None):
    if board_state is None:
        board_state = go.BoardState()
    self.root = MCTreeSearchNode(board_state)
    self.result = 0
    self.logging_buffer = None
    self.game_description_store = []
    self.child_probability_store = []
    self.mean_reward_store = []
```

In each turn, our agent conducts MCTS and picks a move using the `select_move` function. Notice that we allow for some exploration in the early stages of the game by selecting a random node.

The `play_move(coordinates)` method takes in a coordinate returned by `select_move` and updates the MCTS tree and board states:

```
def play_move(self, coordinates):
    if not self.player_v_player:
self.child_probability_store.append(self.root.get_children_as_probability_d
istributions())
        self.mean_reward_store.append(self.root.node_mean_reward)
        self.game_description_store.append(self.root.describe())
    self.root = self.root.record_child_node(utils.to_flat(coordinates))
    self.board_state = self.root.board_state
    del self.root.parent_node.children_moves
    return True

def select_move(self):
    # If we have conducted enough moves and this is single player mode, we
turn off exploration
    if self.root.board_state.n > GLOBAL_PARAMETER_STORE.TEMPERATURE_CUTOFF
and not self.player_v_player:
        self.conduct_exploration = False

    if self.conduct_exploration:
        child_visits_cum_sum = self.root.child_visit_counts.cumsum()
        child_visits_cum_sum /= child_visits_cum_sum[-1]
        coorindate = child_visits_cum_sum.searchsorted(random.random())
    else:
        coorindate = np.argmax(self.root.child_visit_counts)

    return utils.from_flat(coorindate)
```

These functions are encapsulated in the `search_tree` method, which conducts an iteration of MCTS using the network to select the next move:

```
def search_tree(self):
    child_node_store = []
    iteration_count = 0
    while len(child_node_store) < self.workers and iteration_count <
self.workers * 2:
        iteration_count += 1
        child_node = self.root.choose_next_child_node()
        if child_node.is_done():
            result = 1 if child_node.board_state.score() > 0 else -1
            child_node.back_propagate_result(result, start_node=self.root)
            continue
        child_node.propagate_loss(start_node=self.root)
        child_node_store.append(child_node)
    if len(child_node_store) > 0:
        move_probs, values = self.network.predict_on_multiple_board_states(
            [child_node.board_state for child_node in child_node_store])
        for child_node, move_prob, result in zip(child_node_store,
move_probs, values):
            child_node.revert_loss(start_node=self.root)
            child_node.incorporate_results(move_prob, result,
start_node=self.root)
```

Notice that once we have leaf nodes (where we can no longer select a node based on visit count), we use
the `PolicyValueNetwork.predict_on_multiple_board_states(board_states)`
function to output the next move probabilities and value of each leaf node.
This `AlphaGoZeroAgent` is then used for either playing against another network or against itself for self-play. We implement separate functions for each. For `play_match`, we first start by initializing an agent each for black and white pieces:

```
def play_match(black_net, white_net, games, readouts, sgf_dir):

    # Create the players for the game
    black = AlphaGoZeroAgent(black_net, player_v_player=True,
workers=GLOBAL_PARAMETER_STORE.SIMULTANEOUS_LEAVES)
    white = AlphaGoZeroAgent(white_net, player_v_player=True,
workers=GLOBAL_PARAMETER_STORE.SIMULTANEOUS_LEAVES)

    black_name = os.path.basename(black_net.model_path)
    white_name = os.path.basename(white_net.model_path)
```

During the game, we keep track of the number of moves made, which also informs us which agent's turn it is. During each agent's turn, we use MCTS and the network to choose the next move:

```
for game_num in range(games):
    # Keep track of the number of moves made in the game
    num_moves = 0

    black.initialize_game()
    white.initialize_game()

    while True:
        start = time.time()
        active = white if num_moves % 2 else black
        inactive = black if num_moves % 2 else white

        current_readouts = active.root.node_visit_count
        while active.root.node_visit_count < current_readouts + readouts:
            active.search_tree()
```

Once the tree search is done, we see whether the agent has resigned or the game has ended by other means. If so, we write the results and end the game itself:

```
logger.info(active.root.board_state)

# Check whether a player should resign
if active.should_resign():
    active.set_result(-1 * active.root.board_state.to_play,
was_resign=True)
    inactive.set_result(active.root.board_state.to_play, was_resign=True)

if active.is_done():
    sgf_file_path = "{}-{}-vs-{}-{}.sgf".format(int(time.time()),
white_name, black_name, game_num)
    with open(os.path.join(sgf_dir, sgf_file_path), 'w') as fp:
        game_as_sgf_string = make_sgf(active.board_state.recent,
active.logging_buffer,
                        black_name=black_name,
                        white_name=white_name)
        fp.write(game_as_sgf_string)
    print("Game Over", game_num, active.logging_buffer)
    break

move = active.select_move()
active.play_move(move)
inactive.play_move(move)
```

The `make_sgf` method writes the outcome of the game in a format that is commonly used in other Go AIs and computer programs. In other words, the output of this module are compatible with other Go software! Although we won't delve into the technicalities, this would help you create a Go playing bot that can play other agents and even human players.

> **SGF** stands for **Smart Game Format**, and is a popular way of storing the results of board games such as Go. You can find more information here: `https://senseis.xmp.net/?SmartGameFormat`.

The `play_against_self()` is used during the self-play simulations of training, while `play_match()` is used to evaluate the latest model against an earlier version of the model. Again, for a full implementation of the module, please refer to the codebase.

Putting everything together

Now that we have implemented the two main components of AlphaGo Zero—the `PolicyValueNetwork` and the MCTS algorithm—we can build the controller that handles training. At the very beginning of the training procedure, we initialize a model with random weights. Next, we generate 100 self-play games. Five percent of those games and their results are held out for validation. The rest are kept for training the network. After the first initialization and self-play iteration, we essentially loop through the following steps:

1. Generate self-play data
2. Collate self-play data to create `TFRecords`
3. Train network using collated self-play data
4. Validate on `holdout` dataset

After every step 3, the resulting model is stored in a directory as the latest version. The training procedure and logic are handled by `controller.py`.

controller.py

First, we start with some import statements and helper functions that help us check directory paths and find the latest model version:

```
import argparse
import logging
import os
import random
```

```python
import socket
import sys
import time

import argh
import tensorflow as tf
from tensorflow import gfile
from tqdm import tqdm

import alphagozero_agent
import network
import preprocessing
from config import GLOBAL_PARAMETER_STORE
from constants import PATHS
from alphagozero_agent import play_match
from network import PolicyValueNetwork
from utils import logged_timer as timer
from utils import print_flags, generate, detect_model_name,
detect_model_version

logging.basicConfig(
 level=logging.DEBUG,
 handlers=[logging.StreamHandler(sys.stdout)],
 format='%(asctime)s %(name)-12s %(levelname)-8s %(message)s',
)

logger = logging.getLogger(__name__)

def get_models():
    """
    Get all model versions
    """
    all_models = gfile.Glob(os.path.join(PATHS.MODELS_DIR, '*.meta'))
    model_filenames = [os.path.basename(m) for m in all_models]
    model_versionbers_names = sorted([
    (detect_model_version(m), detect_model_name(m))
    for m in model_filenames])
    return model_versionbers_names

def get_latest_model():
    """
    Get the latest model

    Returns:
    Tuple of <int, str>, or <model_version, model_name>
    """
    return get_models()[-1]
```

The first step of every training run is to initialize a random model. Note that we store model definitions and weights in the PATHS.MODELS_DIR directory, while checkpoint results outputted by the estimator object are stored in PATHS.ESTIMATOR_WORKING_DIR:

```
def initialize_random_model():
    bootstrap_name = generate(0)
    bootstrap_model_path = os.path.join(PATHS.MODELS_DIR, bootstrap_name)
    logger.info("Bootstrapping with working dir {}\n Model 0 exported to
{}".format(
        PATHS.ESTIMATOR_WORKING_DIR, bootstrap_model_path))
    maybe_create_directory(PATHS.ESTIMATOR_WORKING_DIR)
    maybe_create_directory(os.path.dirname(bootstrap_model_path))
    network.initialize_random_model(PATHS.ESTIMATOR_WORKING_DIR)
    network.export_latest_checkpoint_model(PATHS.ESTIMATOR_WORKING_DIR,
bootstrap_model_path)
```

We next implement the function for executing self-play simulations. As mentioned earlier, the output of a self-play consist of each board state and the associated moves and game outcomes produced by the MCTS algorithm. Most output are stored in PATHS.SELFPLAY_DIR, while some are stored in PATHS.HOLDOUT_DIR for validation. Self-play involves initializing one AlphaGoZeroAgent and having it play against itself. This is where we use the play_against_self function that we implemented in alphagozero_agent.py. In our implementation, we conduct self-play games according to the GLOBAL_PARAMETER_STORE.NUM_SELFPLAY_GAMES parameter specified. More self-play games allow our neural network to learn from more experience, but do bear in mind that the training time increases accordingly:

```
def selfplay():
    _, model_name = get_latest_model()
    try:
        games = gfile.Glob(os.path.join(PATHS.SELFPLAY_DIR, model_name,
'*.zz'))
        if len(games) > GLOBAL_PARAMETER_STORE.MAX_GAMES_PER_GENERATION:
            logger.info("{} has enough games ({})".format(model_name,
len(games)))
            time.sleep(600)
            sys.exit(1)
    except:
        pass

    for game_idx in range(GLOBAL_PARAMETER_STORE.NUM_SELFPLAY_GAMES):
        logger.info('=============================================')
        logger.info("Playing game {} with model {}".format(game_idx,
model_name))
        logger.info('=============================================')
        model_save_path = os.path.join(PATHS.MODELS_DIR, model_name)
```

```
game_output_dir = os.path.join(PATHS.SELFPLAY_DIR, model_name)
game_holdout_dir = os.path.join(PATHS.HOLDOUT_DIR, model_name)
sgf_dir = os.path.join(PATHS.SGF_DIR, model_name)

clean_sgf = os.path.join(sgf_dir, 'clean')
full_sgf = os.path.join(sgf_dir, 'full')
os.makedirs(clean_sgf, exist_ok=True)
os.makedirs(full_sgf, exist_ok=True)
os.makedirs(game_output_dir, exist_ok=True)
os.makedirs(game_holdout_dir, exist_ok=True)
```

During self-play, we instantiate an agent with weights of a previously-generated model and make it play against itself for a number of games defined by GLOBAL_PARAMETER_STORE.NUM_SELFPLAY_GAMES:

```
with timer("Loading weights from %s ... " % model_save_path):
    network = PolicyValueNetwork(model_save_path)

with timer("Playing game"):
    agent = alphagozero_agent.play_against_self(network,
GLOBAL_PARAMETER_STORE.SELFPLAY_READOUTS)
```

After the agent plays against itself, we store the moves it has generated as game data, which we use to train our policy and value networks:

```
output_name = '{}-{}'.format(int(time.time()), socket.gethostname())
game_play = agent.extract_data()
with gfile.GFile(os.path.join(clean_sgf, '{}.sgf'.format(output_name)),
'w') as f:
    f.write(agent.to_sgf(use_comments=False))
with gfile.GFile(os.path.join(full_sgf, '{}.sgf'.format(output_name)), 'w')
as f:
    f.write(agent.to_sgf())

tf_examples = preprocessing.create_dataset_from_selfplay(game_play)

# We reserve 5% of games played for validation
holdout = random.random() < GLOBAL_PARAMETER_STORE.HOLDOUT
if holdout:
    to_save_dir = game_holdout_dir
else:
    to_save_dir = game_output_dir
tf_record_path = os.path.join(to_save_dir,
"{}.tfrecord.zz".format(output_name))

preprocessing.write_tf_examples(tf_record_path, tf_examples)
```

Notice that we reserve a percentage of the games played as the validation set.

After generating self-play data, we expect roughly five percent of the self-play games to be in the holdout directory, to be used in validation. The majority of self-play data is used to train the neural network. We add another step, called **aggregate**, which takes the latest model version and its self-play data to construct TFRecords with the format that our neural network specifies. This is where we use the functions we implemented in preprocessing.py:

```python
def aggregate():
    logger.info("Gathering game results")

    os.makedirs(PATHS.TRAINING_CHUNK_DIR, exist_ok=True)
    os.makedirs(PATHS.SELFPLAY_DIR, exist_ok=True)
    models = [model_dir.strip('/')
              for model_dir in
    sorted(gfile.ListDirectory(PATHS.SELFPLAY_DIR))[-50:]]

    with timer("Finding existing tfrecords..."):
        model_gamedata = {
            model: gfile.Glob(
                os.path.join(PATHS.SELFPLAY_DIR, model, '*.zz'))
            for model in models
        }
    logger.info("Found %d models" % len(models))
    for model_name, record_files in sorted(model_gamedata.items()):
        logger.info("    %s: %s files" % (model_name, len(record_files)))

    meta_file = os.path.join(PATHS.TRAINING_CHUNK_DIR, 'meta.txt')
    try:
        with gfile.GFile(meta_file, 'r') as f:
            already_processed = set(f.read().split())
    except tf.errors.NotFoundError:
        already_processed = set()

    num_already_processed = len(already_processed)

    for model_name, record_files in sorted(model_gamedata.items()):
        if set(record_files) <= already_processed:
            continue
        logger.info("Gathering files for %s:" % model_name)
        for i, example_batch in enumerate(
    tqdm(preprocessing.shuffle_tf_examples(GLOBAL_PARAMETER_STORE.EXAMPLES_PER_
    RECORD, record_files))):
            output_record = os.path.join(PATHS.TRAINING_CHUNK_DIR,
                                         '{}-
    {}.tfrecord.zz'.format(model_name, str(i)))
            preprocessing.write_tf_examples(
                output_record, example_batch, serialize=False)
```

```
            already_processed.update(record_files)

        logger.info("Processed %s new files" %
            (len(already_processed) - num_already_processed))
        with gfile.GFile(meta_file, 'w') as f:
            f.write('\n'.join(sorted(already_processed)))
```

After we generate the training data, we train a new version of the neural network. We search for the latest version of the model, load an estimator using the weights of the latest version, and execute another iteration of training:

```
def train():
    model_version, model_name = get_latest_model()
    logger.info("Training on gathered game data, initializing from
{}".format(model_name))
    new_model_name = generate(model_version + 1)
    logger.info("New model will be {}".format(new_model_name))
    save_file = os.path.join(PATHS.MODELS_DIR, new_model_name)

    try:
        logger.info("Getting tf_records")
        tf_records =
sorted(gfile.Glob(os.path.join(PATHS.TRAINING_CHUNK_DIR, '*.tfrecord.zz')))
        tf_records = tf_records[
                        -1 * (GLOBAL_PARAMETER_STORE.WINDOW_SIZE //
GLOBAL_PARAMETER_STORE.EXAMPLES_PER_RECORD):]

        print("Training from:", tf_records[0], "to", tf_records[-1])

        with timer("Training"):
                network.train(PATHS.ESTIMATOR_WORKING_DIR, tf_records,
model_version+1)
        network.export_latest_checkpoint_model(PATHS.ESTIMATOR_WORKING_DIR,
save_file)

    except:
        logger.info("Got an error training")
        logging.exception("Train error")
```

Finally, after every training iteration, we would like to validate the model with the holdout dataset. When enough data is available, we take the holdout data from the last five versions:

```
def validate(model_version=None, validate_name=None):
    if model_version is None:
        model_version, model_name = get_latest_model()
    else:
        model_version = int(model_version)
```

```
        model_name = get_model(model_version)

    models = list(
        filter(lambda num_name: num_name[0] < (model_version - 1),
get_models()))

    if len(models) == 0:
        logger.info('Not enough models, including model N for validation')
        models = list(
            filter(lambda num_name: num_name[0] <= model_version,
get_models()))
    else:
        logger.info('Validating using data from following models:
{}'.format(models))

    tf_record_dirs = [os.path.join(PATHS.HOLDOUT_DIR, pair[1])
                    for pair in models[-5:]]

    working_dir = PATHS.ESTIMATOR_WORKING_DIR
    checkpoint_name = os.path.join(PATHS.MODELS_DIR, model_name)

    tf_records = []
    with timer("Building lists of holdout files"):
        for record_dir in tf_record_dirs:
            tf_records.extend(gfile.Glob(os.path.join(record_dir, '*.zz')))

    with timer("Validating from {} to
{}".format(os.path.basename(tf_records[0]),
os.path.basename(tf_records[-1]))):
        network.validate(working_dir, tf_records,
checkpoint_path=checkpoint_name, name=validate_name)
```

Lastly, we implement the `evaluate` function, which has one model play multiple games against another:

```
def evaluate(black_model, white_model):
    os.makedirs(PATHS.SGF_DIR, exist_ok=True)

    with timer("Loading weights"):
        black_net = network.PolicyValueNetwork(black_model)
        white_net = network.PolicyValueNetwork(white_model)

    with timer("Playing {}
games".format(GLOBAL_PARAMETER_STORE.EVALUATION_GAMES)):
        play_match(black_net, white_net,
GLOBAL_PARAMETER_STORE.EVALUATION_GAMES,
                    GLOBAL_PARAMETER_STORE.EVALUATION_READOUTS,
PATHS.SGF_DIR)
```

The `evaluate` method takes two parameters, `black_model` and `white_model`, where each argument refers to the path of the agent used to play a game. We use `black_model` and `white_model` to instantiate two `PolicyValueNetworks`. Typically, we want to evaluate the latest model version, which would play as either black or white.

train.py

Finally, `train.py` is where all the functions we implemented in the controller are called and coordinated. More specifically, we execute each step as `subprocess`:

```
import subprocess
import sys
from utils import timer

import os

from constants import PATHS

import logging

logger = logging.getLogger(__name__)

def main():

    if not os.path.exists(PATHS.SELFPLAY_DIR):
        with timer("Initialize"):
            logger.info('=========================================')
            logger.info("============ Initializing...=============")
            logger.info('=========================================')
            res = subprocess.call("python controller.py initialize-random-model", shell=True)

        with timer('Initial Selfplay'):
            logger.info('=====================================')
            logger.info('============ Selplaying...=============')
            logger.info('=====================================')
            subprocess.call('python controller.py selfplay', shell=True)
```

Assuming that no model has been trained yet, we initialize a model with random weights and make it play against itself to generate some data for our policy and value networks. After rewards, we repeat the following:

1. Aggregate data self-play data
2. Train networks

3. Make the agent play against itself
4. Validate on validation data

This is implemented as follows:

```
while True:
    with timer("Aggregate"):
        logger.info('=========================================')
        logger.info("=========== Aggregating...==============")
        logger.info('=========================================')
        res = subprocess.call("python controller.py aggregate", shell=True)
        if res != 0:
            logger.info("Failed to gather")
            sys.exit(1)

    with timer("Train"):
        logger.info('=========================================')
        logger.info("=========== Training...=================")
        logger.info('=========================================')
        subprocess.call("python controller.py train", shell=True)

    with timer('Selfplay'):
        logger.info('=========================================')
        logger.info('=========== Selplaying...=============')
        logger.info('=========================================')
        subprocess.call('python controller.py selfplay', shell=True)

    with timer("Validate"):
        logger.info('=========================================')
        logger.info("=========== Validating...=============")
        logger.info('=========================================')
        subprocess.call("python controller.py validate", shell=True)
```

Finally, since this is the main module, we add the following at the end of the file:

```
if __name__ == '__main__':
    main()
```

And at long last, we're done!

To run the training of AlphaGo Zero, all you need to do is call this command:

```
$ python train.py
```

If everything has been implemented correctly, you should start to see the model train. However, the reader is to be warned that training will take a long, long time. To put things into perspective, DeepMind used 64 GPU workers and 19 CPU servers to train AlphaGo Zero for 40 days. If you wish to see your model attain a high level of proficiency, expect to wait a long time.

> Note that training AlphaGo Zero takes a very long time. Do not expect the model to reach professional-level proficiency any time soon!

You should be able to see output that looks such as the following:

```
2018-09-14 03:41:27,286 utils INFO Playing game: 342.685 seconds
2018-09-14 03:41:27,332 __main__ INFO
==================================================
2018-09-14 03:41:27,332 __main__ INFO Playing game 9 with model 000010-
pretty-tetra
2018-09-14 03:41:27,332 __main__ INFO
==================================================
INFO:tensorflow:Restoring parameters from models/000010-pretty-tetra
2018-09-14 03:41:32,352 tensorflow INFO Restoring parameters from
models/000010-pretty-tetra
2018-09-14 03:41:32,624 utils INFO Loading weights from models/000010-
pretty-tetra ... : 5.291 seconds
```

You will also be able to see the board state as the agent plays against itself or against other agents:

```
   A B C D E F G H J
9 . . . . . . . X 9
8 . . . X . . O . . 8
7 . . . . X O O . . 7
6 O . X X X<. . . . 6
5 X . O O . . O X . 5
4 . . X X . . . O . 4
3 . . X . X . O O . 3
2 . . . O . . . . X 2
1 . . . . . . . . . 1
   A B C D E F G H J
Move: 25. Captures X: 0 O: 0
 -5.5
   A B C D E F G H J
9 . . . . . . . X 9
8 . . . X . . O . . 8
7 . . . . X O O . . 7
6 O . X X X . . . . 6
```

```
5 X . O O . . O X . 5
4 . . X X . . . O . 4
3 . . X . X . O O . 3
2 . . . O . . . . X 2
1 . . . . . . . . . 1
  A B C D E F G H J
Move: 26. Captures X: 0 O: 0
```

If you want to play one model against another, you can run the following command (assuming that the models are stored in `models/`):

```
python controller.py evaluate models/{model_name_1} models/{model_name_2}
```

Summary

In this chapter, we studied reinforcement learning algorithms for one of the most complex and difficult games in the world, Go. In particular, we explored Monte Carlo tree search, a popular algorithm that learns the best moves over time. In AlphaGo, we observed how MCTS can be combined with deep neural networks to make learning more efficient and powerful. Then we investigated how AlphaGo Zero revolutionized Go agents by learning solely and entirely from self-play experience while outperforming all existing Go software and players. We then implemented this algorithm from scratch.

We also implemented AlphaGo Zero, which is the lighter version of AlphaGo since it does not depend on human game data. However, as noted, AlphaGo Zero requires enormous amounts of computational resources. Moreover, as you may have noticed, AlphaGo Zero depends on a myriad of hyperparameters, all of which require fine-tuning. In short, training AlphaGo Zero fully is a prohibitive task. We don't expect the reader to implement a state-of-the-art Go agent; rather, we hope that through this chapter, the reader has a better understanding of how Go playing deep reinforcement learning algorithms work. A firmer comprehension of these techniques and algorithms is already a valuable takeaway and outcome from this chapter. But of course, we encourage the reader to continue their exploration on this topic and build an even better version of AlphaGo Zero.

For more in-depth information and resources on the topics we covered in this chapter, please refer to the following links:

- **AlphaGo home page**: https://deepmind.com/research/alphago/
- **AlphaGo paper**: https://storage.googleapis.com/deepmind-media/alphago/AlphaGoNaturePaper.pdf
- **AlphaGo Zero paper**: https://www.nature.com/articles/nature24270
- **AlphaGo Zero blog post by DeepMind**: https://deepmind.com/blog/alphago-zero-learning-scratch/
- **A survey of MCTS methods**: http://mcts.ai/pubs/mcts-survey-master.pdf

Now that computers have surpassed human performance in board games, one may ask, What's next? What are the implications of these results? There remains much to be done; Go, which has complete information and is played turn by turn, is still considered simple compared to many real-life situations. One can imagine that the problem of self-driving cars poses a more difficult challenge given the lack of complete information and a larger number of variables. Nevertheless, AlphaGo and AlphaGo Zero have provided a crucial step toward achieving these tasks, and one can surely be excited about further developments in this field.

References

1. Silver, D., Huang, A., Maddison, C. J., Guez, A., Sifre, L., Van Den Driessche, G., ... and Dieleman, S. (2016). *Mastering the game of Go with deep neural networks and tree search*. Nature, 529(7587), 484.
2. Silver, D., Schrittwieser, J., Simonyan, K., Antonoglou, I., Huang, A., Guez, A., ... and Chen, Y. (2017). *Mastering the game of Go without human knowledge*. Nature, 550(7676), 354.
3. Browne, C. B., Powley, E., Whitehouse, D., Lucas, S. M., Cowling, P. I., Rohlfshagen, P., ... and Colton, S. (2012). *A survey of Monte Carlo tree search methods*. IEEE Transactions on Computational Intelligence and AI in games, 4(1), 1-43.

Creating a Chatbot

Dialogue agents and chatbots have been on the rise in recent years. Many businesses have resorted to chatbots to answer customer inquiries, and this has been largely successful. Chatbots have been growing quickly, at 5.6x in the last year (https://chatbotsmagazine. com/chatbot-report-2018-global-trends-and-analysis-4d8bbe4d924b). Chatbots can help organizations to communicate and interact with customers without any human intervention, at a very minimal cost. Over 51% of customers have stated that they want businesses to be available 24/7, and they expect replies in less than one hour. For businesses to achieve this kind of success in an affordable manner, especially with a large customer base, they must resort to chatbots.

The background problem

Many chatbots are created with regular machine learning natural language processing algorithms, and these focus on immediate responses. A new concept is to create chatbots with the use of deep reinforcement learning. This would mean that the future implications of our immediate responses would be considered to maintain coherence.

In this chapter, you will learn how to apply deep reinforcement learning to natural language processing. Our reward function will be a future-looking function, and you will learn how to think probabilistically through the creation of this function.

Dataset

The dataset that we will use mainly consists of conversations from selected movies. This dataset will help to stimulate and understand conversational methods in the chatbot. Also, there are movie lines, which are essentially the same as the movie conversations, albeit shorter exchanges between people. Other data sets that will be used include some containing movie titles, movie characters, and raw scripts.

Step-by-step guide

Our solution will use modeling and will focus on the future direction of a dialogue agent, so as to generate coherent and interesting dialogue. The model will simulate the dialogue between two virtual agents, with the use of policy gradient methods. These methods are designed to reward the sequences of interaction that display three important properties of conversation: informativeness (non-repeating turns), high coherence, and simplicity in answering (this is related to the forward-looking function). In our solution, an action will be defined as the dialogue or communication utterance that the chatbot generates. Also, a state will be defined as the two previous interaction turns. In order to achieve all of this, we will use the scripts in the following sections.

Data parser

The data parser script is designed to help with the cleaning and preprocessing of our datasets. There are a number of dependencies in this script, such as `pickle`, `codecs`, `re`, `os`, `time`, and `numpy`. This script contains three functions. The first function helps to filter words, by preprocessing word counts and creating vocabulary based on word count thresholds. The second function helps to parse all words into this script, and the third function helps to extract only the defined vocabulary from the data:

```
import pickle
import codecs
import re
import os
import time
import numpy as np
```

The following module cleans and preprocesses the text in the training dataset:

```
def preProBuildWordVocab(word_count_threshold=5,
all_words_path='data/all_words.txt'):
    # borrowed this function from NeuralTalk

    if not os.path.exists(all_words_path):
        parse_all_words(all_words_path)

    corpus = open(all_words_path, 'r').read().split('\n')[:-1]
    captions = np.asarray(corpus, dtype=np.object)

    captions = map(lambda x: x.replace('.', ''), captions)
    captions = map(lambda x: x.replace(',', ''), captions)
    captions = map(lambda x: x.replace('"', ''), captions)
    captions = map(lambda x: x.replace('\n', ''), captions)
```

```
captions = map(lambda x: x.replace('?', ''), captions)
captions = map(lambda x: x.replace('!', ''), captions)
captions = map(lambda x: x.replace('\\', ''), captions)
captions = map(lambda x: x.replace('/', ''), captions)
```

Next, iterate through the captions and create the vocabulary.

```
print('preprocessing word counts and creating vocab based on word count
threshold %d' % (word_count_threshold))
word_counts = {}
nsents = 0
for sent in captions:
    nsents += 1
    for w in sent.lower().split(' '):
        word_counts[w] = word_counts.get(w, 0) + 1
vocab = [w for w in word_counts if word_counts[w] >=
word_count_threshold]
print('filtered words from %d to %d' % (len(word_counts), len(vocab)))

ixtoword = {}
ixtoword[0] = '<pad>'
ixtoword[1] = '<bos>'
ixtoword[2] = '<eos>'
ixtoword[3] = '<unk>'

wordtoix = {}
wordtoix['<pad>'] = 0
wordtoix['<bos>'] = 1
wordtoix['<eos>'] = 2
wordtoix['<unk>'] = 3

for idx, w in enumerate(vocab):
    wordtoix[w] = idx+4
    ixtoword[idx+4] = w

word_counts['<pad>'] = nsents
word_counts['<bos>'] = nsents
word_counts['<eos>'] = nsents
word_counts['<unk>'] = nsents

bias_init_vector = np.array([1.0 * word_counts[ixtoword[i]] for i in
ixtoword])
bias_init_vector /= np.sum(bias_init_vector) # normalize to frequencies
bias_init_vector = np.log(bias_init_vector)
bias_init_vector -= np.max(bias_init_vector) # shift to nice numeric
range

return wordtoix, ixtoword, bias_init_vector
```

Next, parse all the words from the movie lines.

```
def parse_all_words(all_words_path):
    raw_movie_lines = open('data/movie_lines.txt', 'r', encoding='utf-8',
errors='ignore').read().split('\n')[:-1]

    with codecs.open(all_words_path, "w", encoding='utf-8',
errors='ignore') as f:
        for line in raw_movie_lines:
            line = line.split(' +++$+++ ')
            utterance = line[-1]
            f.write(utterance + '\n')
```

Extract only the vocabulary part of the data, as follows:

```
def refine(data):
    words = re.findall("[a-zA-Z'-]+", data)
    words = ["".join(word.split("'")) for word in words]
    # words = ["".join(word.split("-")) for word in words]
    data = ' '.join(words)
    return data
```

Next, the utterance dictionary is created and stored.

```
if __name__ == '__main__':
    parse_all_words('data/all_words.txt')

    raw_movie_lines = open('data/movie_lines.txt', 'r', encoding='utf-8',
errors='ignore').read().split('\n')[:-1]
    utterance_dict = {}
    with codecs.open('data/tokenized_all_words.txt', "w", encoding='utf-8',
errors='ignore') as f:
        for line in raw_movie_lines:
            line = line.split(' +++$+++ ')
            line_ID = line[0]
            utterance = line[-1]
            utterance_dict[line_ID] = utterance
            utterance = " ".join([refine(w) for w in
utterance.lower().split()])
            f.write(utterance + '\n')
    pickle.dump(utterance_dict, open('data/utterance_dict', 'wb'), True)
```

The data is parsed and can be utilized in further steps.

Data reader

The data reader script helps to generate trainable batches from the preprocessed training text from the data parser script. Let's start by importing the required methods:

```
import pickle
import random
```

This helper module helps generate trainable batches from the preprocessed training text:

```
class Data_Reader:
    def __init__(self, cur_train_index=0, load_list=False):
        self.training_data =
pickle.load(open('data/conversations_lenmax22_formersents2_with_former ,
'rb'))
        self.data_size = len(self.training_data)
        if load_list:
            self.shuffle_list = pickle.load(open('data/shuffle_index_list',
'rb'))
        else:
            self.shuffle_list = self.shuffle_index()
        self.train_index = cur_train_index
```

The following code gets the batch number from the data:

```
    def get_batch_num(self, batch_size):
        return self.data_size // batch_size
```

The following code shuffles the index from the data:

```
    def shuffle_index(self):
        shuffle_index_list = random.sample(range(self.data_size),
self.data_size)
        pickle.dump(shuffle_index_list, open('data/shuffle_index_list'.
'wb'), True)
        return shuffle_index_list
```

The following code generates the batch indices, based on the batch number that was obtained earlier:

```
    def generate_batch_index(self, batch_size):
        if self.train_index + batch_size > self.data_size:
            batch_index =
self.shuffle_list[self.train_index:self.data_size]
            self.shuffle_list = self.shuffle_index()
            remain_size = batch_size - (self.data_size - self.train_index)
            batch_index += self.shuffle_list[:remain_size]
            self.train_index = remain_size
```

```
        else:
            batch_index =
self.shuffle_list[self.train_index:self.train_index+batch_size]
            self.train_index += batch_size

        return batch_index
```

The following code generates the training batch:

```
    def generate_training_batch(self, batch_size):
        batch_index = self.generate_batch_index(batch_size)
        batch_X = [self.training_data[i][0] for i in batch_index]   #
batch_size of conv_a
        batch_Y = [self.training_data[i][1] for i in batch_index]   #
batch_size of conv_b

        return batch_X, batch_Y
```

The following function generates training batch with the former.

```
    def generate_training_batch_with_former(self, batch_size):
        batch_index = self.generate_batch_index(batch_size)
        batch_X = [self.training_data[i][0] for i in batch_index]   #
batch_size of conv_a
        batch_Y = [self.training_data[i][1] for i in batch_index]   #
batch_size of conv_b
        former = [self.training_data[i][2] for i in batch_index]    #
batch_size of former utterance

        return batch_X, batch_Y, former
```

The following code generates the testing batch:

```
    def generate_testing_batch(self, batch_size):
        batch_index = self.generate_batch_index(batch_size)
        batch_X = [self.training_data[i][0] for i in batch_index]   #
batch_size of conv_a

        return batch_X
```

This concludes the data reading part.

Helper methods

This script consists of a `Seq2seq` dialogue generator model, which is used for the reverse model of the backward entropy loss. This will determine the semantic coherence reward for the policy gradients dialogue. Essentially, this script will help us to represent our future reward function. The script will achieve this via the following actions:

- Encoding
- Decoding
- Generating builds

All of the preceding actions are based on **long short-term memory (LSTM)** units.

The feature extractor script helps with the extraction of features and characteristics from the data, in order to help us train it better. Let us start by importing the required modules.

```
import tensorflow as tf
import numpy as np
import re
```

Next, define the model inputs. If reinforcement learning is set to True, a scalar is computed based on semantic coherence and ease of answering loss caption.

```
def model_inputs(embed_dim, reinforcement= False):
    word_vectors = tf.placeholder(tf.float32, [None, None, embed_dim], name
= "word_vectors")
    reward = tf.placeholder(tf.float32, shape = (), name = "rewards")
    caption = tf.placeholder(tf.int32, [None, None], name = "captions")
    caption_mask = tf.placeholder(tf.float32, [None, None], name =
"caption_masks")
    if reinforcement: #Normal training returns only the word_vectors,
caption and caption_mask placeholders,
        #With reinforcement learning, there is an extra placeholder for
rewards
        return word_vectors, caption, caption_mask, reward
    else:
        return word_vectors, caption, caption_mask
```

Next, define the encoding layers which perform encoding for the sequence to sequence network. The input sequence is passed into the encoder and returns the output of RNN output and the state.

```
def encoding_layer(word_vectors, lstm_size, num_layers, keep_prob,
                   vocab_size):
    cells =
tf.contrib.rnn.MultiRNNCell([tf.contrib.rnn.DropoutWrapper(tf.contrib.rnn.L
```

```
STMCell(lstm_size), keep_prob) for _ in range(num_layers)])
    outputs, state = tf.nn.dynamic_rnn(cells,
                                        word_vectors,
                                        dtype=tf.float32)
    return outputs, state
```

Next, define the training process for decoder using LSTMS cells with the encoder state together with the decoder inputs.

```
def decode_train(enc_state, dec_cell, dec_input,
                    target_sequence_length,output_sequence_length,
                    output_layer, keep_prob):
    dec_cell = tf.contrib.rnn.DropoutWrapper(dec_cell,
#Apply dropout to the LSTM cell
                                        output_keep_prob=keep_prob)
    helper = tf.contrib.seq2seq.TrainingHelper(dec_input,
#Training helper for decoder
                                        target_sequence_length)
    decoder = tf.contrib.seq2seq.BasicDecoder(dec_cell,
                                        helper,
                                        enc_state,
                                        output_layer)

    # unrolling the decoder layer
    outputs, _, _ = tf.contrib.seq2seq.dynamic_decode(decoder,
                                        impute_finished=True,
maximum_iterations=output_sequence_length)
    return outputs
```

Next, define an inference decoder similar to the one used for the training. Makes use of a greedy helper which feeds the last output of the decoder as the next decoder input. The output returned contains the training logits and the sample id.

```
def decode_generate(encoder_state, dec_cell, dec_embeddings,
                    target_sequence_length,output_sequence_length,
                    vocab_size, output_layer, batch_size, keep_prcb):
    dec_cell = tf.contrib.rnn.DropoutWrapper(dec_cell,
                                        output_keep_prob=keep_prob)
    helper = tf.contrib.seq2seq.GreedyEmbeddingHelper(dec_embeddings,
                                        tf.fill([batch_size,
1),  #Decoder helper for inference
                                        2)
    decoder = tf.contrib.seq2seq.BasicDecoder(dec_cell,
                                        helper,
                                        encoder_state,
                                        output_layer)
    outputs, _, _ = tf.contrib.seq2seq.dynamic_decode(decoder,
                                        impute_finished=True,
```

```
        maximum_iterations=output_sequence_length)
            return outputs
```

Next, create a decoding layer.

```
def decoding_layer(dec_input, enc_state,
                   target_sequence_length,output_sequence_length,
                   lstm_size,
                   num_layers,n_words,
                   batch_size, keep_prob,embedding_size, Train = True):
    target_vocab_size = n_words
    with tf.device("/cpu:0"):
        dec_embeddings =
tf.Variable(tf.random_uniform([target_vocab_size,embedding_size], -0.1,
0.1), name='Wemb')
    dec_embed_input = tf.nn.embedding_lookup(dec_embeddings, dec_input)
    cells = tf.contrib.rnn.MultiRNNCell([tf.contrib.rnn.LSTMCell(lstm_size)
for _ in range(num_layers)])
    with tf.variable_scope("decode"):
        output_layer = tf.layers.Dense(target_vocab_size)
    if Train:
        with tf.variable_scope("decode"):
            train_output = decode_train(enc_state,
                                        cells,
                                        dec_embed_input,
                                        target_sequence_length,
output_sequence_length,
                                        output_layer,
                                        keep_prob)

    with tf.variable_scope("decode", reuse=tf.AUTO_REUSE):
        infer_output = decode_generate(enc_state,
                                       cells,
                                       dec_embeddings,
target_sequence_length,
                                       output_sequence_length,
                                       target_vocab_size,
                                       output_layer,
                                       batch_size,
                                       keep_prob)
    if Train:
        return train_output, infer_output
    return infer_output
```

Next, create the bos inclusion which appends the index corresponding to <bos> referring to the beginning of a sentence to the first index of the caption tensor for every batch.

```
def bos_inclusion(caption,batch_size):

    sliced_target = tf.strided_slice(caption, [0,0], [batch_size, -1],
[1,1])
    concat = tf.concat([tf.fill([batch_size, 1],1), sliced_target],1)
    return concat
```

Next, define pad sequences which creates an array of size maxlen from every question by padding with zeros or truncating where necessary.

```
def pad_sequences(questions, sequence_length =22):
    lengths = [len(x) for x in questions]
    num_samples = len(questions)
    x = np.zeros((num_samples, sequence_length)).astype(int)
    for idx, sequence in enumerate(questions):
        if not len(sequence):
            continue  # empty list/array was found
        truncated  = sequence[-sequence_length:]

        truncated = np.asarray(truncated, dtype=int)

        x[idx, :len(truncated)] = truncated
    return x
```

Ignore non-vocabulary parts if the data and take only all alphabets.

```
def refine(data):
    words = re.findall("[a-zA-Z'-]+", data)
    words = ["".join(word.split("'")) for word in words]
    data = ' '.join(words)
    return data
```

Next, create batches to be fed into the network from in word vector representation.

```
def make_batch_input(batch_input, input_sequence_length, embed_dims,
word2vec):
    for i in range(len(batch_input)):
        batch_input[i] = [word2vec[w] if w in word2vec else
np.zeros(embed_dims) for w in batch_input[i]]
        if len(batch_input[i]) >input_sequence_length:
            batch_input[i] = batch_input[i][:input_sequence_length]
        else:
            for _ in range(input_sequence_length - len(batch_input[i])):
                batch_input[i].append(np.zeros(embed_dims))
```

```
        return np.array(batch_input)

def replace(target,symbols):    #Remove symbols from sequence
    for symbol in symbols:
        target = list(map(lambda x: x.replace(symbol,''),target))
    return target
def make_batch_target(batch_target, word_to_index, target_sequence_length):
    target = batch_target
    target = list(map(lambda x: '<bos> ' + x, target))
    symbols = ['.', ',', '"',  '\n','?','!','\\','/']
    target = replace(target, symbols)

    for idx, each_cap in enumerate(target):
        word = each_cap.lower().split(' ')
        if len(word) < target_sequence_length:
            target[idx] = target[idx] + ' <eos>'   #Append the end of symbol
symbol
        else:
            new_word = ''
            for i in range(target_sequence_length-1):
                new_word = new_word + word[i] + ' '
            target[idx] = new_word + '<eos>'
    target_index = [[word_to_index[word] if word in word_to_index else
word_to_index['<unk>'] for word in
                        sequence.lower().split(' ')] for sequence in
target]
    #print(target_index[0])
    caption_matrix = pad_sequences(target_index,target_sequence_length)
    caption_matrix = np.hstack([caption_matrix,
np.zeros([len(caption_matrix), 1])]).astype(int)
    caption_masks = np.zeros((caption_matrix.shape[0],
caption_matrix.shape[1]))
    nonzeros = np.array(list(map(lambda x: (x != 0).sum(),
caption_matrix)))
    #print(nonzeros)
    #print(caption_matrix[1])
    for ind, row in enumerate(caption_masks): #Set the masks as an array of
ones where actual words exist and zeros otherwise
        row[:nonzeros[ind]] = 1
        #print(row)
    print(caption_masks[0])
    print(caption_matrix[0])
    return caption_matrix,caption_masks

def generic_batch(generic_responses, batch_size, word_to_index,
target_sequence_length):
    size = len(generic_responses)
    if size > batch_size:
```

```
            generic_responses = generic_responses[:batch_size]
        else:
            for j in range(batch_size - size):
                generic_responses.append('')
        return make_batch_Y(generic_responses, word_to_index,
    target_sequence_length)
```

Next, generate sentences from the predicted indices. Replace <unk>, <pad> with the word
with the next highest probability whenever predicted.

```
def index2sentence(generated_word_index, prob_logit, ixtoword):
    generated_word_index = list(generated_word_index)
    for i in range(len(generated_word_index)):
        if generated_word_index[i] == 3 or generated_word_index[i] == 0:
            sort_prob_logit = sorted(prob_logit[i])
            curindex = np.where(prob_logit[i] == sort_prob_logit[-2])[0][0]
            count = 1
            while curindex <= 3:
                curindex = np.where(prob_logit[i] == sort_prob_logit[(-2)-
    count])[0][0]
                count += 1

            generated_word_index[i] = curindex

    generated_words = []
    for ind in generated_word_index:
        generated_words.append(ixtoword[ind])
    generated_sentence = ' '.join(generated_words)
    generated_sentence = generated_sentence.replace('<bos> ', '')   #Replace
the beginning of sentence tag
    generated_sentence = generated_sentence.replace('<eos>', '')     #Replace
the end of sentence tag
    generated_sentence = generated_sentence.replace('--', '')        #Replace
the other symbols predicted
    generated_sentence = generated_sentence.split('  ')
    for i in range(len(generated_sentence)):       #Begin sentences with
Upper case
        generated_sentence[i] = generated_sentence[i].strip()
        if len(generated_sentence[i]) > 1:
            generated_sentence[i] = generated_sentence[i][0].upper() +
generated_sentence[i][1:] + '.'
        else:
            generated_sentence[i] = generated_sentence[i].upper()
    generated_sentence = ' '.join(generated_sentence)
    generated_sentence = generated_sentence.replace(' i ', ' I ')
    generated_sentence = generated_sentence.replace("i'm", "I'm")
    generated_sentence = generated_sentence.replace("i'd", "I'd")
```

```
            return generated_sentence
```

This concludes all the helper functions.

Chatbot model

The following script contains the policy gradient model, which will be used where it combines reinforcement learning rewards with the cross-entropy loss. The dependencies include numpy and tensorflow. Our policy gradient is based on an LSTM encoder-decoder. We will use a stochastic demonstration of our policy gradient, which will be a probability distribution of actions over specified states. The script represents all of these, and specifies the policy gradient loss to be minimized.

Run the output of the first cell through the second cell; the input is concatenated with zeros. The final state for the responses mostly consists of two components—the latent representation of the input by the encoder, and the state of the decoder, based on the selected words. The return includes placeholder tensors and other tensors, such as losses and training optimization operation. Let's start by importing the required libraries.

```
import tensorflow as tf
import numpy as np
import helper as h
```

We will create a chatbot class to create the model.

```
class Chatbot():
    def __init__(self, embed_dim, vocab_size, lstm_size, batch_size,
input_sequence_length, target_sequence_length, learning_rate =0.0001,
keep_prob = 0.5, num_layers = 1, policy_gradients = False, Training =
True):
        self.embed_dim = embed_dim
        self.lstm_size = lstm_size
        self.batch_size = batch_size
        self.vocab_size = vocab_size
        self.input_sequence_length =
tf.fill([self.batch_size],input_sequence_length+1)
        self.target_sequence_length =
tf.fill([self.batch_size],target_sequence_length+1)
        self.output_sequence_length = target_sequence_length +1
        self.learning_rate = learning_rate
        self.keep_prob = keep_prob
        self.num_layers = num_layers
        self.policy_gradients = policy_gradients
        self.Training = Training
```

Next, create a method that builds the model. If policy gradients are requested, then get the input accordingly.

```
def build_model(self):
    if self.policy_gradients:
        word_vectors, caption, caption_mask, rewards =
h.model_inputs(self.embed_dim, True)
        place_holders = {'word_vectors': word_vectors,
            'caption': caption,
            'caption_mask': caption_mask, "rewards": rewards
                        }
    else:
        word_vectors, caption, caption_mask =
h.model_inputs(self.embed_dim)
        place_holders = {'word_vectors': word_vectors,
            'caption': caption,
            'caption_mask': caption_mask}
    enc_output, enc_state = h.encoding_layer(word_vectors,
self.lstm_size, self.num_layers,
                                    self.keep_prob, self.vocab_size)
    #dec_inp = h.bos_inclusion(caption, self.batch_size)
    dec_inp = caption
```

Next, get the inference layer.

```
    if not self.Training:
        print("Test mode")
        inference_out = h.decoding_layer(dec_inp,
enc_state,self.target_sequence_length,
self.output_sequence_length,
                                        self.lstm_size,
self.num_layers,
                                        self.vocab_size,
self.batch_size,
                                        self.keep_prob,
self.embed_dim, False)
        logits = tf.identity(inference_out.rnn_output, name =
"train_logits")
        predictions = tf.identity(inference_out.sample_id, name =
"predictions")
        return place_holders, predictions, logits
```

Next, get the loss layers.

```
    train_out, inference_out = h.decoding_layer(dec_inp,
enc_state,self.target_sequence_length,
self.output_sequence_length,
                                        self.lstm_size,
```

```
self.num_layers,
                                                    self.vocab_size,
self.batch_size,
                                                    self.keep_prob,
self.embed_dim)
        training_logits = tf.identity(train_out.rnn_output, name =
"train_logits")
        prediction_logits = tf.identity(inference_out.sample_id, name =
"predictions")
        cross_entropy = tf.contrib.seq2seq.sequence_loss(training_logits,
caption, caption_mask)
        losses = {"entropy": cross_entropy}
```

Depending on the state of the policy gradient, either minimize cross entropy loss or policy gradient loss.

```
        if self.policy_gradients:
            pg_loss = tf.contrib.seq2seq.sequence_loss(training_logits.
caption, caption_mask*rewards)
            with tf.variable_scope(tf.get_variable_scope(), reuse=False):
                optimizer =
tf.train.AdamOptimizer(self.learning_rate).minimize(pg_loss)
            losses.update({"pg":pg_loss})
        else:
            with tf.variable_scope(tf.get_variable_scope(), reuse=False):
                optimizer =
tf.train.AdamOptimizer(self.learning_rate).minimize(cross_entropy)
        return optimizer, place_holders,prediction_logits,training_logits,
losses
```

Now we have all the methods that are required for training.

Training the data

The scripts that were written previously were combined with training the dataset. Let's start the training by importing all the modules that are developed in the previous sections as shown here:

```
from data_reader import Data_Reader
import data_parser
from gensim.models import KeyedVectors
import helper as h
from seq_model import Chatbot
import tensorflow as tf
import numpy as np
```

Next, let's create a set of generic responses observed in the original `seq2seq` model which the policy gradients are trained to avoid:

```
generic_responses = [
    "I don't know what you're talking about.",
    "I don't know.",
    "You don't know.",
    "You know what I mean.",
    "I know what you mean.",
    "You know what I'm saying.",
    "You don't know anything."
]
```

Next, we will define all the constants that are required for the training. Tha

```
checkpoint = True
forward_model_path = 'model/forward'
reversed_model_path = 'model/reversed'
rl_model_path = "model/rl"
model_name = 'seq2seq'
word_count_threshold = 20
reversed_word_count_threshold = 6
dim_wordvec = 300
dim_hidden = 1000
input_sequence_length = 22
output_sequence_length = 22
learning_rate = 0.0001
epochs = 1
batch_size = 200
forward_ = "forward"
reverse_ = "reverse"
forward_epochs = 50
reverse_epochs = 50
display_interval = 100
```

Next, define the training function. Based on the type, either the forward or reverse sequence to sequence model is loaded. The data is also read in reverse model based on the model as shown here:

```
def train(type_, epochs=epochs, checkpoint=False):
    tf.reset_default_graph()
    if type_ == "forward":
        path = "model/forward/seq2seq"
        dr = Data_Reader(reverse=False)
    else:
        dr = Data_Reader(reverse=True)
        path = "model/reverse/seq2seq"
```

Next, create the vocabulary as shown here:

```
    word_to_index, index_to_word, _ =
data_parser.preProBuildWordVocab(word_count_threshold=word_count_threshold)
```

The above command print should print the following indicated the vocabulary size that is filtered.

```
preprocessing word counts and creating vocab based on word count threshold
20
filtered words from 76029 to 6347
```

The `word_to_index` variable is filled with the map of filtered words to an integer as shown here:

```
{'': 4,
'deposition': 1769,
'next': 3397,
'dates': 1768,
'chance': 2597,
'slipped': 4340,...
```

The `index_to_word` variable is filled with the map of integer to the filtered works which will work as a reverse lookup.

```
5: 'tastes',
6: 'shower',
7: 'agent',
8: 'lack',
```

Next, load the word to vector model from `gensim` library.

```
    word_vector =
KeyedVectors.load_word2vec_format('model/word_vector.bin', binary=True)
```

Next, instantiate and build the model the Chatbot model with all the constants that were defined. Restore a checkpoint, if present from the previous run or initialize the graph.

```
    model = Chatbot(dim_wordvec, len(word_to_index), dim_hidden,
batch_size,
                        input_sequence_length, output_sequence_length,
learning_rate)
    optimizer, place_holders, predictions, logits, losses =
model.build_model()
    saver = tf.train.Saver()
    sess = tf.InteractiveSession()
    if checkpoint:
        saver.restore(sess, path)
```

```
        print("checkpoint restored at path: {}".format(path))
    else:
        tf.global_variables_initializer().run()
```

Next, start the training by iterating through the epochs and start the batches.

```
    for epoch in range(epochs):
        n_batch = dr.get_batch_num(batch_size=batch_size)
        for batch in range(n_batch):

            batch_input, batch_target =
dr.generate_training_batch(batch_size)
```

The `batch_input` has the list of words from the training set. The `batch_target` has the list of sentences for the input which will be the target. The list of words is converted to vector form using the helper functions. Make the feed dictionary for the graph using the transformed inputs, masks and targets.

```
            inputs_ = h.make_batch_input(batch_input,
input_sequence_length, dim_wordvec, word_vector)

            targets, masks = h.make_batch_target(batch_target,
word_to_index, output_sequence_length)
            feed_dict = {
                place_holders['word_vectors']: inputs_,
                place_holders['caption']: targets,
                place_holders['caption_mask']: masks
            }
```

Next, train the model by calling the optimizer by feeding the training data. Log the loss value at certain intervals to see the progress of the training. Save the model at the end.

```
            _, loss_val, preds = sess.run([optimizer, losses["entropy"],
predictions],
                                          feed_dict=feed_dict)

            if batch % display_interval == 0:
                print(preds.shape)
                print("Epoch: {}, batch: {}, loss: {}".format(epoch, batch,
loss_val))
    print("=======================================================")

        saver.save(sess, path)

        print("Model saved at {}".format(path))
    print("Training done")

    sess.close()
```

The output should appear as shown here.

```
(200, 23)
Epoch: 0, batch: 0, loss: 8.831538200378418
==========================================================
```

The model is trained for both forward and reverse and the corresponding models are stored. In the next function, the models are restored and trained again to create the chatbot.

```
def pg_train(epochs=epochs, checkpoint=False):
    tf.reset_default_graph()
    path = "model/reinforcement/seq2seq"
    word_to_index, index_to_word, _ =
data_parser.preProBuildWordVocab(word_count_threshold=word_count_threshold)
    word_vector =
KeyedVectors.load_word2vec_format('model/word_vector.bin', binary=True)
    generic_caption, generic_mask = h.generic_batch(generic_responses,
batch_size, word_to_index,
                                                output_sequence_length)

    dr = Data_Reader()
    forward_graph = tf.Graph()
    reverse_graph = tf.Graph()
    default_graph = tf.get_default_graph()
```

Two graphs are created to load the trained models.

```
    with forward_graph.as_default():
        pg_model = Chatbot(dim_wordvec, len(word_to_index), dim_hidden.
batch_size,
                                input_sequence_length, output_sequence_length,
learning_rate, policy_gradients=True)
        optimizer, place_holders, predictions, logits, losses =
pg_model.build_model()

        sess = tf.InteractiveSession()
        saver = tf.train.Saver()
        if checkpoint:
            saver.restore(sess, path)
            print("checkpoint restored at path: {}".format(path))
        else:
            tf.global_variables_initializer().run()
            saver.restore(sess, 'model/forward/seq2seq')
    # tf.global_variables_initializer().run()
    with reverse_graph.as_default():
        model = Chatbot(dim_wordvec, len(word_to_index), dim_hidden,
batch_size,
                            input_sequence_length, output_sequence_length,
```

```
learning_rate)
        _, rev_place_holders, _, _, reverse_loss = model.build_model()
        sess2 = tf.InteractiveSession()
        saver2 = tf.train.Saver()

        saver2.restore(sess2, "model/reverse/seq2seq")
        print("reverse model restored")

    dr = Data_Reader(load_list=True)
```

Next, the data is loaded to train the data in batches.

```
    for epoch in range(epochs):
        n_batch = dr.get_batch_num(batch_size=batch_size)
        for batch in range(n_batch):

            batch_input, batch_caption, prev_utterance =
dr.generate_training_batch_with_former(batch_size)
            targets, masks = h.make_batch_target(batch_caption,
word_to_index, output_sequence_length)
            inputs_ = h.make_batch_input(batch_input,
input_sequence_length, dim_wordvec, word_vector)

            word_indices, probabilities = sess.run([predictions, logits],
feed_dict={place_holders['word_vectors']: inputs_

                                                                      ,
place_holders["caption"]: targets})

            sentence = [h.index2sentence(generated_word, probability,
index_to_word) for
                            generated_word, probability in zip(word_indices,
probabilities)]

            word_list = [word.split() for word in sentence]

            generic_test_input = h.make_batch_input(word_list,
input_sequence_length, dim_wordvec, word_vector)

            forward_coherence_target, forward_coherence_masks =
h.make_batch_target(sentence,
word_to_index,
output_sequence_length)

            generic_loss = 0.0
```

Also, learn when to say generic texts as shown here:

```
for response in generic_test_input:
    sentence_input = np.array([response] * batch_size)
    feed_dict = {place_holders['word_vectors']: sentence_input,
                 place_holders['caption']: generic_caption,
                 place_holders['caption_mask']: generic_mask,
                 }
    generic_loss_i = sess.run(losses["entropy"],
feed_dict=feed_dict)
    generic_loss -= generic_loss_i / batch_size

# print("generic loss work: {}".format(generic_loss))

    feed_dict = {place_holders['word_vectors']: inputs_,
                 place_holders['caption']:
forward_coherence_target,
                 place_holders['caption_mask']:
forward_coherence_masks,
                 }

    forward_entropy = sess.run(losses["entropy"],
feed_dict=feed_dict)

    previous_utterance, previous_mask =
h.make_batch_target(prev_utterance,
word_to_index, output_sequence_length)

    feed_dict = {rev_place_holders['word_vectors']:
generic_test_input,
                 rev_place_holders['caption']: previous_utterance,
                 rev_place_holders['caption_mask']: previous_mask,
                 }
    reverse_entropy = sess2.run(reverse_loss["entropy"],
feed_dict=feed_dict)

    rewards = 1 / (1 + np.exp(-reverse_entropy - forward_entropy -
generic_loss))

    feed_dict = {place_holders['word_vectors']: inputs_,
                 place_holders['caption']: targets,
                 place_holders['caption_mask']: masks,
                 place_holders['rewards']: rewards
                 }

    _, loss_pg, loss_ent = sess.run([optimizer, losses["pg"],
losses["entropy"]], feed_dict=feed_dict)
```

```
                    if batch % display_interval == 0:
                         print("Epoch: {}, batch: {}, Entropy loss: {}, Policy
gradient loss: {}".format(epoch, batch, loss_ent,
loss_pg))

                    print("rewards: {}".format(rewards))
print("===========================================================")
        saver.save(sess, path)
        print("Model saved at {}".format(path))
    print("Training done")
```

Next, call the functions defined in sequence. First train a forward model, followed by reverse model and policy gradient at the end.

```
train(forward_, forward_epochs, False)
train(reverse_, reverse_epochs, False)
pg_train(100, False)
```

This concludes the training of the chatbot. The model is trained in forward and reverse manner to

Testing and results

After training the model, we tested it against our test dataset and obtained reasonably coherent dialogue. There is one very important issue: the context of the communication. Hence, depending on the dataset that is used, the result will be in its context. For our context, the results that were obtained were very reasonable, and they satisfied our three measures of performance—informativeness (non-repeating turns), high coherence, and simplicity in answering (this is related to the forward-looking function).

```
import data_parser
from gensim.models import KeyedVectors
from seq_model import Chatbot
import tensorflow as tf
import numpy as np
import helper as h
```

Next, declare the paths to the various model that are already trained.

```
reinforcement_model_path = "model/reinforcement/seq2seq"
forward_model_path = "model/forward/seq2seq"
reverse_model_path = "model/reverse/seq2seq"
```

Next, declare the path of the files consisting of questions and responses.

```
path_to_questions = 'results/sample_input.txt'
responses_path = 'results/sample_output_RL.txt'
```

Next, declare the constants required for the model.

```
word_count_threshold = 20
dim_wordvec = 300
dim_hidden = 1000

input_sequence_length = 25
target_sequence_length = 22

batch_size = 2
```

Next, load the data and the model as shown here:

```
def test(model_path=forward_model_path):
    testing_data = open(path_to_questions, 'r').read().split('\n')
    word_vector =
KeyedVectors.load_word2vec_format('model/word_vector.bin', binary=True)

    _, index_to_word, _ =
data_parser.preProBuildWordVocab(word_count_threshold=word_count_threshold)

    model = Chatbot(dim_wordvec, len(index_to_word), dim_hidden,
batch_size,
                                input_sequence_length, target_sequence_length,
Training=False)

    place_holders, predictions, logits = model.build_model()

    sess = tf.InteractiveSession()

    saver = tf.train.Saver()

    saver.restore(sess, model_path)
```

Next, open the responses file and prepare the list of questions as shown here:

```
    with open(responses_path, 'w') as out:

        for idx, question in enumerate(testing_data):
            print('question =>', question)

            question = [h.refine(w) for w in question.lower().split()]
            question = [word_vector[w] if w in word_vector else
np.zeros(dim_wordvec) for w in question]
```

```
                 question.insert(0, np.random.normal(size=(dim_wordvec,)))   #
insert random normal at the first step

             if len(question) > input_sequence_length:
                 question = question[:input_sequence_length]
             else:
                 for _ in range(input_sequence_length - len(question)):
                     question.append(np.zeros(dim_wordvec))

             question = np.array([question])

             feed_dict = {place_holders["word_vectors"]:
np.concatenate([question] * 2, 0),
                             }

             word_indices, prob_logit = sess.run([predictions, logits],
feed_dict=feed_dict)

             # print(word_indices[0].shape)
             generated_sentence = h.index2sentence(word_indices[0],
prob_logit[0], index_to_word)

             print('generated_sentence =>', generated_sentence)
             out.write(generated_sentence + '\n')


     test(reinforcement_model_path)
```

By passing the path to the model, we can test the chatbot for various responses.

Summary

Chatbots are taking the world by storm, and are predicted to become more prevalent in the coming years. The coherence of the results obtained from dialogues with these chatbots has to constantly improve if they are to gain widespread acceptance. One way to achieve this would be via the use of reinforcement learning.

In this chapter, we implemented reinforcement learning in the creation of a chatbot. The learning was based on a policy gradient method that focused on the future direction of a dialogue agent, in order to generate coherent and interesting interactions. The datasets that we used were from movie conversations. We proceeded to clean and preprocess the datasets, obtaining the vocabulary from them. We then formulated our policy gradient method. Our reward functions were represented by a sequence to sequence model. We then trained and tested our data and obtained very reasonable results, proving the viability of using reinforcement learning for dialogue agents.

8
Generating a Deep Learning Image Classifier

Over the past decade, deep learning has made a name for itself by producing state-of-the-heart results across computer vision, natural language processing, speech recognition, and many more such applications. Some of the models that human researchers have designed and engineered have also gained popularity, including AlexNet, Inception, VGGNet, ResNet, and DenseNet; some of them are now the go-to standard for their respective tasks. However, it seems that the better the model gets, the more complex the architecture becomes, especially with the introduction of residual connections between convolutional layers. The task of designing a high-performance neural network has thus become a very arduous one. Hence the question arises: is it possible for an algorithm to learn how to generate neural network architectures?

As the title of this chapter suggests, it is indeed possible to train a neural network to generate neural networks that perform well on a given task. In this chapter, we will examine **Neural Architecture Search** (referred to as **NAS** henceforth), a novel framework developed by Barret Zoph and Quoc V. Le from the Google Brain team that uses deep reinforcement learning to train a Controller to produce child networks that learn to accomplish tasks. We will learn how policy gradient methods (REINFORCE in particular) can train such a Controller. We will then implement a Controller that uses NAS to generate child networks that train on `CIFAR-10` data.

In this chapter, we will cover the following:

- Understanding NAS and how it learns to generate other neural networks
- Implementing a simple NAS framework that generates neural networks for training on `CIFAR-10` data

You can find the original sources of the ensuing topics from the following sources:

1. Zoph, B., and Le, Q. V. (2016). *Neural Architecture Search with reinforcement learning*. arXiv preprint arXiv:1611.01578.
2. Pham, H., Guan, M. Y., Zoph, B., Le, Q. V., and Dean, J. (2018). *Efficient Neural Architecture Search via Parameter Sharing*. arXiv preprint arXiv:1802.03268.

Neural Architecture Search

The next few sections will describe the NAS framework. You will learn about how the framework learns to generate other neural networks to complete tasks using a popular reinforcement learning scheme called **REINFORCE**, which is a type of policy gradient algorithm.

Generating and training child networks

Research on algorithms that generate neural architectures has been around since the 1970's. What sets NAS apart from previous works is its ability to cater to large-scale deep learning algorithms and its formulation of the task as a reinforcement learning problem. More specifically, the agent, which we will refer to as the Controller, is a recurrent neural network that generates a sequence of values. You can think of these values as a sort of genetic code of the child network that defines its architecture; it sets the sizes of each convolutional kernel, the length of each kernel, the number of filters in each layer, and so on. In more advanced frameworks, the values also determine the connections between layers to generate residual layers:

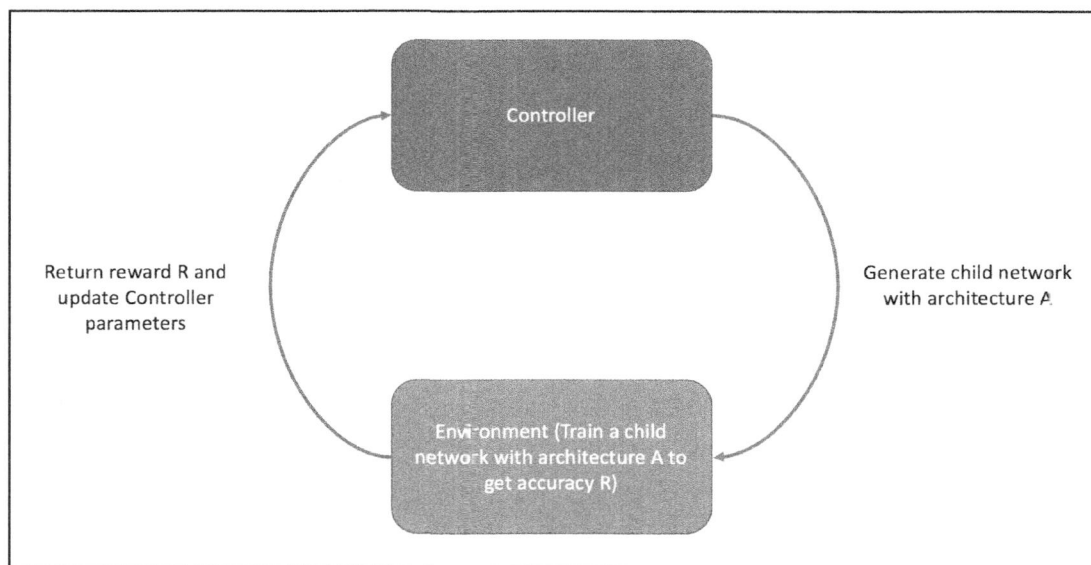

Figure 1: Overview of the NAS framework

Moreover, each value of the genetic code that the Controller outputs counts as an action, a, that is sampled with probability, p. Because the Controller is a recurrent neural network, we can represent the tth action as $p(a_t|a_{t-1})$. Once we have a list of $A = a_1, a_2, \ldots, a_T$ actions, —where T is some predefined parameter that sets the maximum size of the genetic code—we can generate the child network with the specified architecture, A:

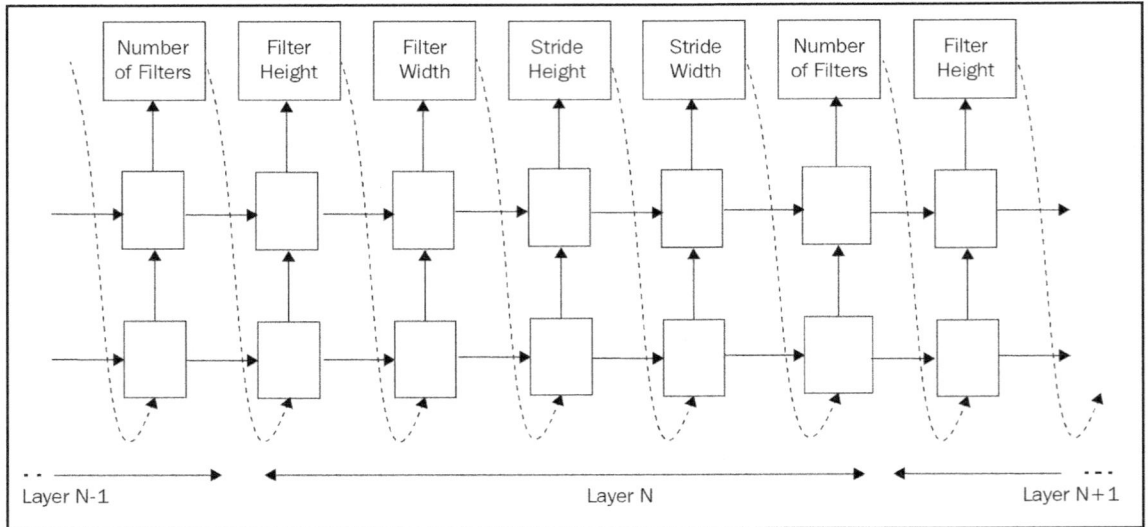

Figure 2: The architecture of the Controller

Once the Controller generates a child network, we train it on a given task until either some termination criteria is met (for example, after a specified number of epochs). We then evaluate the child network on the validation set to produce some validation accuracy, R. The validation accuracy acts as the reward signal for the Controller. So, the objective of the Controller is to maximize the expected reward:

$$J(\theta_c) = E_A[R]$$

Here, J is the reward function (also referred to as the fit function), θ_c is the parameters of the Controller, and the right-hand side of the equation is the expectation of the reward given a child network architecture, A. In practice, this expectation is calculated by averaging the rewards over m child network models that the Controller produces in one batch:

$$\bar{J}(\theta_c) = \frac{1}{m} \sum_{k=1}^{m} R_k$$

Training the Controller

How do we use this reward signal to update the Controller? Remember, this reward signal is not differentiable like a loss function in supervised learning; we may not backpropagate this through the Controller on its own. Instead, we employ a policy gradient method called **REINFORCE** to iteratively update the Controller parameters, θ_c. In REINFORCE, the gradient of the reward function, J, with respect to the parameters of the Controller, θ_c, is defined as follows:

$$\nabla_{\theta_c} J(\theta_c) = \frac{1}{m} \sum_{k=1}^{m} \sum_{t=1}^{T} \nabla_{\theta_c} \log P(a_t | a_{(t-1):1} ; \theta_c) R_k$$

You may recall seeing a similar expression in Chapter 6, *Learning to Play Go*. Indeed, this is the policy gradient method that AlphaGo and AlphaGo Zero use to update the weights of their reinforcement learning policy networks. We briefly introduced the method then, but we will go a bit more in-depth here.

Let's break the preceding equation down. On the right-hand side, we would like to represent the probability of choosing some architecture, A. In particular, $P(a_t | a_{(t-1):1} ; \theta_c)$ represents the probability that the Controller takes action a_t given all the previous actions, $a_{(t-1):1}$, and the parameters of the Controller, θ_c. Again, action a_t corresponds to the tth value in the genetic sequence that represents the child network's architecture. The joint probability of choosing all actions, $a_1, a_2, \ldots, a_T$, can be formulated as follows:

$$P(A) = P(a_1 ; \theta_c) \prod_{t=2}^{T} P(a_t | a_{(t-1):1} ; \theta_c)$$

By transforming this joint probability to the log space, we can turn the product into a sum of probabilities:

$$\log P(A) = \sum_{t=1}^{T} \log P(a_t | a_{(t-1):1}; \theta_c)$$

In general, we want to maximize this log conditional probability for taking some action. In other words, we want to increase the likelihood of the Controller generating a particular sequence of genetic codes. Hence we perform gradient ascent on this objective with respect to the Controller's parameters by taking the derivative of the log probability of sampling architecture A:

$$\nabla_{\theta_c} \log P(A) = \sum_{t=1}^{T} \nabla_{\theta_c} \log P(a_t | a_{(t-1):1}; \theta_c)$$

But how do we update the Controller parameters so that better architectures are generated? This is where we make use of the reward signal, R. By multiplying the preceding with the reward signal, we can control the size of the policy gradient. In other words, if a particular architecture achieved high validation accuracy (with the highest possible being 1.0), the gradients for that policy will be relatively strong and the Controller will learn to produce similar architectures. On the other hand, smaller validation accuracies will mean smaller gradients, which helps the Controller ignore those architectures.

One problem with the REINFORCE algorithm is that the reward signal R can have high variance, which can lead to unstable training curves. To reduce the variance, it is common to subtract the reward with some value, b, which we refer to as the baseline function. In Zoph et al., the baseline function is defined as the exponential moving average of the past rewards. Hence our REINFORCE policy gradient is now defined as follows:

$$\nabla_{\theta_c} J(\theta_c) = \frac{1}{m} \sum_{k=1}^{m} \sum_{t=1}^{T} \nabla_{\theta_c} \log P(a_t | a_{(t-1):1}; \theta_c)(R_k - b)$$

Once we have this gradient, we apply the usual backpropagation algorithm to update the Controller parameters, θ_c.

Training algorithm

The training steps for the Controller is as follows:

- For each episode, do the following:
    1. Generate m child network architectures
    2. Train child networks on given task and obtain m validation accuracies
    3. Calculate $\nabla_{\theta_c} J(\theta_c)$
    4. Update θ_c

In Zoph et al., the training procedure is done with several copies of the Controller. Each Controller is parameterized by θ_c, which itself is stored in a distributed manner among multiple servers, which we call parameter servers.

In each episode of training, the Controller creates several child architectures and trains them independently. The policy gradient calculated as a result is then sent to the parameter servers to update the Controller's parameters:

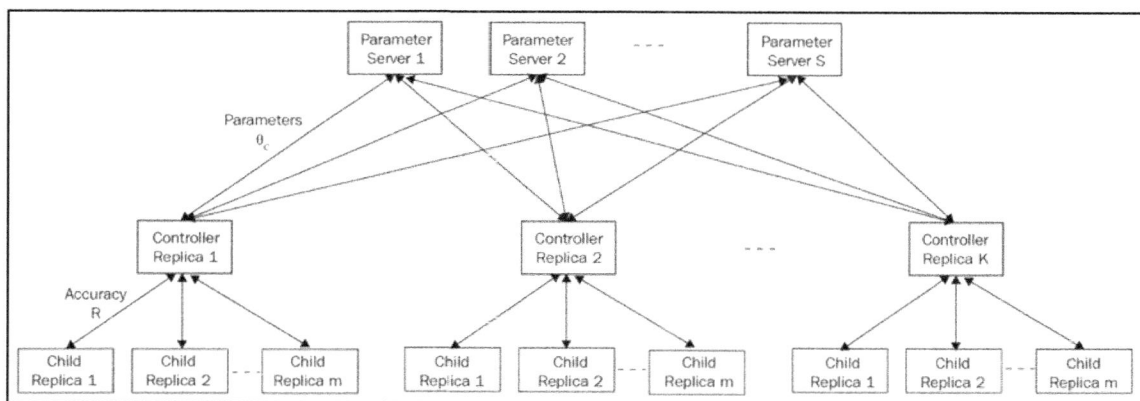

Figure 3: The training architecture

The Controller's parameters are shared among a number of parameter servers. Moreover, multiple copies of the Controller are trained in parallel, each one calculating rewards and gradients for its respective batches of child network architectures.

This architecture allows the Controller to be trained quickly given enough resources. For our purposes, however, we will stick to one Controller that generates m child network architectures. Once we have trained the Controller for a specified number of episodes, we calculate the test accuracy by choosing the child network architecture that had the best validation accuracy and measuring its performance on the test set.

Implementing NAS

In this section, we will implement NAS. In particular, our Controller is tasked with generating child network architectures that learn to classify images from the CIFAR-10 dataset. The architecture of the child network will be represented by a list of numbers. Every four values in this list represent a convolutional layer in the child network, each describing the kernel size, stride length, number of filters, and the pooling window size in the subsequent pooling layer. Moreover, we specify the number of layers in a child network as a hyper-parameters. For example, if our child network has three layers, its architecture is represented as a vector of length 12. If we have an architecture represented as [3, 1, 12, 2, 5, 1, 24, 2], then the child network is a two-layer network where the first layer has kernel size of 3, stride length of 1, 12 filters, and a max-pooling window size of 2, and the second layer has kernel size of 5, stride length of 1, 24 filters, and max-pooling window size of 2. We set the activation function between each layer as ReLU. The final layer involves flattening the last convolutional layer output and applying a linear layer with the number of classes as its width, followed by a Softmax activation. The following sections will walk you through the implementation.

child_network.py

We will first implement our child network module. This module contains a class called ChildCNN, which constructs a child network given some architecture configuration, which we call cnn_dna. As mentioned previously, cnn_dna is simply a list of numbers, with each value representing a parameter of its respective convolutional layer. In our config.py, we specify the max number of layers a child network can have. For our implementation, each convolutional layer is represented by four parameters, where each corresponds to the kernel size, stride length, number of filters, and subsequent max-pooling window size.

Our ChildCNN is a class that takes the following parameters in its constructor:

- cnn_dna: The network architecture
- child_id: A string that simply identifies the child network architecture
- beta: Weight parameter for L2 regularization
- drop_rate: Dropout rate

```
import logging

import tensorflow as tf
```

```
logger = logging.getLogger(__name__)

class ChildCNN(object):

    def __init__(self, cnn_dna. child_id, beta=1e-4, drop_rate=0.2,
**kwargs):
        self.cnn_dna = self.process_raw_controller_output(cnn_dna)
        self.child_id = child_id
        self.beta = beta
        self.drop_rate = drop_rate
        self.is_training = tf.placeholder_with_default(True, shape=None,
name="is_training_{}".format(self.child_id))
        self.num_classes = 10
```

We also implement a helper function called `proces_raw_controller_output()`, which
parses `cnn_dna` that the Controller outputs:

```
def process_raw_controller_output(self, output):
    """
    A helper function for preprocessing the output of the NASCell
    Args:
        output (numpy.ndarray) The output of the NASCell

    Returns:
        (list) The child network's architecture
    """
    output = output.ravel()
    cnn_dna = [list(output[x:x-4]) for x in range(0, len(output), 4)]
    return cnn_dna
```

Finally, we include the `build` method, which builds our child network using the
given `cnn_dna`. You will notice that, although we are letting the Controller decide the
architecture of our child network, we are still hardcoding several things, such as the
activation function, `tf.nn.relu`, and the way we initialize the kernels. The fact that we are
adding a max-pooling layer after each convolutional layer is also hardcoded. A more
sophisticated NAS framework would also let the Controller decide these components of the
architecture as well, with the trade off being longer training time:

```
def build(self, input_tensor):
    """
    Method for creating the child neural network
    Args:
        input_tensor: The tensor which represents the input

    Returns:
        The tensor which represents the output logit (pre-softmax
activation)
```

```
    """
    logger.info("DNA is: {}".format(self.cnn_dna))
    output = input_tensor
    for idx in range(len(self.cnn_dna)):
        # Get the configuration for the layer
        kernel_size, stride, num_filters, max_pool_size = self.cnn_dna[idx]
        with tf.name_scope("child_{}_conv_layer_{}".format(self.child_id,
idx)):
            output = tf.layers.conv2d(output,
                    # Specify the number of filters the convolutional layer
will output
                    filters=num_filters,
                    # This specifies the size (height, width) of the
convolutional kernel
                    kernel_size=(kernel_size, kernel_size),
                    # The size of the stride of the kernel
                    strides=(stride, stride),
                    # We add padding to the image
                    padding="SAME",
                    # It is good practice to name your layers
                    name="conv_layer_{}".format(idx),
                    activation=tf.nn.relu,
        kernel_initializer=tf.contrib.layers.xavier_initializer(),
                    bias_initializer=tf.zeros_initializer(),
        kernel_regularizer=tf.contrib.layers.l2_regularizer(scale=self.beta))
```

Each convolutional layer is followed by a max-pooling layer and a dropout layer:

```
                # We apply 2D max pooling on the output of the conv layer
                output = tf.layers.max_pooling2d(
                    output, pool_size=(max_pool_size, max_pool_size),
        strides=1,
                    padding="SAME", name="pool_out_{}".format(idx)
                )
                # Dropout to regularize the network further
                output = tf.layers.dropout(output, rate=self.drop_rate,
        training=self.is_training)
```

Finally, after several blocks of convolutional, pooling, and dropout layers, we flatten the output volume and a fully connected layer:

```
        # Lastly, we flatten the outputs and add a fully-connected layer
        with tf.name_scope("child_{}_fully_connected".format(self.child_id)):
            output = tf.layers.flatten(output, name="flatten")
            logits = tf.layers.dense(output, self.num_classes)

        return logits
```

The argument to our `build` method is an input tensor, which has by default a shape cf (32, 32, 3), which is the `CIFAR-10` data shape. The reader is free to tweak the architecture of this network, including adding a few more fully connected layers or inserting batch normalization layers in between convolutions.

cifar10_processor.py

This module contains code for processing `CIFAR-10` data, which we use to train our child networks. In particular, we construct an input data pipeline using TensorFlow's native `tf.data.Dataset` API. Those who have used TensorFlow for some time may be more familiar with creating `tf.placeholder` tensors and feeding data via `sess.run(..., feed_dict={...})`. However, this is no longer the preferred way of feeding data into the network; in fact, it is the slowest way to train a network, for the repetitive conversions from data in `numpy` format to a native TensorFlow format cause significant computational overhead. `tf.data.Dataset` alleviates this problem by turning the input pipeline into TensorFlow operations that are part of the symbolic graph. In other words, the data is converted into tensors right from the get-go. This allows for a much smoother input pipeline that can speed up training.

Refer to this official tutorial (https://www.tensorflow.org/guide/datasets_for_estimators) for more information on the `tf.data.Dataset` API.

The `cifar10_processor.py` contains a single method to create `CIFAR-10` data into tensors. We first implement a helper function for creating a `tf.data.Dataset` object:

```
import logging

import numpy as np
import tensorflow as tf
from keras.datasets import cifar10
from keras.utils import np_utils

logger = logging.getLogger(__name__)

def _create_tf_dataset(x, y, batch_size):
    return tf.data.Dataset.zip((tf.data.Dataset.from_tensor_slices(x),
tf.data.Dataset.from_tensor_slices(y))).shuffle(500).repeat().batch(batch_s
ize)
```

In the main data processor function, we first load `CIFAR-10` data. We use the `keras.datasets` API to do this (run `pip install keras` in your Terminal if you don't have Keras):

```
def get_tf_datasets_from_numpy(batch_size, validation_split=0.1):
    """
    Main function getting tf.Data.datasets for training, validation, and
testing

    Args:
        batch_size (int): Batch size
        validation_split (float): Split for partitioning training and
validation sets. Between 0.0 and 1.0.
    """
    # Load data from keras datasets api
    (X, y), (X_test, y_test) = cifar10.load_data()

    logger.info("Dividing pixels by 255")
    X = X / 255.
    X_test = X_test / 255.

    X = X.astype(np.float32)
    X_test = X_test.astype(np.float32)
    y = y.astype(np.float32)
    y_test = y_test.astype(np.float32)

    # Turn labels into onehot encodings
    if y.shape[1] != 10:
        y = np_utils.to_categorical(y, num_classes=10)
        y_test = np_utils.to_categorical(y_test, num_classes=10)

    logger.info("Loaded data from keras")

    split_idx = int((1.0 - validation_split) * len(X))
    X_train, y_train = X[:split_idx], y[:split_idx]
    X_valid, y_valid = X[split_idx:], y[split_idx:]
```

We then turn these NumPy arrays into TensorFlow tensors, which we can feed directly to our network. What actually happens in our `_create_tf_dataset` helper function? We use the `tf.dataset.Dataset.from_tensor_slices()` function to turn the data and the labels, both of which are NumPy arrays, into TensorFlow tensors. We then create the native dataset by zipping these tensors. The `shuffle`, `repeat`, and `batch` functions after zipping the data and labels define how we want the input pipeline to work. In our case, we are shuffling the input data, repeating the dataset once we reach the end, and batching the data with a given batch size. We also calculate the number of batches that each dataset has and return them:

```
train_dataset = _create_tf_dataset(X_train, y_train, batch_size)
valid_dataset = _create_tf_dataset(X_valid, y_valid, batch_size)
test_dataset = _create_tf_dataset(X_test, y_test, batch_size)

# Get the batch sizes for the train, valid, and test datasets
num_train_batches = int(X_train.shape[0] // batch_size)
num_valid_batches = int(X_valid.shape[0] // batch_size)
num_test_batches = int(X_test.shape[0] // batch_size)

return train_dataset, valid_dataset, test_dataset, num_train_batches,
num_valid_batches, num_test_batches
```

And with that, we have an optimized input data pipeline that is much faster than using `feed_dict`.

controller.py

The `controller.py` module is where everything comes together. We will implement the Controller, which handles training each child network as well as its own parameter updates. We first implement a helper function that calculates an exponential moving average of a list of numbers. We use this as the baseline function for our REINFORCE gradient calculation, as mentioned previously, to calculate the exponential moving average of the past rewards:

```
import logging

import numpy as np
import tensorflow as tf

from child_network import ChildCNN
from cifar10_processor import get_tf_datasets_from_numpy
from config import child_network_params, controller_params

logger = logging.getLogger(__name__)
```

```
def ema(values):
    """
    Helper function for keeping track of an exponential moving average of a
list of values.
    For this module, we use it to maintain an exponential moving average of
rewards
    Args:
        values (list): A list of rewards

    Returns:
        (float) The last value of the exponential moving average
    """
    weights = np.exp(np.linspace(-1., 0., len(values)))
    weights /= weights.sum()
    a = np.convolve(values, weights, mode="full")[:len(values)]
    return a[-1]
```

Next, we define our `Controller` class:

```
class Controller(object):

    def __init__(self):
        self.graph = tf.Graph()
        self.sess = tf.Session(graph=self.graph)
        self.num_cell_outputs = controller_params['components_per_layer'] *
controller_params['max_layers']
        self.reward_history = []
        self.architecture_history = []
        self.divison_rate = 100
        with self.graph.as_default():
            self.build_controller()
```

There are several attributes to note: `self.num_cell_outputs` refers to the number of values that our **recurrent neural network (RNN)** should output and corresponds to the length of the child network architecture configuration. `self.reward_history` and `self.ar chitecture_history` are simply buffers that allow us to keep track of rewards and child network architectures that the RNN generated.

Method for generating the Controller

We next implement a method for generating the Controller, which we
call `build_controller`. The first step in constructing our Controller is defining the input
placeholders. We create two of these—one is for the child network DNA, which is fed as
input to the RNN for generating a new child network DNA, and the second is a list for
storing discounted rewards when calculating the gradients for REINFORCE:

```
def build_controller(self):
    logger.info('Building controller network')
    # Build inputs and placeholders
    with tf.name_scope('controller_inputs'):
        # Input to the NASCell
        self.child_network_architectures = tf.placeholder(tf.float32,
[None, self.num_cell_outputs],
name='controller_input')
        # Discounted rewards
        self.discounted_rewards = tf.placeholder(tf.float32, (None, ),
name='discounted_rewards')
```

We then define the output tensors of our RNN (to be implemented here). Note that the
outputs of the RNN are small, in the range of (-1, 1). So, we multiply the output by 10 in
order to create the child network DNA:

```
# Build controller
with tf.name_scope('network_generation'):
    with tf.variable_scope('controller'):
        self.controller_output =
tf.identity(self.network_generator(self.child_network_architectures),
                                          name='policy_scores')
        self.cnn_dna_output = tf.cast(tf.scalar_mul(self.divison_rate,
self.controller_output), tf.int32,
                                          name='controller_prediction')
```

We then define the loss function and optimizer. We use `RMSPropOptimizer` as our
backpropagation algorithm, where the learning rate decays exponentially. Rather than
calling `optimizer.minimize(loss)` as is usually done with other neural network
models, we call the `compute_gradients` method to obtain gradients for calculating
REINFORCE gradients:

```
# Set up optimizer
self.global_step = tf.Variable(0, trainable=False)
self.learning_rate = tf.train.exponential_decay(0.99, self.global_step,
500, 0.96, staircase=True)
self.optimizer =
tf.train.RMSPropOptimizer(learning_rate=self.learning_rate)
```

```
# Gradient and loss computation
with tf.name_scope('gradient_and_loss'):
    # Define policy gradient loss for the controller
    self.policy_gradient_loss =
tf.reduce_mean(tf.nn.softmax_cross_entropy_with_logits(
        logits=self.controller_output[:, -1, :],
        labels=self.child_network_architectures))
    # L2 weight decay for Controller weights
    self.l2_loss = tf.reduce_sum(tf.add_n([tf.nn.l2_loss(v) for v in
tf.trainable_variables(scope="controller")]))
    # Add the above two losses to define total loss
    self.total_loss = self.policy_gradient_loss + self.l2_loss *
controller_params["beta"]
    # Compute the gradients
    self.gradients = self.optimizer.compute_gradients(self.total_loss)

    # Gradients calculated using REINFORCE
    for i, (grad, var) in enumerate(self.gradients):
        if grad is not None:
            self.gradients[i] = (grad * self.discounted_rewards, var)
```

Finally, we apply the REINFORCE gradients on the Controller parameters:

```
with tf.name_scope('train_controller'):
    # The main training operation. This applies REINFORCE on the weights of
the Controller
    self.train_op = self.optimizer.apply_gradients(self.gradients,
global_step=self.global_step)

logger.info('Successfully built controller')
```

The actual Controller network is created via the network_generator function. As mentioned, the Controller is a recurrent neural network with a special kind of cell. However, we don't have to implement this from scratch, as the developers behind TensorFlow have already implemented a custom tf.contrib.rnn.NASCell. We simply need to use this to construct our recurrent neural network and obtain the outputs:

```
def network_generator(self, nas_cell_hidden_state):
    # number of output units we expect from a NAS cell
    with tf.name_scope('network_generator'):
        nas = tf.contrib.rnn.NASCell(self.num_cell_outputs)
        network_architecture, nas_cell_hidden_state =
tf.nn.dynamic_rnn(nas, tf.expand_dims(
            nas_cell_hidden_state, -1), dtype=tf.float32)
        bias_variable = tf.Variable([0.01] * self.num_cell_outputs)
        network_architecture = tf.nn.bias_add(network_architecture,
bias_variable)
        return network_architecture[:, -1:, :]
```

Generating a child network using the Controller

Now, we implement a method that generates a child network using the Controller:

```
def generate_child_network(self, child_network_architecture):
    with self.graph.as_default():
        return self.sess.run(self.cnn_dna_output,
{self.child_network_architectures: child_network_architecture})
```

Once we generate our child network, we call the `train_child_network` function to train it. This function takes `child_dna` and `child_id` and returns the validation accuracy that the child network achieves. First, we instantiate a new `tf.Graph()` and a new `tf.Session()` so that the child network is separated from the Controller's graph:

```
def train_child_network(self, cnn_dna, child_id):
    """
    Trains a child network and returns reward, or the validation accuracy
    Args:
        cnn_dna (list): List of tuples representing the child network's DNA
        child_id (str): Name of child network

    Returns:
        (float) validation accuracy
    """
    logger.info("Training with dna: {}".format(cnn_dna))
    child_graph = tf.Graph()
    with child_graph.as_default():
        sess = tf.Session()

        child_network = ChildCNN(cnn_dna=cnn_dna, child_id=child_id,
**child_network_params)
```

We then define the input data pipeline, which uses the `tf.data.Dataset` creator we implemented here. In particular, we use `tf.data.Iterator` to create a generator that yields a batch of input tensors every time we call `iterator.get_next()`. We initialize an iterator for the training and validation datasets respectively. The batch of input tensors contains the `CIFAR-10` images and the corresponding labels, which we unpack at the end:

```
# Create input pipeline
train_dataset, valid_dataset, test_dataset, num_train_batches,
num_valid_batches, num_test_batches = \
get_tf_datasets_from_numpy(batch_size=child_network_params["batch_size'])

# Generic iterator
iterator = tf.data.Iterator.from_structure(train_dataset.output_types,
train_dataset.output_shapes)
next_tensor_batch = iterator.get_next()
```

```
# Separate train and validation set init ops
train_init_ops = iterator.make_initializer(train_dataset)
valid_init_ops = iterator.make_initializer(valid_dataset)

# Build the graph
input_tensor, labels = next_tensor_batch
```

The `input_tensor` becomes the argument to the child network's `build` method. We then define all the TensorFlow operations needed for training, including the prediction, loss, optimizer, and accuracy operations:

```
# Build the child network, which returns the pre-softmax logits of the
child network
logits = child_network.build(input_tensor)

# Define the loss function for the child network
loss_ops = tf.nn.softmax_cross_entropy_with_logits_v2(labels=labels,
logits=logits, name="loss")

# Define the training operation for the child network
train_ops =
tf.train.AdamOptimizer(learning_rate=child_network_params["learning_rate"])
.minimize(loss_ops)

# The following operations are for calculating the accuracy of the child
network
pred_ops = tf.nn.softmax(logits, name="preds")
correct = tf.equal(tf.argmax(pred_ops, 1), tf.argmax(labels, 1),
name="correct")
accuracy_ops = tf.reduce_mean(tf.cast(correct, tf.float32),
name="accuracy")

initializer = tf.global_variables_initializer()
```

We then train the child network. Notice that when calling `sess.run(...)`, we are no longer passing an argument for the `feed_dict` parameter. Instead, we are simply calling the operations we want to run (`loss_ops`, `train_ops`, and `accuracy_ops`). This is because the inputs are already represented as tensors in the child network's graph:

```
# Training
sess.run(initializer)
sess.run(train_init_ops)

logger.info("Training child CNN {} for {} epochs".format(child_id,
child_network_params["max_epochs"]))
for epoch_idx in range(child_network_params["max_epochs"]):
    avg_loss, avg_acc = [], []
```

```
for batch_idx in range(num_train_batches):
    loss, _, accuracy = sess.run([loss_ops, train_ops, accuracy_ops])
    avg_loss.append(loss)
    avg_acc.append(accuracy)

logger.info("\tEpoch {}:\tloss - {:.6f}\taccuracy -
{:.3f}".format(epoch_idx,
np.mean(avg_loss), np.mean(avg_acc)))
```

Once training finishes, we calculate the validation accuracy and return it:

```
# Validate and return reward
logger.info("Finished training, now calculating validation accuracy")
sess.run(valid_init_ops)
avg_val_loss, avg_val_acc = [], []
for batch_idx in range(num_valid_batches):
    valid_loss, valid_accuracy = sess.run([loss_ops, accuracy_ops])
    avg_val_loss.append(valid_loss)
    avg_val_acc.append(valid_accuracy)
logger.info("Valid loss - {:.6f}\tValid accuracy -
{:.3f}".format(np.mean(avg_val_loss),
np.mean(avg_val_acc)))

return np.mean(avg_val_acc)
```

Finally, we implement a method for training the Controller. Due to computational resource constraints, we will not parallelize the training procedure (that is, *m* child networks trained in parallel per Controller epoch). Instead, we will sequentially generate these child networks and keep track of the mean validation accuracy among them.

train_controller method

The `train_controller` method is called after we build the Controller. The first step is thus to initialize all the variables and the first state:

```
def train_controller(self):
    with self.graph.as_default():
        self.sess.run(tf.global_variables_initializer())

    step = 0
    total_rewards = 0
    child_network_architecture = np.array([[10.0, 128.0, 1.0, 1.0] *
controller_params['max_layers']], dtype=np.float32)
```

The first `child_network_architecture` is a list that resembles an architecture configuration and will be the argument to `NASCell`, which would output the first child DNA.

The training procedure consists of two `for` loops: one for the number of epochs for the Controller, and another for each child network the Controller generates per epoch. In the inner `for` loop, we generate a new `child_network_architecture` using `NASCell` and train a child network based on it to obtain a validation accuracy:

```
for episode in range(controller_params['max_episodes']):
    logger.info('==============> Episode {} for Controller'.format(episode))
    step += 1
    episode_reward_buffer = []

    for sub_child in range(controller_params["num_children_per_episode"]):
        # Generate a child network architecture
        child_network_architecture =
self.generate_child_network(child_network_architecture)[0]

        if np.any(np.less_equal(child_network_architecture, 0.0)):
            reward = -1.0
        else:
            reward =
self.train_child_network(cnn_dna=child_network_architecture,
child_id='child/{}'.format("{}_{}".format(episode, sub_child)))
        episode_reward_buffer.append(reward)
```

After we obtain *m* validation accuracies, we update our Controller using the mean reward and the gradients computed with respect to the last child network's DNA. We also keep track of past mean rewards. Using the `ema` method implemented previously, we calculate the baseline, which we then subtract from the latest mean reward. We then call `self.sess.run([self.train_op, self.total_loss]...)` to update the Controller and calculate the Controller's loss:

```
mean_reward = np.mean(episode_reward_buffer)

self.reward_history.append(mean_reward)
self.architecture_history.append(child_network_architecture)
total_rewards += mean_reward

child_network_architecture = np.array(self.architecture_history[-
step:]).ravel() / self.divison_rate
child_network_architecture = child_network_architecture.reshape((-1,
self.num_cell_outputs))
baseline = ema(self.reward_history)
last_reward = self.reward_history[-1]
```

```
rewards = [last_reward - baseline]
logger.info("Buffers before loss calculation")
logger.info("States: {}".format(child_network_architecture))
logger.info("Rewards: {}".format(rewards))

with self.graph.as_default():
    _, loss = self.sess.run([self.train_op, self.total_loss],
                            {self.child_network_architectures:
child_network_architecture,
                            self.discounted_rewards: rewards})

logger.info('Episode: {} | Loss: {} | DNA: {} | Reward : {}'.format(
    episode, loss, child_network_architecture.ravel(), mean_reward))
```

And that's it! You can find the full implementation of `controller.py` in the main GitHub repository.

Testing ChildCNN

Now that we have implemented both `child_network` and `controller`, it would be great to test the training of `ChildCNN` via our `Controller` with custom child network configurations. We would like to make sure that, with a sensible architecture, `ChildCNN` can learn sufficiently.

To do this, first open up your favorite Terminal and start a Jupyter console:

```
$ ipython
Python 3.6.4 (default, Jan 6 2018, 11:49:38)
Type 'copyright', 'credits' or 'license' for more information
IPython 6.4.0 -- An enhanced Interactive Python. Type '?' for help.
```

We first configure our logger so we can see the outputs on the Terminal:

```
In [1]: import sys

In [2]: import logging

In [3]: logging.basicConfig(stream=sys.stdout,
   ...: level=logging.DEBUG,
   ...: format='%(asctime)s %(name)-12s %(levelname)-8s %(message)s')
   ...:

In [4]:
```

Next, we import the `Controller` class from `controller.py`:

```
In [4]: import numpy as np

In [5]: from controller import Controller

In [6]:
```

We then handcraft some child network architecture to be passed to the Controller's `train_child_network` function:

```
In [7]: dna = np.array([[3, 1, 30, 2], [3, 1, 30, 2], [3, 1, 40, 2]])
```

Finally, we instantiate our `Controller` and call the `train_child_network` method:

```
In [8]: controller = Controller()

...

2018-09-16 01:58:54,978 controller INFO Successfully built controller

In [9]: controller.train_child_network(dna, "test")

2018-09-16 01:58:59,208 controller INFO Training with dna: [[ 3 1 30 2]
 [ 3 1 30 2]
 [ 3 1 40 2]]
2018-09-16 01:58:59,605 cifar10_processor INFO Dividing pixels by 255
2018-09-16 01:59:01,289 cifar10_processor INFO Loaded data from keras
2018-09-16 01:59:03,150 child_network INFO DNA is: [[3, 1, 30, 2], [3, 1,
30, 2], [3, 1, 40, 2]]
2018-09-16 01:59:14,270 controller INFO Training child CNN first for 1000
epochs
```

If successful, you should be seeing decent accuracy scores after several epochs of training:

```
2018-09-16 06:25:01,927 controller INFO Epoch 436: loss - 1.119608 accuracy
- 0.663
2018-09-16 06:25:19,310 controller INFO Epoch 437: loss - 0.634937 accuracy
- 0.724
2018-09-16 06:25:36,438 controller INFO Epoch 438: loss - 0.769766 accuracy
- 0.702
2018-09-16 06:25:53,413 controller INFO Epoch 439: loss - 0.760520 accuracy
- 0.711
2018-09-16 06:26:10,530 controller INFO Epoch 440: loss - 0.606741 accuracy
- 0.812
```

config.py

The `config.py` module includes configurations used by the Controller and the child networks. Here, you can adjust several training parameters, such as the number of episodes, the learning rate, and the number of child networks generated by the Controller per epoch. You can also experiment with child network sizes, but do note that the larger the child network, the longer training takes for both the Controller and the child network:

```
child_network_params = {
    "learning_rate": 3e-5,
    "max_epochs": 100,
    "beta": 1e-3,
    "batch_size": 20
}

controller_params = {
    "max_layers": 3,
    "components_per_layer": 4,
    'beta': 1e-4,
    'max_episodes': 2000,
    "num_children_per_episode": 10
}
```

Some of these numbers (such as `max_episodes`) are arbitrarily chosen. We encourage the reader to tweak these numbers to understand how they affect the training of both the Controller and the child networks.

train.py

This `train.py` module acts as our top-level entry to training the Controller:

```
import logging
import sys

from .controller import Controller

if __name__ == '__main__':
    # Configure the logger
    logging.basicConfig(stream=sys.stdout,
                        level=logging.DEBUG,
                        format='%(asctime)s %(name)-12s %(levelname)-8s
%(message)s')
    controller = Controller()
    controller.train_controller()
```

And there we have it; a neural network that generates other neural networks! Make sure your implementation has the following directory structure:

```
src
|-- __init__.py
|-- child_network.py
|-- cifar10_processor.py
|-- config.py
|-- constants.py
|-- controller.py
`-- train.py
```

To execute training, simply run the following command:

```
$ python train.py
```

If all works well, you should be seeing output like the following:

```
2018-09-16 04:13:45,484 src.controller INFO Successfully built controller
2018-09-16 04:13:45,542 src.controller INFO =============> Episode 0 for
Controller
2018-09-16 04:13:45,952 src.controller INFO Training with dna: [[ 2 10 2 4
1 1 12 14 7 1 1 1]] 2018-09-16 04:13:45.953482: I
tensorflow/core/common_runtime/gpu/gpu_device.cc:1484] Adding visible gpu
devices: 0
2018-09-16 04:13:45.953530: I
tensorflow/core/common_runtime/gpu/gpu_device.cc:965] Device interconnect
StreamExecutor with strength 1 edge matrix:
2018-09-16 04:13:45.953543: I
tensorflow/core/common_runtime/gpu/gpu_device.cc:971] 0
2018-09-16 04:13:45.953558: I
tensorflow/core/common_runtime/gpu/gpu_device.cc:984] 0: N
2018-09-16 04:13:45.953840: I
tensorflow/core/common_runtime/gpu/gpu_device.cc:1097] Created TensorFlow
device (/job:localhost/replica:0/task:0/device:GPU:0 wi th 21618 MB memory)
-> physical GPU (device: 0, name: Tesla M40 24GB, pci bus id: 0000:03:00.0,
compute capability: 5.2)
2018-09-16 04:13:47,143 src.cifar10_processor INFO Dividing pixels by 255
2018-09-16 04:13:55,119 src.cifar10_processor INFO Loaded data from keras
2018-09-16 04:14:09,050 src.child_network INFO DNA is: [[2, 10, 2, 4], [1,
1, 12, 14], [7, 1, 1, 1]]
2018-09-16 04:14:21,326 src.controller INFO Training child CNN child/0_0
for 100 epochs
2018-09-16 04:14:32,830 src.controller INFO Epoch 0: loss - 2.351300
accuracy - 0.100
2018-09-16 04:14:43,976 src.controller INFO Epoch 1: loss - 2.202928
accuracy - 0.180
2018-09-16 04:14:53,412 src.controller INFO Epoch 2: loss - 2.102713
```

```
accuracy - 0.220
2018-09-16 04:15:03,704 src.controller INFO Epoch 3: loss - 2.092676
accuracy - 0.232
2018-09-16 04:15:14,349 src.controller INFO Epoch 4: loss - 2.092633
accuracy - 0.240
```

You should see logging statements for each child network architecture its CIFAR-10 training logs. During CIFAR-10 training, we print the loss and accuracy for each epoch as well as the validation accuracy which we return to the Controller.

Additional exercises

In this section, we have implemented the NAS framework for CIFAR-10 data. While this is a great start, there are additional features one can implement, which we will leave to the reader as exercises:

- How can we make the Controller create child networks that solve problems in other domains, such as text and speech recognition?
- How can we make the Controller train multiple child networks in parallel in order to speed up the training process?
- How can we visualize the training process using TensorBoard?
- How can we make the Controller design child networks that include residual connections?

Some of these exercises may require significant changes in the code base but are beneficial for deepening your understanding of NAS. We definitely recommend giving these a try!

Advantages of NAS

The biggest advantage of NAS is that one does not need to spend copious amounts of time designing a neural network for a particular problem. This also means that those who are not data scientists can also create machine learning agents as long as they can prepare data. In fact, Google has already productized this framework as Cloud AutoML, which allows anyone to train customized machine learning models with minimum effort. According to Google, Cloud AutoML provides the following benefits:

- Users only need to interact with a simple GUI to create machine learning models.
- Users can have Cloud AutoML annotate their own datasets if they are not labeled already. This is similar to Amazon's Mechanical Turk service.

- Models generated by Cloud AutoML are guaranteed to have high accuracy and fast performance.
- Easy end-to-end pipeline for uploading data, training and validating the model, deploying the model, and creating a REST endpoint for fetching predictions.

Currently, Cloud AutoML can be used for image classification/detection, natural language processing (text classification), and translation.

> For more information on Cloud AutoML, check out their official page here: https://cloud.google.com/automl/

Another advantage that NAS provides is the ability to generate more compact models than those designed by humans. According to *Efficient Neural Architecture Search via Parameter Sharing* by Hieu Pham et. al., whereas the most recent state-of-the-art neural network for CIFAR-10 classification had 26.2 million parameters, a NAS-generated neural network that achieved comparable test accuracy (97.44% for human-designed network versus 97.35% for the NAS-generated network) only had 3.3 million parameters. Note that older, less-accurate models such as VGG16, ResNet50, and InceptionV3 have 138 million, 25 million, and 23 million parameters respectively. The vast reduction in parameter size allows for more efficient inference time and model storage, both of which are important aspects when deploying models into production.

Summary

In this chapter, we have implemented NAS, a framework where a reinforcement learning agent (the Controller) generates child neural networks to complete a certain task. We studied the theory behind how the Controller learns to generate better child network architectures via policy gradient methods. We then implemented a simplified version of NAS that generates child networks that learn to classify CIFAR-10 images.

For more information on related topics, refer to the following list of links:

- NAS with reinforcement learning: https://arxiv.org/abs/1611.01578
- Efficient NAS via parameter sharing: https://arxiv.org/pdf/1802.03268
- Google Cloud AutoML: https://cloud.google.com/automl/
- Awesome Architecture Search—a curated list of papers related to generating neural networks: https://github.com/markdtw/awesome-architecture-search

The NAS framework marks an exciting development in the deep learning field, for we have figured out how to automatically design neural network architectures, a decision previously made by humans. There are now improved versions of NAS and other kinds of algorithms that generate neural networks automatically, which we encourage the reader to look into as well.

Predicting Future Stock Prices

9

The financial market is a very important part of any economy. For an economy to thrive, its financial market must be solid. Since the advent of machine learning, companies have begun to adopt algorithmic trading in the purchase of stocks and other financial assets. There has been proven successful with this method, and it has risen in prominence over time. Given its rise, several machine models have been developed and adopted for algorithmic trading. One popular machine learning model for trading is the time series analysis. You have already learned about reinforcement learning and Keras, and in this chapter, they will be used to develop a model that can predict stock prices.

Background problem

Automation is taking over in almost every sector, and the financial market is no exception. Creating automated algorithmic trading models will provide for a faster and more accurate analysis of stocks before purchase. Multiple indicators can be analyzed at a speed that humans are incapable of. Also, in trading, it is dangerous to operate with emotions. Machine learning models can solve that problem. There is also a reduction in transaction costs, as there is no need for continuous supervision.

In this tutorial, you will learn how to combine reinforcement learning with time series modeling, in order to predict the prices of stocks, based on real-life data.

Data used

The data that we will use will be the standard and poor's 500. According to Wikipedia, it is *An American stock market index based on the market capitalizations of 500 large companies having common stock listed on the NYSE or NASDAQ*. Here is a link to the data (`https://ca.finance.yahoo.com/quote/%255EGSPC/history?p=%255EGSPC`).

The data has the following columns:

1. **Date**: This indicates the date under consideration
2. **Open**: This indicates the price at which the market opens on the date
3. **High**: This indicates the highest market price on the date
4. **Low**: This indicates the lowest market price on the date
5. **Close**: This indicates the price at which the market closes on the date, adjusted for the split
6. **Adj Close**: This indicates the adjusted closing price for both the split and dividends
7. **Volume**: This indicates the total volume of shares available

The date under consideration for training the data is as follows:

```
Start: 14 August 2006
End: 13th August 2015
```

On the website, filter the date as follows, and download the dataset:

Summary	Chart	Conversations	**Historical Data**	Options	Components		
Time Period: Aug. 14, 2006 - Aug. 13, 2015 ⌄			**Show:** Historical Prices ⌄		**Frequency:** Daily ⌄		Apply
Currency in USD							⤓ Download Data

For testing, we will use the following date range:

```
Start: 14 August 2015
End: 14 August 2018
```

Change the dates on the website accordingly, and download the dataset for testing, as follows:

Summary	Chart	Conversations	**Historical Data**	Options	Components		
Time Period: Aug. 14, 2015 - Aug. 14, 2018 ⌄			**Show:** Historical Prices ⌄		**Frequency:** Daily ⌄		Apply
Currency in USD							⤓ Download Data

In the next section, we will define some possible actions that the agent can carry out.

Step-by-step guide

Our solution uses an actor-critic reinforcement learning model, along with an infused time series, to help us predict the best action, based on the stock prices. The possible actions are as follows:

1. **Hold**: This means that based on the price and projected profit, the trader should hold a stock
2. **Sell**: This means that based on the price and projected profit, the trader should sell a stock
3. **Buy**: This means that based on the price and projected profit, the trader should buy a stock

The actor-critic network is a family of reinforcement learning methods premised on two interacting network models. These models have two components: the actor and the critic. In our case, the network models that we will use will be neural networks. We will use the Keras package, which you have already learned about, to create the neural networks. The reward function that we are looking to improve is the profit.

The actor takes in the state of the environment, then returns the best action, or a policy that refers to a probability distribution over actions. This seems like a natural way to perform reinforcement learning, as policies are directly returned as a function of the state.

The critic evaluates the actions returned by the actor-network. This is similar to the traditional deep Q network; in the environment state and an action to return a score representing the value of taking that action given the state. The job of the critic is to compute an approximation, which is then used to update the actor in the direction of its gradient. The critic is trained itself temporal difference algorithm.

These two networks are trained simultaneously. With time, the critic network is able to improve its Q_value prediction, and the actor also learns how to make better decisions, given the state.

There are five scripts that make up this solution, and they will be described in the next sections.

Actor script

The actor script is where the policy model is defined. We begin by importing certain modules from Keras: layers, optimizers, models, and the backend. These modules will help us to construct our neural network: Let's start by importing the required functions from Keras.

```
from keras import layers, models, optimizers
from keras import backend as K
```

1. We create a class called `Actor`, whose object takes in the parameters of the `state` and `action` size:

```
class Actor:
  # """Actor (policy) Model. """

    def __init__(self, state_size, action_size):
        self.state_size = state_size
        self.action_size = action_size
```

2. The preceding code shows the state size, which represents the dimension of each state, and the action size, which represents the dimensions of the actions. Next, call a function to build the model, as follows:

```
self.build_model()
```

3. Build a policy model that maps the states to actions, and start by defining the input layer, as follows:

```
def build_model(self):
    states = layers.Input(shape=(self.state_size,), name='states')
```

4. Add hidden layers to the model. There are two dense layers, each one followed by a batch normalization and an activation layer. The dense layers are regularized. The two layers have 16 and 32 hidden units, respectively:

```
        net =
layers.Dense(units=16,kernel_regularizer=layers.regularizers.l2(1e-
6))(states)
        net = layers.BatchNormalization()(net)
        net = layers.Activation("relu")(net)
        net =
layers.Dense(units=32,kernel_regularizer=layers.regularizers.l2(1e-
6))(net)
        net = layers.BatchNormalization()(net)
        net = layers.Activation("relu")(net)
```

5. The final output layer will predict the action probabilities that have an activation of `softmax`:

```
actions = layers.Dense(units=self.action_size,
activation='softmax', name = 'actions')(net)
    self.model = models.Model(inputs=states, outputs=actions)
```

6. Define the loss function by using the action value (`Q_value`) gradients, as follows:

```
action_gradients = layers.Input(shape=(self.action_size,))
loss = K.mean(-action_gradients * actions)
```

7. Define the `optimizer` and training function, as follows:

```
optimizer = optimizers.Adam(lr=.00001)
updates_op =
optimizer.get_updates(params=self.model.trainable_weights,
loss=loss)
    self.train_fn = K.function(
        inputs=[self.model.input, action_gradients,
K.learning_phase()],
        outputs=[],
        updates=updates_op)
```

The custom training function for the actor-network that makes use of the Q gradients with respect to the action probabilities. With this custom function, the training aims to maximize the profits (in other words, minimize the negatives of the `Q_values`).

Critic script

We begin by importing certain modules from Keras: layers, optimizers, models, and the backend. These modules will help us to construct our neural network:

```
from keras import layers, models, optimizers
from keras import backend as K
```

1. We create a class called `Critic`, whose object takes in the following parameters:

```
class Critic:
    """Critic (Value) Model."""

    def __init__(self. state_size, action_size):
        """Initialize parameters and build model.
        Params
        ======
```

```
        state_size (int): Dimension of each state
        action_size (int): Dimension of each action
    """
    self.state_size = state_size
    self.action_size = action_size

    self.build_model()
```

2. Build a critic (value) network that maps `state` and `action` pairs (`Q_values`), and define input layers, as follows:

```
def build_model(self):
    states = layers.Input(shape=(self.state_size,),
name='states')
    actions = layers.Input(shape=(self.action_size,),
name='actions')
```

3. Add the hidden layers for the state pathway, as follows:

```
    net_states =
layers.Dense(units=16,kernel_regularizer=layers.regularizers.l2(1e-
6))(states)
    net_states = layers.BatchNormalization()(net_states)
    net_states = layers.Activation("relu")(net_states)

    net_states = layers.Dense(units=32,
kernel_regularizer=layers.regularizers.l2(1e-6))(net_states)
```

4. Add the hidden layers for the action pathway, as follows:

```
    net_actions =
layers.Dense(units=32,kernel_regularizer=layers.regularizers.l2(1e-
6))(actions)
```

5. Combine the state and action pathways, as follows:

```
net = layers.Add()([net_states, net_actions])
net = layers.Activation('relu')(net)
```

6. Add the final output layer to produce the action values (`Q_values`):

```
    Q_values = layers.Dense(units=1,
name='q_values',kernel_initializer=layers.initializers.RandomUnifor
m(minval=-0.003, maxval=0.003))(net)
```

7. Create the Keras model, as follows:

```
self.model = models.Model(inputs=[states, actions],
outputs=Q_values)
```

8. Define the `optimizer` and compile a model for training with the built-in loss function:

```
optimizer = optimizers.Adam(lr=0.001)
self.model.compile(optimizer=optimizer, loss='mse')
```

9. Compute the action gradients (the derivative of `Q_values`, with respect to `actions`):

```
action_gradients = K.gradients(Q_values, actions)
```

10. Define an additional function to fetch the action gradients (to be used by the actor model), as follows:

```
self.get_action_gradients = K.function(
    inputs=[*self.model.input, K.learning_phase()],
    outputs=action_gradients)
```

This concludes the critic script.

Agent script

In this section, we will train an agent that will perform reinforcement learning based on the actor and critic networks. We will perform the following steps to achieve this:

1. Create an agent class whose initial function takes in the batch size, state size, and an evaluation Boolean function, to check whether the training is ongoing.
2. In the agent class, create the following methods:
3. Import the `actor` and `critic` scripts:

```
from actor import Actor
from critic import Critic
```

4. Import `numpy`, `random`, `namedtuple`, and `deque` from the `collections` package:

```
import numpy as np
from numpy.random import choice
import random

from collections import namedtuple, deque
```

5. Create a `ReplayBuffer` class that adds, samples, and evaluates a buffer:

```
class ReplayBuffer:
    #Fixed sized buffer to stay experience tuples
    def __init__(self, buffer_size, batch_size):
    #Initialize a replay buffer object.
    #parameters
    #buffer_size: maximum size of buffer. Batch size: size of each
batch
        self.memory = deque(maxlen = buffer_size)  #memory size of
replay buffer
        self.batch_size = batch_size                #Training batch
size for Neural nets
        self.experience = namedtuple("Experience", field_names =
["state", "action", "reward", "next_state", "done"])
    #Tuple containing experienced replay
```

6. Add a new experience to the replay buffer memory:

```
def add(self, state, action, reward, next_state, done):
    e = self.experience(state, action, reward, next_state,
done)
    self.memory.append(e)
```

7. Randomly sample a batch of experienced tuples from the memory. In the following function, we randomly sample states from a memory buffer. We do this so that the states that we feed to the model are not temporally correlated. This will reduce overfitting:

```
def sample(self, batch_size = 32):
    return random.sample(self.memory, k=self.batch_size)
```

8. Return the current size of the buffer memory, as follows:

```
def __len__(self):
    return len(self.memory)
```

9. The reinforcement learning agent that learns using the actor-critic network is as follows:

```
class Agent:
    def __init__(self. state_size, batch_size, is_eval = False):
        self.state_size = state_size #
```

10. The number of actions are defined as 3: sit, buy, sell

```
self.action_size = 3
```

11. Define the replay memory size

```
self.buffer_size = 1000000
self.batch_size = batch_size
self.memory = ReplayBuffer(self.buffer_size, self.batch_size)
self.inventory = []
```

12. Define whether or not training is ongoing. This variable will be changed during the training and evaluation phase:

```
self.is_eval = is_eval
```

13. Discount factor in Bellman equation:

```
self.gamma = 0.99
```

14. A soft update of the actor and critic networks can be done as follows:

```
self.tau = 0.001
```

15. The actor policy model maps states to actions and instantiates the actor networks (local and target models, for soft updates of parameters):

```
self.actor_local = Actor(self.state_size, self.action_size)
self.actor_target = Actor(self.state_size, self.action_size)
```

16. The critic (value) model that maps the state-action pairs to Q_values is as follows:

```
self.critic_local = Critic(self.state_size, self.action_size)
```

17. Instantiate the critic model (the local and target models are utilized to allow for soft updates), as follows:

```
self.critic_target = Critic(self.state_size,
self.action_size)
self.critic_target.model.set_weights(self.critic_local.model.get_we
ights())
```

18. The following code sets the target model parameters to local model parameters:

```
self.actor_target.model.set_weights(self.actor_local.model.get_weig
hts()
```

19. Returns an action, given a state, using the actor (policy network) and the output of the softmax layer of the actor-network, returning the probability for each action. An action method that returns an action, given a state, using the actor (policy network) is as follows:

```
def act(self, state):
    options = self.actor_local.model.predict(state)
    self.last_state = state
    if not self.is_eval:
        return choice(range(3), p = options[0])
    return np.argmax(options[0])
```

20. Returns a stochastic policy, based on the action probabilities in the training model and a deterministic action corresponding to the maximum probability during testing. There is a set of actions to be carried out by the agent at every step of the episode. A method (step) that returns the set of actions to be carried out by the agent at every step of the episode is as follows:

```
def step(self, action, reward, next_state, done):
```

21. The following code adds a new experience to the memory:

```
self.memory.add(self.last_state, action, reward, next_state,
    done)
```

22. The following code asserts that enough experiences are present in the memory to train:

```
if len(self.memory) > self.batch_size:
```

23. The following code samples a random batch from the memory to train:

```
experiences = self.memory.sample(self.batch_size)
```

24. Learn from the sampled experiences, as follows:

```
self.learn(experiences)
```

25. The following code updates the state to the next state:

```
self.last_state = next_state
```

26. Learning from the sampled experiences through the actor and the critic. Create a method to learn from the sampled experiences through the actor and the critic, as follows:

```
def learn(self, experiences):
    states = np.vstack([e.state for e in experiences if e is
not None]).astype(np.float32).reshape(-1,self.state_size)
    actions = np.vstack([e.action for e in experiences if e is
not None]).astype(np.float32).reshape(-1,self.action_size)
    rewards = np.array([e.reward for e in experiences if e is
not None]).astype(np.float32).reshape(-1,1)
    dones = np.array([e.done for e in experiences if e is not
None]).astype(np.float32).reshape(-1,1)
    next_states = np.vstack([e.next_state for e in experiences
if e is not None]).astype(np.float32).reshape(-1,self.state_size)
```

27. Return a separate array for each experience in the replay component and predict actions based on the next states, as follows:

```
actions_next =
self.actor_target.model.predict_on_batch(next_states)
```

28. Predict the Q_value of the actor output for the next state, as follows:

```
Q_targets_next =
self.critic_target.model.predict_on_batch([next_states,
actions_next])
```

29. Target the Q_value to serve as a label for the critic network, based on the temporal difference, as follows:

```
Q_targets = rewards + self.gamma * Q_targets_next * (1 - dones)
```

30. Fit the critic model to the time difference of the target, as follows:

```
self.critic_local.model.train_on_batch(x = [states,
actions], y = Q_targets)
```

31. Train the actor model (local) using the gradient of the critic network output with respect to the action probabilities fed from the actor-network:

```
action_gradients =
np.reshape(self.critic_local.get_action_gradients([states, actions,
0]),(-1, self.action_size))
```

32. Next, define a custom training function, as follows:

```
self.actor_local.train_fn([states, action_gradients, 1])
```

33. Next, initiate a soft update of the parameters of both networks, as follows:

```
self.soft_update(self.actor_local.model,
self.actor_target.model)
```

34. This performs soft updates on the model parameters, based on the parameter `tau` to avoid drastic model changes. A method that updates the model by performing soft updates on the model parameters, based on the parameter `tau` (to avoid drastic model changes), is as follows:

```
def soft_update(self, local_model, target_model):
    local_weights = np.array(local_model.get_weights())
    target_weights = np.array(target_model.get_weights())
    assert len(local_weights) == len(target_weights)
    new_weights = self.tau * local_weights + (1 - self.tau) *
target_weights
    target_model.set_weights(new_weights)
```

This concludes the agent script.

Helper script

In this script, we will create functions that will be helpful for training, via the following steps:

1. Import the numpy and math modules, as follows:

```
import numpy as np
import math
```

2. Next, define a function to format the price to two decimal places, to reduce the ambiguity of the data:

```
def formatPrice(n):
    if n>=0:
        curr = "$"
    else:
        curr = "-$"
    return (curr +"{0:.2f}".format(abs(n)))
```

3. Return a vector of stock data from the CSV file. Convert the closing stock prices from the data to vectors, and return a vector of all stock prices, as follows:

```
def getStockData(key):
    datavec = []
    lines = open("data/" + key + ".csv", "r").read().splitlines()
    for line in lines[1:]:
        datavec.append(float(line.split(",")[4]))
    return datavec
```

4. Next, define a function to generate states from the input vector. Create the time series by generating the states from the vectors created in the previous step. The function for this takes three parameters: the data; a time, *t* (the day that you want to predict); and a window (how many days to go back in time). The rate of change between these vectors will then be measured and based on the sigmoid function:

```
def getState(data, t, window):
    if t - window >= -1:
        vec = data[t - window+ 1:t+ 1]
    else:
        vec = -(t-window+1)*[data[0]]+data[0: t + 1]
    scaled_state = []
    for i in range(window - 1):
```

5. Next, scale the state vector from 0 to 1 with a sigmoid function. The sigmoid function can map any input value, from 0 to 1. This helps to normalize the values to probabilities:

```
        scaled_state.append(1/(1 + math.exp(vec[i] - vec[i+1])))
    return np.array([scaled_state])
```

All of the necessary functions and classes are now defined, so we can start the training process.

Training the data

We will proceed to train the data, based on our agent and helper methods. This will provide us with one of three actions, based on the states of the stock prices at the end of the day. These states can be to buy, sell, or hold. During training, the prescribed action for each day is predicted, and the price (profit, loss, or unchanged) of the action is calculated. The cumulative sum will be calculated at the end of the training period, and we will see whether there has been a profit or a loss. The aim is to maximize the total profit.

Let's start with the imports, as follows:

```
from agent import Agent
from helper import getStockData, getState
import sys
```

1. Next, define the number of market days to consider as the window size, and define the batch size with which the neural network will be trained, as follows:

   ```
   window_size = 100
   batch_size = 32
   ```

2. Instantiate the stock agent with the window size and batch size, as follows:

   ```
   agent = Agent(window_size, batch_size)
   ```

3. Next, read the training data from the CSV file, using the helper function:

   ```
   data = getStockData("^GSPC")
   l = len(data) - 1
   ```

4. Next, the episode count is defined as 300. The agent will look at the data for so many numbers of times. An episode represents a complete pass over the data:

   ```
   episode_count = 300
   ```

5. Next, we can start to iterate through the episodes, as follows:

   ```
   for e in range(episode_count):
       print("Episode " + str(e) + "/" + str(episode_count))
   ```

6. Each episode has to be started with a state based on the data and window size. The inventory of stocks is initialized before going through the data:

   ```
   state = getState(data, 0, window_size + 1)
   agent.inventory = []
   total_profit = 0
   done = False
   ```

7. Next, start to iterate over every day of the stock data. The action probability is predicted by the agent, based on the `state`:

```
for t in range(l):
    action = agent.act(state)
    action_prob = agent.actor_local.model.predict(state)

    next_state = getState(data, t + 1, window_size + 1)
    reward = 0
```

8. The `action` can be held, if the agent decides not to do anything with the stock. Another possible action is to buy (hence, the stock will be added to the inventory), as follows:

```
if action == 1:
    agent.inventory.append(data[t])
    print("Buy:" + formatPrice(data[t]))
```

9. If the `action` is 2, the agent sells the stocks and removes it from the inventory. Based on the sale, the profit (or loss) is calculated:

```
elif action == 2 and len(agent.inventory) > 0:  # sell
    bought_price = agent.inventory.pop(0)
    reward = max(data[t] - bought_price, 0)
    total_profit += data[t] - bought_price
    print("sell: " + formatPrice(data[t]) + "| profit: " +
        formatPrice(data[t] - bought_price))

if t == l - 1:
    done = True
agent.step(action_prob, reward, next_state, done)
state = next_state

if done:
    print("--------------------------------------------")
    print("Total Profit: " + formatPrice(total_profit))
    print("--------------------------------------------")
```

10. You can see logs similar to those that follow during the training process. The stocks are bought and sold at certain prices:

```
sell: $2102.15| profit: $119.30
sell: $2079.65| profit: $107.36
Buy:$2067.64
sell: $2108.57| profit: $143.75
Buy:$2108.63
Buy:$2093.32
```

```
Buy:$2099.84
Buy:$2083.56
Buy:$2077.57
Buy:$2104.18
sell: $2084.07| profit: $115.18
sell: $2086.05| profit: $179.92
--------------------------------------------
Total Profit: $57473.53
```

11. Next, the test data is read from the CSV file. The initial state is inferred from the data. The steps are very similar to a single episode of the training process:

```
test_data = getStockData("^GSPC Test")
l_test = len(test_data) - 1
state = getState(test_data, 0, window_size + 1)
```

12. The profit starts at 0. The agent is initialized with a zero inventory and in test mode:

```
total_profit = 0
agent.inventory = []
agent.is_eval = False
done = False
```

13. Next, every day of trading is iterated, and the agent can act upon the data. Every day, the agent decides an action. Based on the action, the stock is held, sold, or bought:

```
for t in range(l_test):
    action = agent.act(state)
```

14. If the action is 0, then there is no trade. The state can be called **holding** during that period:

```
next_state = getState(test_data, t + 1, window_size + 1)
reward = 0
```

15. If the action is 1, buy the stock by adding it to the inventory, as follows:

```
if action == 1:

    agent.inventory.append(test_data[t])
    print("Buy: " + formatPrice(test_data[t]))
```

16. If the action is 2, the agent sells the stock by removing it from the inventory. The difference in price is recorded as a profit or a loss:

```
elif action == 2 and len(agent.inventory) > 0:
    bought_price = agent.inventory.pop(0)
    reward = max(test_data[t] - bought_price, 0)
    total_profit += test_data[t] - bought_price
    print('Sell: ' + formatPrice(test_data[t]) + " | profit: '
+ formatPrice(test_data[t] - bought_price))

    if t == l_test - 1:
        done = True
    agent.step(action_prob, reward, next_state, done)
    state = next_state

    if done:
        print("---------------------------------------------")
        print('Total Profit: " + formatPrice(total_profit))
        print("---------------------------------------------")
```

17. Once the script starts to run, the model will get better over time through training. You can see the logs, as follows:

```
Sell: $2818.82 | profit: $44.80
Sell: $2802.60 | profit: $4.31
Buy: $2816.29
Sell: $2827.22 | profit: $28.79
Buy: $2850.40
Sell: $2857.70 | profit: $53.21
Buy: $2853.58
Buy: $2833.28
------------------------------------------
Total Profit: $10427.24
```

The model has traded and made a total profit of $10,427. Please note that this style of trading is not suitable for the real world, as trading involves more costs and uncertainty; hence, this trading style could have adverse effects.

Final result

After training the data, we tested it against the `test` dataset. Our model resulted in a total profit of `$10427.24`. The best thing about the model was that the profits kept improving over time, indicating that it was learning well and taking better actions.

Summary

In conclusion, machine learning can be applied to several industries and can be applied very efficiently in financial markets, as you saw in this chapter. We can combine different models, as we did with reinforcement learning and time series, to produce stronger models that suit our use cases. We discussed the use of reinforcement learning and time series to predict the stock market. We worked with an actor-critic model that determined the best action, based on the state of the stock prices, with the aim of maximizing profits. In the end, we obtained a result that boasted an overall profit and included increasing profits over time, indicating that the agent learned more with each state.

In the next chapter, you will learn about the future areas of work.

10
Looking Ahead

Over the past few hundred pages, we have faced numerous challenges, to which we applied reinforcement and deep learning algorithms. To conclude our **reinforcement learning (RL)** journey, this chapter will look at several aspects of the field that we have not covered yet. We will start by looking at several of the drawbacks of reinforcement learning, which any practitioner or researcher should be aware of. To end on a positive note, we will follow up by describing numerous exciting academic developments and achievements the field has seen in recent years.

The shortcomings of reinforcement learning

So far, we have only covered what reinforcement learning algorithms can do. To the reader, reinforcement learning may seem like the panacea for all kinds of problems. But why do we not see a ubiquitous application of reinforcement learning algorithms in real-life situations? The reality is that the field has a myriad of shortcomings that hinder commercial adoption.

Why is it necessary to talk about the field's flaws? We think this will help you build a more holistic, less biased view of reinforcement learning. Moreover, understanding the weaknesses of reinforcement learning and machine learning is an important quality of a good machine learning researcher or practitioner. In the following subsections, we will discuss a few of the most important limitations that reinforcement learning is currently facing.

Resource efficiency

Current deep reinforcement learning algorithms require vast amounts of time, training data, and computational resources in order to reach a desirable level of proficiency. For algorithms such as AlphaGo Zero, where our reinforcement learning algorithm learns to play Go with zero prior knowledge and experience, resource efficiency becomes a major bottleneck for taking such algorithms to commercial scales. Recall that when DeepMind implemented AlphaGo Zero, they needed to train the agent on tens of millions of games using hundreds of GPUs and thousands of CPUs. For AlphaGo Zero to reach a reasonable proficiency, it needs to play a number of games, equivalent to what hundreds of thousands of humans would play in their lifetimes.

Unless, in the future, the average consumer can readily leverage vast amounts of computational power that only the likes of Google and Nvidia can offer today, the ability to develop superhuman reinforcement learning algorithms will continue to be way beyond the public's reach. This means that powerful, resource-hungry reinforcement learning algorithms will be monopolized by a small consortium of institutions, which is probably not a great thing.

Thus, making reinforcement learning algorithms trainable under limited resources will continue to be an important issue that the community must address.

Reproducibility

In numerous fields of scientific research, a prevalent problem has been the inability to reproduce the experimental results claimed in academic papers and journals. In a 2016 survey conducted by Nature, the world's most renowned scientific journal, 70% of respondents claimed that they have failed to reproduce their own or another researcher's experimental results. Moreover, the attitude toward the inability to reproduce experimental results was a stark one, with 90% of researchers thinking that there is indeed a reproducibility crisis.

The original work reported by nature can be found here: `https://www.nature.com/news/1-500-scientists-lift-the-lid-on-reproducibility-1.19970`.

While this survey targeted researchers across a number of disciplines, including biology and chemistry, reinforcement learning is also facing a similar problem. In the paper *Deep Reinforcement Learning Matters* (reference at the end of this chapter; you can view it at https://arxiv.org/pdf/1709.06560.pdf for the online version), Peter Henderson et al. study the effects of different configurations of a deep reinforcement learning algorithm on experimental outcomes. These configurations include hyperparameters, seeds for the random number generator, and network architecture.

In extreme cases, they found that, when training the same model on two sets of five different random seed configurations, the resulting average return for the two sets of models diverged significantly. Moreover, changing other settings, such as the architecture of the CNN, activation functions, and learning rates, have profound effects on the outcome.

What are the implications of inconsistent, unreproducible results? As the adoption and popularity of reinforcement learning and machine learning continues to grow at near exponential rates, the number of implementations of reinforcement learning algorithms freely available on the internet also increases. If those implementations cannot reproduce the results they claim to be able to achieve, this would cause major issues and potential danger in real-life applications. Certainly, no one would want their self-driving car to be implemented so that it cannot produce consistent decisions!

Explainability/accountability

We have seen how an agent's policy can return either a single action or a probability distribution over a set of possible actions and how its value function can return how desirable a certain state is. But how can a model explain how it arrived at such predictions? As reinforcement learning becomes more popular and potentially more prevalent in real-life applications, there will be an ever-increasing need to be able to explain the output of reinforcement learning algorithms.

Today, most advanced reinforcement learning algorithms incorporate deep neural networks, which, as of now, can only be represented as a set of weights and a sequence of non-linear functions. Moreover, due to its high dimensional nature, neural networks are not able to provide any meaningful, intuitive relationships between input and their corresponding output that can be understood easily by humans. Hence, deep learning algorithms are often referred to as black boxes, for it is difficult for us to understand what is really going on inside a neural network.

Why is it important for a reinforcement learning algorithm to be explainable? Suppose an autonomous car is involved in a car accident (let's assume it was just an innocuous bump between two cars and the drivers are not hurt). Human drivers would be able to explain what led to the crash; they can give reasons for why they performed a particular maneuver and what exactly happened when the accident occurred. This would help law enforcement ascertain the cause of the accident and potentially determine who or what was accountable. However, even if we create an agent that can drive cars sufficiently well using algorithms available today, this is simply not possible.

Without the ability to explain predictions, it will be difficult for users and the general public to trust software that uses any kind of machine learning, especially in use cases where the algorithms are accountable for making important decisions. This is a serious impediment to the adoption of reinforcement learning algorithms in practical applications.

Susceptibility to attacks

Deep learning algorithms have shown incredible results across numerous tasks, including computer vision, natural language processing, and speech recognition. In several tasks, deep learning has already surpassed human capabilities. However, recent work has shown that these algorithms are incredibly vulnerable to attacks. By attacks, we mean attempts to make imperceptible modifications to the input which causes the model to behave differently. Take the following example:

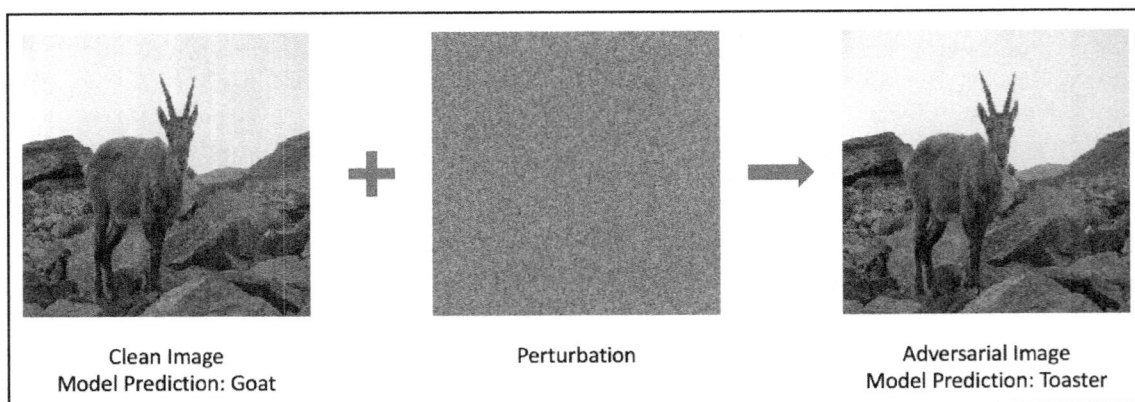

Clean Image	Perturbation	Adversarial Image
Model Prediction: Goat		Model Prediction: Toaster

An illustration of adversarial attacks. By adding imperceptible perturbations to an image, an attacker can easily fool deep learning image classifiers.

The rightmost image is the result of adding the left image, which is the original image, and the middle image, which represents the perturbations added to the original image. Even the most accurate, well-performing deep neural network image classifier fails to identify the right image as a goat and instead predicts it to be a toaster.

These examples have shocked many in the research community, for people did not expect that deep learning algorithms can be incredibly brittle and susceptible to such attacks. This field is now called **adversarial machine learning** and has been rapidly increasing in prominence and importance as more researchers around the world are investigating the robustness and vulnerabilities of deep learning algorithms.

Reinforcement learning algorithms are also no stranger to these results and attacks. According to the paper titled *Robust Deep Reinforcement Learning with Adversarial Attacks* (https://arxiv.org/abs/1712.03632) by Anay Pattanaik et. al., adversarial attacks to reinforcement learning algorithms can be defined as any possible perturbation that leads the agent into an increased probability of taking the worst possible action in that state. For example, we can add noise to the screen of an Atari game with the intention of tricking the RL agent playing the game to make a poor decision, which leads to a lower score.

More serious applications include adding noise to street signs to trick a self-driving car into thinking that a STOP sign is a speed sign, making an ATM recognize a $100 check as a $1,000,000 one, or even fooling a facial-recognition system to identify an attacker's face as that of another user.

Needless to say, these vulnerabilities further add to the risks of adopting deep learning algorithms in practical, safety-critical use cases. While there are numerous ongoing efforts to countervail adversarial attacks, there is still a long way to go for deep learning algorithms to become robust enough for such use cases.

Upcoming developments in reinforcement learning

The past few sections may have painted a stark outlook for deep learning and reinforcement learning. However, there is no need to feel entirely discouraged; this is, in fact, an exciting time for DL and RL, where many significant advances in research are continuing to shape the field and cause it to evolve at a rapid pace. With increasing availability of computational resources and data, the possibilities of expanding and improving deep learning and reinforcement learning algorithms continue to expand.

Addressing the limitations

For one, the issues raised in the preceding section are recognized and acknowledged by the research community. There are several efforts being made to address them. In the work by Pattanaik et. al., not only do the authors demonstrate that current deep reinforcement learning algorithms are susceptible to adversarial attacks, they also propose techniques that can make the same algorithms more robust toward such attacks. In particular, by training deep RL algorithms on examples that were adversarially perturbed, the model can improve its robustness against similar attacks. This technique is commonly referred to as adversarial training.

Moreover, the research community is actively taking actions to solve the reproducibility problem. ICLR and ICML, two of the biggest conferences in machine learning, have hosted challenges where participants are invited to reimplement and re-run experiments conducted by submitted papers to reproduce the reported results. Participants are then required to critique the original work by writing a reproducibility report that describes the problem statement, experimental methodology, implementation details, analyses, and the reproducibility of the original paper. Organized by Joelle Pineau and McGill University, this challenge aims to promote transparency in experiments and academic work as well as to ensure the reproducibility and integrity of results.

More information on the ICLR 2018 reproducibility challenge can be found here: `https://www.cs.mcgill.ca/~jpineau/ICLR2018-ReproducibilityChallenge.html`. Similarly, the original ICML workshop on reproducibility can be found here: `https://sites.google.com/view/icml-reproducibility-workshop/home`.

Transfer learning

Another important topic that is increasing in importance and attention is transfer learning. Transfer learning is a paradigm in machine learning, where a model trained on one task is fine-tuned to accomplish another.

For example, we can train a model to recognize images of cars and use the weights of that model to initialize an identical model that learns to recognize trucks. The main intuition is that certain abstract concepts and features learned by training on one task are transferable to other similar tasks. This idea is applicable to many reinforcement learning problems as well. An agent that learns to play a particular Atari game should be able to play other Atari games proficiently without training entirely from scratch, much like how a human can.

Demis Hassabis, the founder of DeepMind and a pioneer in deep reinforcement learning, said in a recent talk that transfer learning is the key to general intelligence. And I think the key to doing transfer learning will be the acquisition of conceptual knowledge that is abstracted away from perceptual details of where you learned it from.

> The Demis Hassabis quote and the talk in which this was mentioned can be found here: https://www.youtube.com/watch?v=YofMOh6_WKo

There have already been several advances in computer vision and natural language processing, where models initialized with knowledge and priors from one domain are used to learn about data from another domain.

This is especially useful when the second domain lacks data. Called **few-shot** or **one-shot** learning, these techniques allow models to learn to perform tasks well, even when the dataset is small, as illustrated in the following diagram:

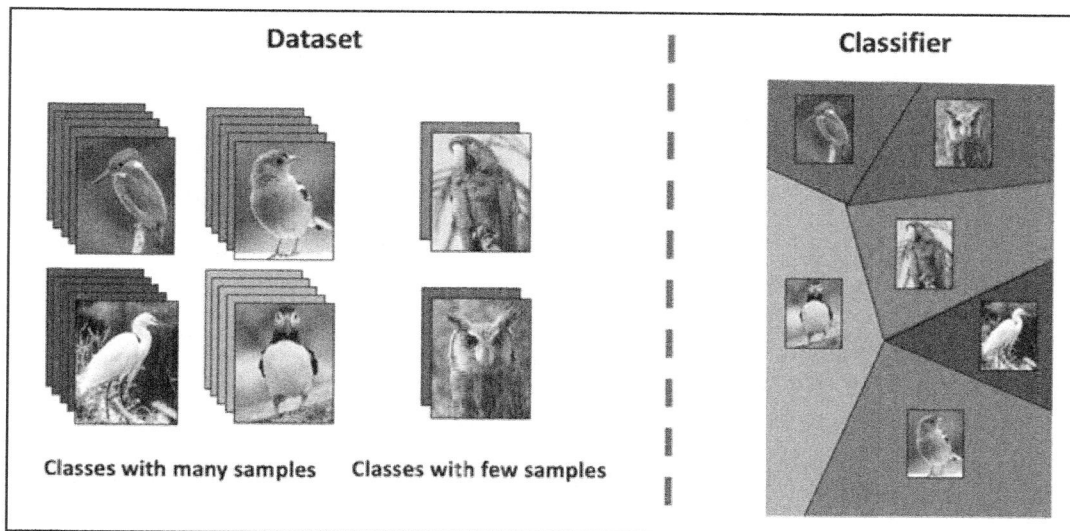

An illustration of a few-shot learning classifier learning good decision boundaries for classes with small volumes of data

Few-shot learning for reinforcement learning would involve having the agent learn to achieve high proficiency on a given task without a high dependence on time, data, and computational resources. Imagine a generalized game-playing agent that can easily be fine-tuned to perform well on any other video game using readily-available computational resources; this would make training RL algorithms a lot more efficient and thus more accessible to a wider audience.

Multi-agent reinforcement learning

Another promising area making significant strides is multi-agent reinforcement learning. Contrary to the problems we've seen where only one agent makes decisions, this topic involves having multiple agents make decisions simultaneously and cooperatively in order to achieve a common objective. One of the most significant works related to this has been OpenAI's Dota2-playing system, called **OpenAI Five**. Dota2 is one of the world's most popular **Massively Multiplayer Online Role Playing Game (MMORPGs)**. Compared to traditional RL games such as Go and Atari, Dota2 is more complex for the following reasons:

- **Multiple agents**: Dota2 games involve two teams of five players, each fighting to destroy the other team's base. Hence there are multiple agents, not just one, making decisions simultaneously.
- **Observability**: The screen only shows the proximity of the agent's character instead of the whole map. This means that the whole game state, including the locations of opponents and what they are doing, is not observable. In reinforcement learning, we call this a *partially-observable* state.
- **High dimensionality**: A Dota2 agent's observations can include 20,000 points, each depicting what a human player may observe on the screen, including health, the location of the controlling character, the location of enemies, and any attacks. Go, on the other hand, requires fewer data points to construct an observation (19 x 19 board, past moves). Hence, observations have high dimensionality and complexity. This also goes for decisions, where a Dota2 AI's action space consists of 170,000 possibilities, which includes decisions on movement, casting spells, and using items.

For more information on OpenAI's Dota2 AI, check out their blogs on the project at https://blog.openai.com/openai-five/.

Moreover, by using novel upgrades on traditional reinforcement learning algorithms, each agent in OpenAI Five was able to learn to cooperate with one another in order to reach the common objective of destroying the enemy's base. They were even able to learn several team strategies that experienced human players employ. The following is a screenshot from a game being played between a team of Dota players and OpenAI Five:

OpenAI versus human players (source: https://www.youtube.com/watch?v=eaBYhLttETw)

Despite the extreme levels of resource requirements (240 GPUs, 120,000 CPU cores, ~200 human years of gameplay in a single day), this project demonstrates that current AI algorithms are indeed able to cooperate with one another to reach a common objective in a vastly complex environment. This work symbolizes another significant advancement in AI and RL research and demonstrates what the current technology is capable of.

Summary

This concludes our introductory journey into reinforcement learning. Over the course of this book, we learned how to implement agents that can play Atari games, navigate Minecraft, predict stock market prices, play the complex board game of Go, and even generate other neural networks to train on `CIFAR-10` data. In doing so, you acquired and became accustomed to some of the fundamental and state-of-the-art deep learning and reinforcement learning algorithms. In short, you have achieved a lot!

But the journey does not and should not end here. We hope that, with your newfound skills and knowledge, you will continue to utilize deep learning and reinforcement learning algorithms to tackle problems that you face outside of this book. More importantly, we hope that this guide motivates you to explore other fields of machine learning and further develop your knowledge and experience.

There are many obstacles for the reinforcement learning community to overcome. However, there is much to look forward to. With the increasing popularity and development of the field, we can't wait to see what new developments and milestones the field will achieve. We hope the reader, upon completing this guide, will feel more equipped and ready to build reinforcement learning algorithms and make significant contributions to the field.

References

Open Science Collaboration. (2015). *Estimating the reproducibility of psychological science*. Science, 349(6251), aac4716.

Henderson, P., Islam, R., Bachman, P., Pineau, J., Precup, D., and Meger, D. (2017). *Deep reinforcement learning that matters*. arXiv preprint arXiv:1709.06560.

Pattanaik, A., Tang, Z., Liu, S., Bommannan, G., and Chowdhary, G. (2018, July). *Robust deep reinforcement learning with adversarial attacks*. In Proceedings of the 17th International Conference on Autonomous Agents and MultiAgent Systems (pp. 2040-2042). International Foundation for Autonomous Agents and Multiagent Systems.

Other Books You May Enjoy

If you enjoyed this book, you may be interested in these other books by Packt:

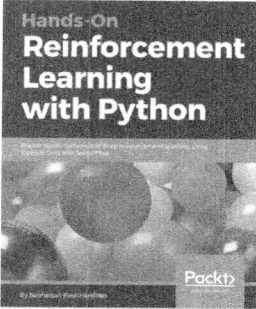

Hands-On Reinforcement Learning with Python
Sudharsan Ravichandiran

ISBN: 978-1-78883-652-4

- Understand the basics of reinforcement learning methods, algorithms, and elements
- Train an agent to walk using OpenAI Gym and Tensorflow
- Understand the Markov Decision Process, Bellman's optimality, and TD learning
- Solve multi-armed-bandit problems using various algorithms
- Master deep learning algorithms, such as RNN, LSTM, and CNN with applications

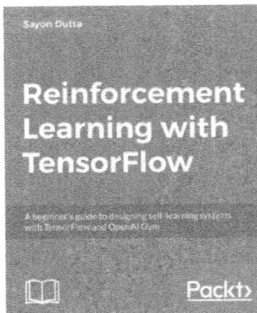

Reinforcement Learning with TensorFlow
Sayon Dutta

ISBN: 978-1-78883-572-5

- Implement state-of-the-art Reinforcement Learning algorithms from the basics
- Discover various techniques of Reinforcement Learning such as MDP, Q Learning and more
- Learn the applications of Reinforcement Learning in advertisement, image processing, and NLP
- Teach a Reinforcement Learning model to play a game using TensorFlow and the OpenAI gym
- Understand how Reinforcement Learning Applications are used in robotics

Leave a review - let other readers know what you think

Please share your thoughts on this book with others by leaving a review on the site that you bought it from. If you purchased the book from Amazon, please leave us an honest review on this book's Amazon page. This is vital so that other potential readers can see and use your unbiased opinion to make purchasing decisions, we can understand what our customers think about our products, and our authors can see your feedback on the title that they have worked with Packt to create. It will only take a few minutes of your time, but is valuable to other potential customers, our authors, and Packt. Thank you!

Index

S

SGF (Smart Game Format) 182
supervised learning 11

T

TensorFlow 27
terminal state 12
TMUX
  about 145
  reference 145
trust region policy optimization (TRPO) algorithm

about 91, 113, 117, 118
experiments, on MuJoCo tasks 119, 120
theory 114, 116

U

unsupervised learning 11
Upper Confidence Bound 1 Applied to Trees (UCT)
  151

V

value function, reinforcement learning 16

Printed in Great Britain
by Amazon